The Food and Cooking of
Scandinavia

The Food and Cooking of
Scandinavia

SWEDEN • NORWAY • DENMARK

150 authentic regional recipes shown in 800 stunning photographs

ANNA MOSESSON, JANET LAURENCE AND JUDITH H. DERN
CONSULTANT: JOHN NIELSEN

LORENZ BOOKS

This edition is published by Lorenz Books,
an imprint of Anness Publishing Ltd,
Blaby Road, Wigston, Leicestershire LE18 4SE

Email: info@anness.com

Web: www.lorenzbooks.com; www.annesspublishing.com

If you like the images in this book and would like
to investigate using them for publishing, promotions
or advertising, please visit our website
www.practicalpictures.com for more information.

Publisher: Joanna Lorenz
Project Editor: Kate Eddison
Copy Editor: Catherine Best
Designer: Nigel Partridge
Illustrators: Anthony Duke and Rob Highton
Photographer: William Lingwood
Food Stylists: Fergal Connolly and Lucy McKelvie
Prop Stylist: Helen Trent
Proofreading Manager: Lindsay Zamponi
Production Controller: Mai-Ling Collyer

ETHICAL TRADING POLICY
Because of our ongoing ecological investment programme,
you, as our customer, can have the pleasure and reassurance
of knowing that a tree is being cultivated on your behalf to
naturally replace the materials used to make the book you are
holding. For further information about this scheme, go to
www.annesspublishing.com/trees

Previously published as *Swedish Food & Cooking*, *Danish
Food & Cooking* and *The Food & Cooking of Norway*.

PUBLISHER'S NOTE
Although the advice and information in this book are believed to
be accurate and true at the time of going to press, neither the
authors nor the publisher can accept any legal responsibility or
liability for any errors or omissions that may have been made
nor for any inaccuracies nor for any loss, harm or injury that
comes about from following instructions or advice in this book.

NOTES
Bracketed terms are intended for American readers.

For all recipes, quantities are given in both metric and
imperial measures and, where appropriate, in standard cups
and spoons. Follow one set of measures, but not a mixture,
because they are not interchangeable.

Standard spoon and cup measures are level.
1 tsp = 5ml, 1 tbsp = 15ml, 1 cup = 250ml/8fl oz.

Australian standard tablespoons are 20ml. Australian readers
should use 3 tsp in place of 1 tbsp for measuring small quantities.

American pints are 16fl oz/2 cups. American readers should
use 20fl oz/2.5 cups in place of 1 pint when measuring liquids.

Electric oven temperatures in this book are for conventional
ovens. When using a fan oven, the temperature will probably
need to be reduced by about 10–20°C/20–40°F. Since ovens
vary, you should check with your manufacturer's instruction
book for guidance.

The nutritional analysis given for each recipe is calculated
per portion (i.e. serving or item), unless otherwise stated.
If the recipe gives a range, such as Serves 4–6, then the
nutritional analysis will be for the smaller portion size, i.e.
6 servings. The analysis does not include optional ingredients,
such as salt added to taste.

Medium (US large) eggs are used unless otherwise stated.

Cover shows Salted Salmon with Potatoes in Dill Sauce,
for recipe see p130.

CONTENTS

INTRODUCTION

The Scandinavian peninsula, situated at the far north of the European continent, comprises Norway, Sweden and Denmark. These three countries are intrinsically connected by cultural bonds and shared histories, mutually understandable languages, an affinity with the surrounding seas, and an ability to create flavoursome and sustaining food in harsh climates and make it last throughout the long, dark winters. Foods such as salted fish, pickled vegetables and dried flatbreads embody the tastes and traditions of Scandinavian cuisine, where preserving food has always been a necessity.

SHARED HISTORIES

The cultural and culinary histories of Sweden, Norway and Denmark are inextricably linked. The region was originally inhabited by the indigenous Sami people (previously known as Lapps). Scandinavian settlers drove them north and, as one of the largest ethnic minorities in Europe, they are

Below: Sami reindeer herders, who are indigenous to northern Scandinavia, have maintained an important relationship with the natural landscape.

Above: In Copenhagen, the capital of Denmark, traditional foods are still enjoyed in many cafés and restaurants.

still found in Norway, Sweden, Finland and Russia, with over 60 per cent in Norway, largely in the most northern region of Finnmark, where they still herd reindeer (caribou). Their economy

has always been based on a strong relationship with the land and its natural resources.

A shared Viking history has influenced the various food cultures of Scandinavia. The Vikings set out from Norway, Sweden, Denmark and the Baltic countries. Initially establishing peaceful farming settlements in Orkney and Shetland off the north coast of Scotland, the adventurous Norsemen soon developed powerful boats capable of crossing oceans. Viking expeditions would have taken many weeks, during which active sailors needed to be fed large quantities of protein in ships with little storage and few cooking facilities. What made the voyages possible were two of the great culinary staples of the Scandinavians, dried cod and pickled herring (a rich source of vitamin C, which was necessary to avoid scurvy).

To preserve food for winter use, many of the cod that teemed in the northern waters were gutted and dried in the wind, first on rocks and then on poles, until they became as hard as a board. The dried fish was first prepared without salt and was known as stockfish. By the 19th century, the Norwegians had perfected a system for salting and drying the cod.

It was during the medieval period that the three distinct Scandinavian kingdoms emerged: Denmark, Norway and Sweden. A period of many civil wars saw land exchanging hands and political control being passed from one country to another. Denmark's royal licence inns, or kroer, date from this time: in 1283, King Erik Klipping decreed that inns should be established at intervals along roads and at ferry landings to guarantee the monach lodgings while travelling around the realm. Many of these old country inns have not changed since the 1700s, and are noted for serving traditional Danish dishes.

THE SCANDINAVIAN DIET

The isolated position of the Scandinavian countries as well as their geography, with numerous separate islands that were difficult to reach, meant that in the past most food had to be seasonal and locally produced. In the far north of the region, particularly in Norway, harsh winter weather meant that efforts had to be made to conserve as much food as possible during the summer months.

To cope with the cold climate and short growing season for crops, the diet of Scandinavians has traditionally been weighted with carbohydrates and fatty, rich foods, meat and fish, with few greens or fresh fruit. Beer and rye bread were staples for both upper and lower classes. Meat was a luxury. Without refrigeration, storing food meant salting, pickling or drying it; smoking was reserved for special foods, such as eel, because wood was available only in limited amounts. Fruit was eaten in season or dried. The large summer catches of herring were pickled or salted, using imported salt.

Today Scandinavian cuisine has remained relatively unchanged. Norway is still very much a seafaring nation, and Norwegians enjoy the countryside and outdoor pursuits, such as hiking, fishing, hunting and skiing. Dried salted cod remains an important part of the cuisine, as do many venison meats.

Although international foods are now enjoyed as part of their cuisine, the Danish also stay loyal to their culinary heritage. The cold table buffet has been adopted by restaurants due to a resurgence of appreciation for classic Danish cuisine, as has the open sandwich, which originated during the 19th-century agricultural reform, from the sandwiches eaten by farm workers.

Above: A royal barge is displayed in the Viking Ship Museum in Bygdoy, Norway, where the seafaring heritage of Scandinavia is celebrated.

In Sweden, the smörgåsbord, which dates back to the 16th century, is still a popular form of eating, with simple bread and butter, cheese and pickled herrings, as well as gravlax, meatballs and sweet dishes.

ABOUT THIS BOOK

This wonderful new book explores the unique tastes and traditions of the Scandinavian countries and gives a fascinating insight into the cultures and peoples behind the food.

The following pages focus in turn on the landscape, cuisine and festivals of Norway, Sweden and Denmark, exploring how each of these factors has influenced the food culture of each country. There is then an imaginative, in-depth look at the range of ingredients used in Scandinavian cooking. A comprehensive recipe section follows, containing 150 authentic step-by-step dishes, providing a perfect introduction to classic Scandinavian cooking.

Left: Wild mushrooms are picked in Swedish forests and used in many dishes.

THE NORWEGIAN LANDSCAPE

Situated on the western part of the Scandinavian peninsula, Norway borders Sweden to the east and the Norwegian Sea to the west. It is a sensationally beautiful country with soaring mountains, peaceful valleys, dark forests, silver lakes, rushing rivers and deep fjords that lead to a coastline fringed with small islands. Some of the highest waterfalls and glacial streams in the world are in Norway. The simple grandeur of the natural world dominates the entire country and affects the whole way of life.

In Norway, the days are very long in summer and short in winter; the relatively brief warm growing season makes both fishing and farming difficult for much of the year despite the abundance of fish in seas, rivers and fjords and the more temperate climate created by the Gulf Stream. Yet the beauty of the country is indisputable, making such hardships incidental for a population that makes much of the outdoors, all year round. Norwegians fiercely guard their ancient law of *allemannsretten*, a law that gives everyone in Norway the right of access to wild areas. The all-too-short summer is spent out of doors, revelling in days filled with a sun that for much of the country never sets. The long, dark and icy winters, though, require preparation as four to six months of the year see much of the country covered in snow.

The Norwegian attitude to food is deeply bound up in their surroundings and history. Food and cooking traditions can be traced back to the days when maintaining regular food supplies involved ensuring that the short summer harvests yielded enough food to last through the long, dark winters.

Despite seasonal extremes, nature is generous in Norway. Both salt and fresh waters teem with high-quality fish. What agricultural land is available is fertile and can be made to produce crops and raise domestic animals. Sheep and goats can feed on green pastures above deep fjords offering a backdrop of dramatic mountains, often with snow-covered peaks, a constant reminder of the shortness of the summer season.

AN EXTREME CLIMATE

Norway hugs the edge of Scandinavia. A bulb shape in southern and central Norway, the land then stretches and elongates itself up the side of Sweden, over into the top of Finland and then curves over to hug the north of Russia. It is as though the coast of Norway, laced with small islands and fringed with fjords, offers protection to the other northern countries from the blast of the Atlantic. In part this is true. However, the coastal regions are also blessed with the softening effect of the Gulf Stream. Although most of Norway lies on the same latitude as Siberia, it enjoys a much more temperate climate than might be expected, which enables a wider range of crops to be grown.

Over one-third of Norway lies within the Arctic Circle, which is the line of latitude linking the places around the world that have at least one full day on which the sun never sets and one day on which it never rises.

As you travel north during the summer, the days when the sun never sets lengthen into weeks. The midnight sun gradually approaches the horizon then, instead of vanishing below it, slowly begins an upward trajectory towards another day. The light around

Left: Norway's coastline is long and scattered with many fjords, which has led to an important fishing industry for the country's economy.

midnight is not quite daylight but has a pearly, mystical quality. Even in the very south of Norway, the midsummer sun lingers until almost midnight. Between late May and mid-August, nowhere in the country experiences true darkness.

Endless summer days contrast with polar nights when the sun never rises. Curiously, the periods of sunless days are not as long as those of the midnight sun. And, just as the light at midnight is not that of daylight, so the dark at midday in winter resembles a twilight as if the sun is struggling to break through. Only in a few places in the far north, such as the island of Svalbard, is darkness complete.

Norway offers great variations in both landscape and weather. Most of the country's eastern spine is mountainous, as is the central part of its southern peninsula. Here, winters are bitter and summer temperatures tend to be higher than the coastal regions, which have a milder climate with less dramatic extremes between the summer and winter seasons. Rain falls generously on some coastal areas, while others have hardly any precipitation – the latter still manage to thrive, due to the many rivers that bring water down from the snow-laden mountains.

Below: Soaring mountains provide Norway's fjords with a dramatic backdrop, but limit the amount of land available for agriculture.

Above: The shimmering curtains of the Northern Lights, the phenomenon seen in the sky in northern latitudes, are one of the wonders of the Arctic Circle.

THE NATURAL LANDSCAPE

Norway has distinctive natural features in its landscape, including mountains, rivers, lakes, waterfalls, glaciers and fjords, which were all formed by several prehistoric glaciers. The mountain areas typically run from north to south, and consist of plateaus, lakes and peaks. Notable ranges include Dovrefjell and Trollheimen in the centre, Jotunheimum in the south and the Kjølen mountain range, which runs throughout most of Norway. Fjords, which are narrow inlets between cliffs or steep slopes with their bases eroded significantly below sea level, characterize the Norwegian landscape and provide spectacularly grand views. Together with the extensive coastline, these stunning inlets provide plentiful fish and shellfish, which are used in a multitude of traditional Norwegian dishes.

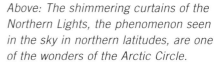

NORWEGIAN CUISINE

The food in Norway is characterized by its simple, delicate flavours. The traditions of preparing food in this region have always been driven by the practical need to ensure that the produce of the short summer is preserved to last all the way through the long winter. Creative ways of using ingredients, to keep them tasting good all year round, have been devised and refined ever since the first cod was dried to make stockfish to sustain Norwegian sailors centuries ago.

The Norwegian cuisine derives from its peasant culture, a simple, wholesome diet where food was harvested from sea and land. Families had their own smallholding and it was common for those who lived along the coast to be both fishermen and farmers, with the men fishing and the women running the farm. As a result, the Norwegian diet has been defined by livestock, grain and fish, with plentiful supplies of milk, butter, buttermilk, cheese, meat, bread and fish, particularly cod and herring. Even in contemporary Norway, the emphasis on outdoor activities such as hunting, walking and skiing have ensured that the traditional, sustaining dishes remain in demand.

PRESERVING FOR WINTER

In Norway, food has always been grown and preserved. Vegetables were selected for their ease of storage, such as beetroot (beet), which can be easily pickled and provides a tasty vegetable accompaniment, and small, plump cucumbers, used to make pickled gherkins. Barley and other grains were great standbys for making sustaining porridge, as well as soups and bread. After the mid-18th century, potatoes appeared and, because they were so easily stored, quickly became a staple food.

Domestic animals, such as cows, sheep and goats, were fattened on plentiful summer feed and then slaughtered during the autumn months, when the cooler temperatures helped with conservation. Techniques such as smoking, salting, drying and curing

were, and still are, all traditionally used in Norway to preserve meat and fish for winter use.

With the introduction of the cooking stove in the 17th century, oven-prepared dishes shifted the balance away from cured products. However, in modern Norway time-honoured dishes using cured ingredients – such as rakefisk, pinnekjøtt and the sour milk cheese gammelost – have once again

Left: A typical 19th-century Norwegian lunchtime scene, with porridge and flatbread, as seen at the Maihaugen Working Museum.

become popular. This reflects an increasing nostagia for the traditional patterns of life, as well as a new awareness of the importance of using local and seasonal foods.

MEALTIME TRADITIONS

The strong farming heritage of Norway dictates that classic Norwegian dishes are based on local produce. This does result in certain regional variations of dishes, although the wide availability of all ingredients now makes such differences less marked.

In the past, eating well in the morning was essential for all families to give energy to those working long hours in the open air. Energy was also needed to stave off the bitter cold brought by the long winters. Frokost, or breakfast, would typically include grøt, a filling porridge that was made by boiling milk with flour, or the richer rømmegrøt, with cream and flour. A sweet version of this is often used for birthdays, summer

Below: Cod is dried on the Lofoten Islands to produce traditional stockfish.

parties and at Christmas. Today breakfast also features cold or cured meats and fish, cheese, eggs, stewed or fresh fruit, fresh and sour milk, and traditional hardbread, all washed down with lots of coffee.

Lunchtime has always been a rushed affair, nowadays usually an open sandwich wrapped in paper called 'matpakke' and a very short break of less than half an hour.

The 5 pm 'middag' for most people is the only hot meal of the day, consisting of a main dish of meat, seafood or pasta, almost always accompanied by potatoes and a small amount of other vegetables.

Dishes for this main meal might include fårikål, a stew with lamb, cabbage and whole peppercorns. In earlier times, this would have been made from mutton, as lamb was expensive and reserved for the wealthy. Another meat dish is pinnekjøtt, made with cured and sometimes smoked mutton ribs, which is also a favourite for Christmas lunch in the west of Norway. Smalahove is another speciality of the west, made with smoked lamb's head.

Preserved meat and sausages are available in a multitude of regional variations. They are typically served with sour cream dishes and flatbread or

Right: A Fat Tuesday buffet, with yellow pea soup, salted and boiled pork and lamb, and smoked sausages with mashed swede.

wheat/potato wraps. Other meat delicacies include an air-dried lamb's leg called fenalår, and mor, a smoked cured sausage.

One of Norway's most recognized fish dishes is smoked salmon, and this is typically served with scrambled eggs and dill or mustard sauce. Then there are the many guises of pickled herring and anchovy, which adorn the main dinner table as well as being eaten for 'aftons', a snack often taken later in the evening.

The ancient seafarers' staple of stockfish (also called tørrfisk or clipfish), the unsalted fish that is dried hard in the open air, is a highly nutritious ingredient used in various fish dishes. The distinctive taste of lutefisk, another long-established speciality, which is created with salted and dried cod soaked in a lye solution, produces a jelly-like substance that is eaten with boiled potatoes and flatbread, traditionally on Christmas Eve or at Easter.

Another classic Scandinavian fish dish is gravlaks, as it is known in Norway (or gravlax in Sweden). This is

made with oily fish smothered with salt, and then buried in the ground to preserve it. Left for under a week, the flesh cures to produce the clean flavour and smooth texture of gravlaks. If the fish is left longer, for up to several months, the flesh ferments into a sour product with an individual smell known as rakefisk, an acquired taste, which is usually served with raw red onion rings, boiled potatoes, butter, lefse (traditional bread) and sour cream.

FRUIT AND SWEETS

Many Norwegian desserts feature fruits and berries, which mature slowly in the cold climate, producing a smaller volume with a rich taste. Fruit soup, a speciality of Scandinavia, is made with seasonal fruits, often cooked with tapioca. Another traditional dessert is rødgrøt, a fruit pudding made from red fruit juices. Norwegians are also big coffee drinkers and an important social pastime is 'kaffe', coffee served with kaffebrød (coffee bread), cakes or waffles with jam and cream in the afternoon or early evening.

Left: Sami reindeer herders brew coffee, one of Norway's favourite drinks, during their long migration across northern Norway.

NORWEGIAN FESTIVALS AND CELEBRATIONS

Norwegian celebrations have much in common with those of other Scandinavian countries. One of the most important Scandinavian celebrations is the day of Santa Lucia, or the festival of light, which originates in Sweden, with light symbolizing a powerful force that combats the long hours of darkness.

Norway is a predominantly Protestant country, and many of its festivals can be traced to the church calendar, as well as to the changing seasons and historical events. They range from the very start of the year with New Year's Day, when people's fortunes were predicted, to Christmas at the end of the year, with the traditional key figure of the Norwegian fjøsnisse, or goblin, as well as the more modern figure of Santa Claus.

These are the main annual holidays and festivities, including ancient traditions, modern interpretations, as well as more recently introduced festivals.

NEW YEAR'S DAY

Historically, this was a traditional day of omens in Norway, when the successful production of crops and food was

predicted, as well as the general fortunes of the forthcoming year. It is still an official flag-flying day that is associated with the making of resolutions.

SHROVETIDE

Fastelavn, or Shrovetide, runs through Shrove Sunday, Shrove Monday (Blåmandag) and Shrove Tuesday or Fat Tuesday (Fetetirsdag), the latter marked by eating a traditional pastry, called semla, filled with marzipan and whipped cream. Officially celebrated on the day before Lent, Shrovetide is also a Norwegian celebration of the approach of spring.

EASTER

The year's most important church festival, Påske, or Easter, is sometimes referred to as the Quiet Week in Norway, linked to the Easter message of the suffering of Jesus and his resurrection. Today the celebration has lost many of its sober connotations and provides another occasion for days in the mountains, activities such as skiing and family celebrations. One traditional activity is decorating Easter eggs and

Above: A Sami couple wear traditional dress at the Easter reindeer races in Kautekeino in northern Norway.

rolling them down a slope. Easter dishes are typically egg dishes and lamb, the latter originating in the sacrifice of lambs during the Jewish celebration of spring.

WHITSUN

Pinse, or Whitsun, in Norwegian means the 50th day after Easter. While less of a tradition, it is still a national holiday in Norway.

CONSTITUTION DAY

Norway's celebration of its independence, also called National Day, falls on 17 May, commemorating the signing of the first constitution in 1814. Breakfast often features spekemat (cured meats), smoked salmon, scrambled eggs and pickled herrings, as well as stewed fruits, bread and coffee. In the morning, citizens assemble to greet the king and royal family as they appear on the balcony of the royal palace in Oslo, or the local mayor in other towns. Citizens'

Left: Constitution Day falls on 17 May. The festival processions include brass bands and school children waving flags.

processions are headed by school brass bands with school children waving Norwegian flags or holding sprays of newly emerged birch leaves.

MIDSUMMER'S EVE

Sankhansaften, Jonsok, or Midsummer's Eve, on 23 June is based on an ancient festival celebrating the summer solstice (21 June). On this night, witches were believed to be abroad, plants picked were thought to have healing powers, and bonfires were lit up along the coast to protect against evil spirits. Now Jonsok is a private celebration where people dance around a bonfire.

ST OLAF'S DAY

Olsok, or St Olaf's Day, on 29 July marks the death of King Olaf Haraldsson in 1030, who brought Christianity to Norway. An important holy day, traditionally bonfires are lit, especially in rural areas.

ALL SAINTS' DAY

Allehelgens Dag, or All Hallows Day, on 1 November commemorated the saints, and Alle Sjeles Dag, or All Souls'

Above: Women on the northern island of Vardö celebrate Midsummer's Eve by dressing up as witches and dancing around the bonfire.

Day, on 2 November commemorated the dead. The first Sunday in November is today celebrated as All Saints' Day, when people in Norway place wreaths and lighted candles on the graves of deceased relatives. The celebrations are now also being influenced by the Halloween customs of the US.

SANTA LUCIA DAY

This custom, which actually originates in Sweden, is celebrated each year on 13 December as a feast of light. Dressed all in white, young Norwegian girls wear a crown of lighted candles and offer coffee and buns or cookies to their neighbours.

CHRISTMAS

The main Christmas celebration is held on Christmas Eve when it is common to attend carol services. Norwegians

Left: This illustration depicts children on a 19th-century Norwegian farm dressing up as gnomes to celebrate the tradition of Yuletide.

observe the traditional celebrations of Advent, the Christmas tree, cards, gifts and Santa Claus, although there is also the more ancient influence of the Norwegian Fjøsnisse (goblin who lives in the barn), a much-seen symbol at this time of year.

Festive fare varies, but sour cream porridge, usually made with rice and traditionally hiding an almond, is a lunchtime favourite inland. Lutefisk is most often eaten on the coast, where it is a speciality, usually followed by a whole cod. Roast rib or loin of pork is eaten in central and eastern Norway. On the west coast, the traditional dish is pinnekjøtt, which is smoked and dried lamb ribs.

On Christmas Day there is usually an elaborate koldt bord, or cold table. A Christmas ham studded with cloves or decorated with mayonnaise provides a festive centrepiece, sometimes given extra flavour by being cured in a beer brine before being smoked. Christmas baking traditions are still strong, and custom used to dictate that seven different kinds of biscuits (cookies) were baked and offered to guests alongside cakes and coffee. Any guest who leaves without eating anything is considered to bring bad luck to the house.

THE SWEDISH LANDSCAPE

Sweden nestles between Norway and Finland, with the Baltic Sea and Gulf of Bothnia to the east and Skagerrak to the west. With cold, dark winters and hot, long summer days, Sweden's climate is similar to Norway's. In the Arctic north there are vast expanses of snow and complete silence and, in the winter, intense darkness, which is only broken by the fantastic Northern Lights that sparkle and dance across the polar skies in shades of red, green, blue and violet.

NATURAL BEAUTY

Despite Sweden being geographically the fourth largest country in Europe, the population has remained relatively small, at around nine million people, and thinly spread across the country. Over half of Sweden's land area is covered in forest and woodland; only seven per cent of the land is arable and just two per cent is grazing land, the latter all in the south. Wildlife such as elk (moose), reindeer (caribou), grouse and hare populate the forests and woodlands, and these areas are also home to many species of wild mushrooms as well as native berries, such as lingonberries and cloudberries. The long coastline of Sweden is dotted with numerous beautiful islands and there are around a staggering 95,000 lakes in the country, in which thrive an amazing 52 species of freshwater fish.

DISTINCT REGIONS

Sweden is traditionally divided into three major regions, each of which contains a number of provinces – 25 provinces in total. Norrland, the largest region, forms northern Sweden; Svealand, the smallest region, is in

Below: The famously beautiful Laponian area in Lappland at the far north of Sweden became a World Heritage Site in 1996.

Above: The Rapa River delta forms a stunning valley in Sarek National Park in northern Sweden, one of the rainiest areas of the country.

central Sweden; and Götaland (or Götland) is the region that makes up southern Sweden.

Stockholm, the capital city, is built on 14 islands, between a large freshwater lake called Mälaren and the Baltic Sea. Stockholm is the most highly populated city of Sweden with around 750,000 inhabitants. Due to the colder temperatures, the north of the country is far less populated.

TEMPERATE CLIMATE

Sweden is a long country from north to south and has eight climatic zones, meaning that the climate varies between

Above: The lush green islands of Stockholm sit on the Stockholm archipelago, creating stunning waterways throughout the capital city.

Left: Sweden is geographically Europe's fourth largest country, which means that the climate can vary greatly between the most northerly and most southerly regions.

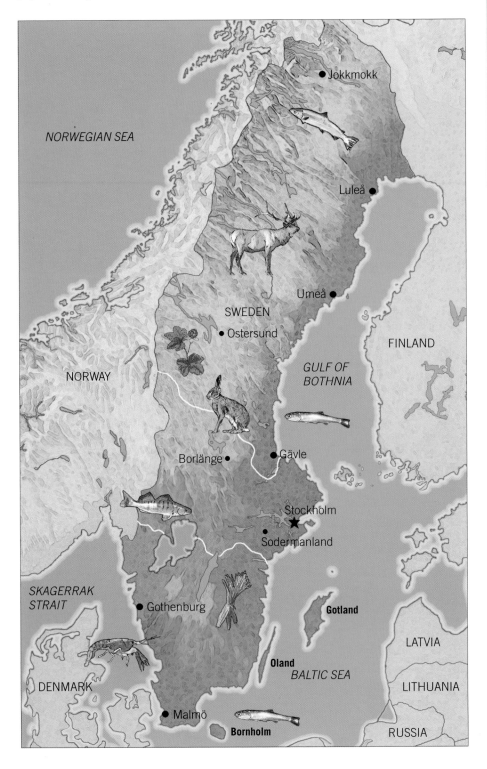

regions. Despite its northern latitude, the southern regions of Sweden have a relatively mild climate with distinct spring, summer, autumn and winter seasons. Like neighbouring Denmark, it is surprisingly warm and dry compared with other countries of the same latitude, partly due to the Gulf Stream. However, the temperatures vary greatly between the north and the south of the country, with the winters getting progressively longer, darker and colder towards the north of the country. As in Norway, there is plenty of snow and ice in the northern provinces of Sweden.

Like Norway, Sweden has seemingly endless hours of sunlight in the summer months, and relentless hours of darkness in the winter. The far north is within the Artic Circle which means there is at least one day in summer when the sun never sets, and a day in winter when the sun never rises.

SWEDISH CUISINE

The traditional Swedish approach to food emphasized the need to preserve and store the fresh produce obtained in the warmer months and make it last throughout the year. Despite modern refrigeration techniques, these preserved ingredients still provide the backbone of the diet.

In the past, people would gather all that they needed during the summer harvest, preserve it and then save it for future use in the less productive times of year. Even eating fresh berries was a real treat, because berries were collected and then cooked into jam for the winter. Fresh vegetables were another rare luxury, since there was always a pressure to preserve or pickle them. The same rule applied to potatoes and other root vegetables, which used to be stacked away in an earth cellar for winter use.

HUSMANSKOST

Swedish home cooking, known as *husmanskost*, was born from the need for such food preservation techniques and is often based on traditional methods of smoking, fermenting, salting, drying, marinating and poaching ingredients such as seafood, poultry, lamb, beef, veal and wild game. Husmanskost consists of plain, rustic

dishes and familiar classics include meatballs, stuffed cabbage rolls and yellow pea soup. The husmanskost is still a strong contemporary tradition and forms the main component of the Swedish smörgåsbord.

In more recent times the best of the traditional recipes have been modernized so that they are less hearty

Below: A variety of seafood and vegetables on display at a Swedish indoor market.

Above: A traditional Christmas buffet on display at Stallmästaregården, which is Stockholm's oldest hotel and restaurant.

and simpler to prepare, and also in keeping with today's lifestyles and different nutritional needs. Fresh fruit and vegetables have been added, traditional fatty dishes have been replaced with steaks and stews, stocks are reduced to give deliciously flavoured jus or gravy, and sauces have been made lighter and created with less cream – but although their fat content has been reduced, none of their other characteristics have been lost. Also, the large quantities of oil-rich salmon and herrings that the Swedes eat have always contained high amounts of the polyunsaturated fats called omega-3 fatty acids, which many recent studies have shown to be essential to good health.

EATING PATTERNS

The daily dietary regime in Sweden is based around three main meals. Breakfast usually consists of open sandwiches with hard cheese or slices of meat, and possibly crispbread (knäckebröd). Swedes don't use sweet spreads on their breads but the traditional Swedish bread, sirapslimpa, is sweet in itself, as it is baked with

syrup. Yogurt and fermented milk (filmjölk) are common breakfast foods, and are usually served in a bowl with cereals such as cornflakes or muesli (granola), sometimes with sugar, fruit or jam. Porridge (US oatmeal), or gröt, is another popular breakfast food often made of rolled oats, and eaten with milk and fruit or jam.

Lunch tends to be a light snack such as a sandwich whereas the evening meal is usually hot. At the table, Swedes like to serve themselves unless it is impractical, and it is therefore considered polite to finish what one has served oneself.

SMÖRGÅSBORD

The most well-known eating style in Sweden is the smörgåsbord, or bread-and-butter table. There was a distinguishable smörgåsbord tradition as far back as the 16th century, when all the food for a meal would be placed on the table at the same time. At the beginning the smörgåsbord dishes were simple, consisting of bread, butter, cheese and herring, but as the custom

Below: Strandvägen is an exclusive boulevard in the Östermalm area of Stockholm – it has many restaurants that overlook the waterfront.

continued, more and more dishes were added. By the 18th century it had become a regular feature in most homes.

The smörgåsbord is now commonly prepared for special occasions such as Christmas, Easter and midsummer. On these occasions, the array of food is set out on a long table and people continue to help themselves.

Diners start with a selection of herring, such as Glasmästarsill, or other fish and shellfish dishes. These are served with boiled potatoes, hard-boiled eggs and bread, and accompanied by snaps. They then proceed to cold, savoury dishes such as cuts of game, poultry and meat, pâtés and salads and then hot dishes, such as the traditional Jansson's Temptation. Sweet desserts are served last, usually with coffee. Every time diners choose their next selection, they change their plate so that the flavours do not intermingle. Diners may return to the table as often as they wish but they must not load their plate with too many foods at the same time.

Because preparing a full smörgåsbord involves considerable work, it is unusual to experience the real smörgåsbord anywhere other than in restaurants, on festival days or on special occasions.

Swedish smörgåsbord
Recipe ideas that could be included in a formal smörgåsbord are listed below.

Chilled fish dishes
Mustard Herrings (Senapsill)
Gravlax with Mustard and Dill
    Sauce (Gravlax med gravlax sås)
Salted Salmon with Potatoes and
    Dill Sauce (Rimmad lax med
    dillstuvad potatis)

Savoury dishes
West Coast Salad (Västkustsalad)
Hare Pâté (Harpâté)
Christmas Ham with Swedish
    Mustard (Julskinka med senap)
Anchovy Terrine (Gubbröra)
Västerbotten Cheese Flan
    (Västerbottenost flan)

Hot dishes
Stuffed Cabbage Rolls (Kåldolmar)
Elk Meatballs with Lingon
    (Algköttbullar med lingon)
Janssons Temptation
    (Jansson's frestelse)
Swedish Hash (Pytt i panna)

Desserts
Rice porridge (Risgrynsgröt)
Wild Berry Tart (Skogsbär flan)
Almond Stuffed Baked Apples
    (Drottningäpplen)
Gingerbread Biscuits
    (Pepparkakor)

SWEDISH FESTIVALS AND CELEBRATIONS

Feasts and festivals play an important part in the Swedish calendar. Many of them are based on peasant traditions and are therefore closely associated with the changing seasons. Summer is celebrated with an understandable intensity by a population who have endured a long, dark winter. Many of the celebrations mentioned below are linked to the farming year, to the welcoming of spring, to the hunting and fishing seasons and to harvest time.

SHROVE TUESDAY

Recipes that regularly feature in the Shrove Tuesday celebrations at the end of February are roasted pork and Fat Tuesday buns (semla). These have a

Below: Dancers in folk costume enjoy the Midsummer's Eve celebrations.

sweet, overpowering almond flavour, intended as a celebratory, rich farewell to good food before the fasting regime of Lent begins.

OUR LADY'S DAY

On 25 March farmers celebrate Vårfrudagen, or Our Lady's Day. Delicious waffles are made with a simple batter of an egg, a little flour and some cream or melted butter and sparkling water, which makes the waffles crispy. Some cooks even use snow if it is on the ground. Toppings for the waffles vary and include fried salty bacon or cloudberry jam and whipped cream.

EASTER

Swedish legend has it that on Maundy Thursday witches would fly off on their broomsticks to a blue mountain where

they would be entertained by the devil. So the tradition is that children dress up as witches, ride on broomsticks and visit their neighbours shouting "Glad Påsk" (Happy Easter) in return for treats. Halibut is often served on Good Friday, on the evening of Easter Saturday most Swedes will have a small smörgåsbord, and the Easter Sunday meal often includes spinach soup and roasted lamb or pork with hasselback potatoes. It is also a good time to eat Nettle Soup with Egg Butterballs as the nettles are just coming up.

VALBORGSMÄSSA

This festival is celebrated on 1 May when the Swedes dance and sing to celebrate the end of winter and the coming of spring and summer. This is considered to be the beginning of summer even though it can still be very cold. The night before, huge bonfires made from juniper bushes are lit all over the country, and the smell creates a magical atmosphere.

MIDSUMMER'S EVE

This major Swedish festival takes place on the weekend nearest to 21 June. Traditionally everyone dances around a flower-bedecked maypole, folk songs are sung and folk music is played. Midsummer's Eve is an all-night indulgence of dancing, eating and drinking, and the celebrations can continue for almost 24 hours as it hardly gets dark at this time of year.

THE CRAYFISH FESTIVAL

During this August festival crayfish are cooked with dill, chilled and served in a large mound on a platter, garnished with fresh dill. The eating ritual is a happy, noisy affair. Paper lanterns are put up and jovial folk songs are sung. The cold crayfish are served with snaps or beer, toast and cheese flavoured with cumin and cloves.

SURSTRÖMMING SEASON

During this short season around August a strange and pungent dish called surströmming is eaten – this Baltic

herring dish from the north of Sweden dates back to the 16th century. The herring is salted and fermented in a large wooden barrel at room temperature for about six weeks and then canned. It is eaten with boiled potatoes and tunnbröd, a thin soft bread, with butter and chopped raw onions. When the can is opened, it releases an unbearable smell, which is caused by the fermenting gas mixing with oxygen.

NOBEL PRIZE DINNER

Sweden is well known for the Nobel Prize, named after the famous scientist Alfred Nobel. The Nobel Prize dinner, a modern tradition, is held every year on 10 December and is an extraordinary feat of culinary skill. The first Nobelfest (Nobel Feast) was given in 1901, in the Mirrored Hall of the Grand Hotel in Stockholm. There were 150 guests and champagne and Russian caviar were served. There were seven courses, which included crêpes fried in olive oil and fillet steak stuffed with foie gras. The dessert was an ice-cream bombe consisting of several different ice creams, or a tart filled with almond paste and topped with glazed fresh

Below: A Day of Santa Lucia celebration takes place at a church in Lekvattnet, Värmland, in the Svealand province.

Above: Swedish children dress up as witches at Easter and collect treats from their neighbours.

apricots. Nowadays, over 1,000 guests attend the dinner, which is held at the Stockholm Town Hall.

THE DAY OF SANTA LUCIA

At the end of the year, the Swedes celebrate light, for the long dark winters can induce a feeling of melancholy. The Day of Santa Lucia, the Queen of Light, falls on 13 December. A young girl (or several young girls) is chosen to

Above: A traditional Swedish Christmas table with cheese, bread, roast ham, marinated herrings, beer and aquavit.

represent the saint and wear a crown of candles in her hair, although these days they are usually electric. After the procession, coffee is served with Lucia Saffron Buns and Gingerbread Biscuits.

CHRISTMAS

The Day of Santa Lucia marks the beginning of the magical Christmas season. The climax is Christmas Eve (Julafton), when smörgåsbord is served at lunchtime. A Christmas ham glazed with mustard and breadcrumbs is the centrepiece and other traditional Christmas dishes include herrings, pork sausage, potatoes and vört bread. The meal ends with coffee and Christmas cookies. In the evening, dishes include lutfisk, a speciality of both Sweden and Norway, which is a dish with a jelly-like consistency made from dried cod or ling soaked in a lye solution and then boiled. It is served with a white sauce, melted butter, peas, new potatoes and mustard. Dessert is typically julgröt, Sweden's traditional creamed rice pudding, which has a lucky almond hidden inside, a sign of marriage or great fortune. Some Swedes make their julgröt more traditionally using barley instead of rice.

THE DANISH LANDSCAPE

Lying at the crossroads between continental Europe and Scandinavia, Denmark is a magical land of low-lying islands and a peninsula stretching into the North Sea. Linked to Norway and Sweden by language and history, the country experiences similar extremes of climate, ranging from blissful, cool summers of endless light to wet, windy and dark winters.

Compared to its Scandinavian neighbours and most other European countries, the Kingdom of Denmark is a small nation and a low one, its land smoothed by receding glaciers in the last Ice Age. In area, the country spans only 43,094 sq km/16,639 sq miles. Of Denmark's 406 named islands, fewer than 100 are inhabited; the three largest are Sjælland (Zealand), Fyn (Funen) and Bornholm. There are 5.4 million Danes, and the country's capital city is København (Copenhagen) on Zealand. Germany lies to the south, while to the east is Sweden, the Kattegat and Øresund Channels and the Baltic Sea. Norway and the Skagerrak Channel lie to the north, while the North Sea

Below: The country's soil, enriched by years of pig and chicken production, yields golden wheat, rye and oats.

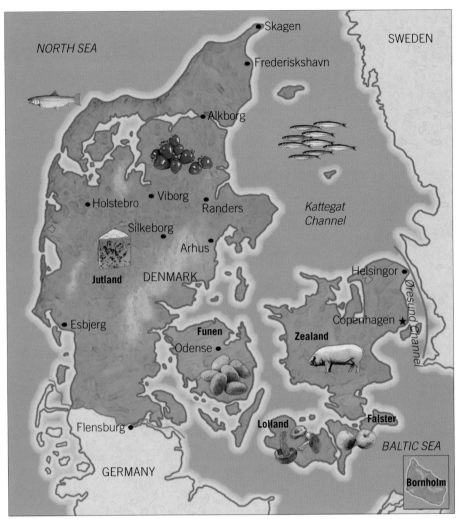

washes the west coast. No doubt the proximity of water and its role in transportation contributed to making the early Danes such superb seafarers and ship designers, not to mention fishermen.

SEA, SKY AND LANDSCAPE

Warmed by the Gulf Stream, Denmark enjoys a mild climate despite its northerly location. The prevailing winds from the west off the North Sea create billowy cumulus clouds. The landscape is flat, but its features vary between marshland, wooded hills, moors, lakes and farmland. Sandy beaches and steep chalk cliffs add another dimension to the terrain.

Barely 150 years ago, Denmark's soil was mostly poor glacier moraine on which farmers scraped out a precarious living and the people's diet was correspondingly limited. But decades

Above: Almost surrounded by the sea, Danes have long relied on fish to supplement what they could produce on their farms.

of raising livestock and tilling in manure have improved the land's fertility, making agriculture a leading industry. The Danish menu has expanded accordingly to include many pork products and a greater variety of grains and seeds as well as eggs, cheese, cream and butter.

Ever since the first Dane sailed off in a boat, the waters surrounding Denmark's islands and peninsula have been important sources of fish. In summer the herring shoals are harvested along the coast, and in past times, during the fallow winter months, farmers turned fishermen would set out to catch cod, halibut and plaice. Denmark has no

Right: Agriculture in Denmark centres around family farms.

major rivers, but fjords reach far inland. These fingers of the sea linking to freshwater streams are where salmon and eels return to spawn in spring.

Denmark's natural vegetation is mixed forest, but just 12 per cent of the country is forested today, due to felling in earlier centuries for building ships and houses. Coniferous trees prevail in the former heath areas of western Jutland, and many dunes along the beaches in north Jutland are forested with spruce and pine. The climate is hospitable to apple orchards, especially on the islands of Lolland and Falster, and plum and cherry trees thrive in gardens.

ZEALAND AND COPENHAGEN

The island of Zealand has gently rolling hills, long sandy beaches, particularly on the west and north coasts, and prosperous dairy and arable farms in the west and south. Low-lying and accessible from the sea, it's where Germanic tribes first settled 8,000 years ago, followed by Norsemen.

Below: Denmark's picturesque coastline has always been a source of fish.

By 1167, when Copenhagen, meaning 'merchants' harbour', was officially founded, the city was a significant trading settlement. It still serves as the country's focus for trade, its waterways echoing those of ancient times.

FUNEN AND BORNHOLM

Denmark's second largest island is Funen. Its west coast is lapped by the Little Belt Channel, and its eastern edge by the Great Belt, both important herring grounds. In the south-west, on a wooded moraine ridge called the Funen Alps, the fertile soil yields an abundance of vegetables including corn, tomatoes and cucumbers, plus flowers and fruit grown in tidy, straight-edged fields and orchards. It is often called the country's granary, and is one of the wealthier regions of Denmark.

Ferries leave nightly from Copenhagen to make the seven-hour voyage to Bornholm, lying south-east of Zealand in the Baltic Sea. For centuries, the island served as a defensive outpost for Copenhagen against Sweden. Today, its fertile, rolling hills are forested or farmed, set with thousand-year-old churches, manor houses and village inns. A temperate climate, with long hours of sunlight, produces lush gardens, fields of mustard, rapeseed and grain, and meadows where figs, cherry, chestnut and mulberry trees flourish.

JUTLAND

The Jutland Peninsula is Denmark's link with the rest of Europe. Jutland is more rugged than Funen and Zealand. A region of thriving pig farms and dairies, Jutland is sliced by the craggy Limfjord, a shallow sound that reaches in from the west coast and bisects its northern tip.

East Jutland features a network of lakes and forests around the town of Silkeborg. In summer, its woodlands are full of wild raspberries, strawberries and blueberries, and later, mushrooms. In the north, beautiful sand dunes and white beaches are a destination for tourists and artists seeking the radiant Nordic light. On the west coast, the soil favours wild pors (bog myrtle) and juniper berries, used in making aquavit.

DANISH CUISINE

The Danish cook's talent for making much out of a little reflects the difficulties of living off the land in a cold climate, but this frugality does not extend to entertaining. Danes have a deep-rooted sense of wellbeing, which is expressed in the enjoyment of dining with family and friends.

It's long been said that Danes love to eat, and eat well. But there's a deeper meaning behind this statement. Underlying the Danish attitude to good food is one of the bedrocks of social culture: the concept of *hygge*. There is no literal English translation for *hygge*. It's best described as mental and physical contentment, the security and warmth connected with good feelings about home and family. *Hygge* includes eating and drinking with family and friends in a convivial atmosphere of generous hospitality and comfort. It includes candles, pleated napkins, a beautifully set table and gracious hosts. It's an essential part of the national psyche.

Hygge also explains why the vast majority of social eating in Denmark takes place at home, which is still the focus of Danish culture. Home is where the host or hostess can spread

Below: The precious first potato crop of the season is watered in Jutland.

Above: Before modern refrigeration, the preserving, pickling, drying and storing of food was essential for surviving the far north's long, harsh winters.

out a *koldt bord* (cold table) with an abundance of assorted dishes, both cold and hot, several varieties of cheese, breads, snaps, coffee and cakes to create a warm and welcoming atmosphere. Restaurants are reserved for business socializing or special

occasions, such as Christmas luncheons, and countryside inns, or *kro*, are very popular for spring or holiday excursions.

RURAL TRADITIONS

No doubt the concept of *hygge* stems from living in a cold, inhospitable climate. In earlier centuries seasonal extremes made survival challenging. Making a living, and having enough food in your storehouse to last until the next harvest, was a source of deep contentment and something worth celebrating, especially when lean times and the need for frugality were never far away.

An appreciation of good food was established during Denmark's pre-industrial era, when the climate acutely affected the life and livelihood of the average labourer. If you were a peasant facing uncertain meals, you ate whatever and whenever you could, but even so, eating was also about creating an atmosphere of wellbeing, whatever your class. The first Danish cookbook, published in 1616, was a directive to aristocrats about how to achieve an elegant courtly table with nationally produced seasonal fare.

A history of living close to nature gives Danes, and most Scandinavians, a special appreciation for seasonal

Above: First built in the 13th century to guarantee lodging for royalty touring the countryside, royal inns (or kro) still serve traditional Danish fare.

Above: Coffee and Danish pastries are enjoyed at any time of day in present-day Denmark, particularly as a late-morning or mid-afternoon snack.

During the week it is generally one course, but soup, a main course and dessert (a pudding or cheese) may be served at weekends. Coffee and pastries generally follow later in the evening, with a small glass of liqueur if there are guests. But Danes have a knack for adding extra meals. Late morning or afternoon coffee with Danish pastry is a favourite for a work break.

DENMARK'S BEER CULTURE

Drinking beer is a Danish custom that dates back to before Viking times, although in pre-Christian history it would have been mead, a fermented honey beverage. For centuries, beer was served with every meal, including breakfast. The brewing cycle started in March, with a waning moon. There was also then a winter brew around 9 December, to be ready by the winter solstice or St Thomas' Eve on 20 December. Food is not a necessary accompaniment to beer for a Dane, but some insist that only with a glass of beer or snaps is the experience of *smørrebrød* complete.

Below: Ablaze with candles, the bars in Denmark promote a cosy, convivial atmosphere to create the feeling of hygge, *or wellbeing and contentment.*

foods even today. The first spring asparagus and the first strawberries of summer are causes for celebration. Copenhagen's finest restaurants annually vie for the prestige of serving the first new potatoes, particularly from the island of Samsø – regardless of cost – and the event is sure to make the evening news.

FROM FIVE MEALS A DAY TO THREE

Rural life is the source for Denmark's plain dishes and straightforward eating traditions. In agrarian times, work schedules meant five meals spaced through the day to maintain energy; the midday meal was typically bread and butter eaten in the fields. Hearty, high-carbohydrate and high-fat meals served as insulation against cold winters and draughty lodgings. Today, with rich country dishes still mainstays of the everyday diet, an active lifestyle – the bicycle is the most common form of transport – means there are few Danes who qualify as overweight.

Three meals per day became the norm with the arrival of the industrial era. *Morgenmad* (breakfast), with bread and butter, sliced cheese, pickled herring and perhaps an egg, is followed by *frokost* (lunch) between 12 and 2 pm. This meal might be *smørrebrød* or a packed lunch from home. *Aftensmad* (dinner), eaten between 6 and 8 pm, is the hot meal, for which families gather.

Danish Festivals and Celebrations

A blend of sacred and secular rituals defines Denmark's key holidays. Many of these annual events have their roots in ancient pagan traditions, while others reflect the country's early Catholic era and subsequent shift to the Lutheran faith.

By law, public holidays fall on the same days as those of the Danish National Church. Other holidays mark historic dates or the seasonal swings from brilliant summer to deep winter darkness. Special foods are part of many celebrations.

NEW YEAR'S EVE

Exchanging visits with family and friends to enjoy wine and small cakes is the traditional pastime as the year winds to a close. The wine, often a home-made vintage made from garden currants or cherries, is served with small cakes or biscuits (cookies) such as mazarins, macaroons and vanilla rings. At 6 pm the monarch delivers the annual speech on television, and families enjoy a supper of baked or poached cod with potatoes, cauliflower, aquavit and beer.

FASTELAVN

Once a period of fasting, Fastelavn (Shrovetide) on the Monday before Lent begins has become a carnival-like event for children. They wake their parents by

'beating' or tickling them with birch branches called Fastelavnsris, wear fancy costumes to school and feast on Fastelavnsboller, sweet, cream-filled Lenten buns, which they are given by their neighbours.

EASTER

When the first snowdrops appear in the spring garden, Påske (Easter) is just around the corner. Danes celebrate by sending anonymous messages called *gækkebreve* (guessing letter), which are

Above: On Store Bededag, Danes walk along the Copenhagen waterfront where the Little Mermaid keeps her vigil.

poems decorated with papercuts and snowdrops. If the recipient can't guess the name of the sender, they owe them an Easter egg. Easter lasts from Wednesday to the following Monday, prompting lavish lunch parties, specially brewed beer and many glasses of aquavit. On Easter Sunday the main meal can include lamb, chicken or fish. If the first asparagus has appeared, it's a special side dish.

STORE BEDEDAG

Celebrated on the fourth Friday after Easter, this exclusively Danish holiday is called Great Prayer Day. In Copenhagen, residents traditionally promenade along the city's ramparts in their new spring clothes, then feast on *varme hveder*, square wheat biscuits served warm.

VALBORGSAFTEN

Celebrated on 30 April in Jutland, Valborgsaften (Walpurgis Eve) is the time when peasant folk believed witches on broomsticks and other demons rode

Left: As in the rest of Europe, the people of Denmark enjoy egg hunts during the Easter holiday.

Above: Girls in national costume cook æbleskiver, *the Danish doughnut.*

through the night to visit the Devil. Building hilltop bonfires kept the evil spirits from stopping to harm farms and villages – as well as burning up the garden's winter refuse.

WHITSUN

'White Sunday', or Pentecost, is marked with songfests by choral societies, plus vigorous cleaning at home. It is considered spring's official beginning when Danes rise early 'to see the sun dance' after the long winter, and coffee must be ready on the table in the garden by 6 am. On the following Monday people go on country walks or bicycle rides to look for the first leaves appearing on the beech trees (the beech is Denmark's national tree). They celebrate with picnics or patio parties, and dine at *kroer*, where the season's first elver or eel, a speciality of these old countryside inns, may be on the menu.

CONSTITUTION DAY

On 5 June 1849, King Frederick VII signed Denmark's first constitution. On the same day in 1953, King Frederick IX signed another that declared Denmark a democratic parliamentary monarchy. The date coincides with early rhubarb,

Above: On Midsummer's Eve bonfires burn along the coast, blazing into the sky.

which inspired the National Day dessert, often served following cold roast chicken, cucumber salad and potato salad.

MIDSUMMER'S EVE

Marking St Hansaften (St John's Eve) and the summer solstice, when daylight in the far north never ends, 23 June is celebrated with folk dancing, speeches, singing, bonfires, feasts and all-night parties. An effigy of a witch (a symbol of winter or death) is sometimes burnt in an ancient ritual condemning evil spirits forever to the fires of hell.

MORTENSAFTEN

An old family holiday, Mortensaften (St Martin's Eve) on 11 November celebrates the harvest and the legend that St Martin, reluctant to become a bishop, hid in a barn until some geese alerted the searchers to his hiding place. Perhaps as retribution, a fine meal with goose as the main course is served on Mortensaften, followed by traditional *æbleskiver* (doughnuts).

CHRISTMAS

In the weeks before 24 December, houses are scrubbed, cakes and biscuits are prepared, farm animals are

tended with extra care, sheaves of grain are put out to feed birds, the fir tree is cut or purchased, and gifts are gathered and wrapped. Danish brewers produce special Christmas beers, and employers host Christmas lunches for their employees and colleagues.

On Lille Julaften (little Christmas Eve), on 23 December, friends and families gather for *glögg* (spiced wine) and *æbleskiver* served with jam and dusted with icing sugar. Christmas candles are lit and every house glows.

On Julaften (Christmas Eve), families gather for three days of celebrations. Following afternoon church services, people enjoy a lavish Christmas feast, featuring roast goose, duck or turkey, gravy, red cabbage, boiled potatoes, mashed parsnips or carrots, and always rice pudding for dessert. The *jule-nisse*, the elusive, red-capped, Christmas farm elf, is remembered and given his own bowl of rice pudding to ensure good luck in the coming year. After dinner, the family sings Christmas carols, dances round the Christmas tree, opens presents and eats marzipan and biscuits with coffee.

Below: Traditional Christmas candles are lit in many Danish homes on 23 December, which is Lille Julaften or 'little Christmas Eve'.

THE SCANDINAVIAN KITCHEN

The traditional foods of Norway, Sweden and Denmark share many similarities. Historically, an extreme climate has led to a cultural emphasis on the need to preserve and store the fresh produce obtained in the warmer months in order to make it last throughout the cold winter. Scandinavians make the most of the fruits and vegetables that flourish in the summer, as well as the fresh fish and shellfish that thrive in the seas, lakes and rivers, and the top-quality meat and game of the region.

FISH AND SHELLFISH

A quick glance at any map will show why the people of Norway, Sweden and Denmark are so reliant on fish as a major part of their diet. Norway's crinkly coastline, dotted with islands, faces the cold Norwegian Sea for hundreds of kilometres (miles), right up through the Arctic Circle; Sweden's slightly smoother outline curves round from the North Sea into the shallow waters of the Baltic; and Denmark sits firmly in the North Sea, a small peninsula of land almost completely surrounded by water. The fishermen from all three countries have traditionally provided food for their families and communities throughout the year, and during the worst of the winter gales, when it is not possible to go to sea, careful housekeepers can still make a good meal from preserved fish that has been salted, smoked, pickled or dried. Traditional fish recipes abound in Scandinavia – this is a part of the culinary heritage that is still enjoyed in many homes.

SEA FISH

The common sea fish such as cod, herring and plaice grow slowly in the cold waters around Scandinavia, reaching their full size only after several years. These fish form part of the staple

Below: Herring is salted as one of the many ways to preserve it – a useful ingredient for thrifty Scandinavian cooks.

Above: Cod is found in the cold waters around the coast of Norway, and is eaten fresh, dried and salted.

diet of the people in all three countries, especially now that they have good transport links and refrigeration. Every coastal town has its favourite recipe for fish soup, made with varying amounts of white fish, oily fish, shellfish, stock, cream and herbs – combining whatever is available from the sea as well as seasonal produce from the garden.

Herring

This medium-sized oily fish is the king of the kitchen, especially in Sweden where the eastern coastline touches the Baltic Sea, a prime fishing ground for this species. Herring is often marinated in vinegar and herbs and then grilled (broiled) or fried and served with potatoes for a balanced meal. But cooked herring is also served cold as part of an appetizer or an open sandwich for lunch, or raw and pickled, with a sliced onion garnish. It has a particular affinity with mustard, which cuts through the slightly greasy texture, and in Scandinavia it is often chased down into the stomach by a thimbleful of aquavit to cleanse the palate.

Cod

While the Swedes and Danes love herring best, the Norwegians focus on cod. This plain, firm-textured white fish is found all round the Norwegian coast, where it thrives in the cold waters. Its subtle flavour means that it blends well with all kinds of other ingredients, particularly dill and cream sauces, but also with delicate vegetables such as asparagus. Unfortunately over-fishing has meant that cod is becoming scarcer

Above: Smoked salmon is a much-loved food in the cuisines of Norway, Denmark and Sweden.

and more expensive. Dried and salted cod is still popular in Norway, although it is an acquired taste to those not brought up on this very stiff, salty, strong-flavoured ingredient.

Salmon

Sea and river salmon are plentiful near the sea coast. They enter the Norwegian fjords and the clear waters of Danish and Swedish rivers to spawn around the time of the summer solstice, when the days in the far north are almost endless. Salmon can be eaten freshly cooked, with cream sauce or accompanied by shellfish such as prawns (shrimp), but the best known product both locally and for export is smoked salmon. The traditional methods of smoking over juniper twigs or pine chips add a distinctive flavour. Thinly cut slices of this tasty pinky-orange fish make the most delicious appetizers, open sandwiches and buffet canapés. A squeeze of lemon cuts through the oily texture and a sprinkling of dill or parsley enhances the flavour. All three countries also have their own version of marinated salmon, known as gravlax (literally, buried salmon), which consists of salmon fillets marinated in salt, sugar and chopped dill for a couple of days, then served sliced, with a sharp mustard and dill sauce.

Above: Crayfish are caught in the rivers and lakes of Sweden, and are traditionally eaten in August and September.

Other sea fish

There are many other varieties of white fish to be found in the teeming waters that surround Scandinavia. Haddock and ling are beginning to rival cod in popularity; mackerel, turbot, plaice and zander are plentiful; and even little sprats are caught and cooked whole, blended with a dish of potatoes, onions and cream in the delightfully named Jansson's Temptation. The people of the seaside towns would normally eat the fish whole, with its head on, freshly grilled or fried and simply topped with melted butter and a few herbs. Further inland, creamy sauces are more popular, making a small amount of fish go further by using dairy produce to eke out the precious protein in the meal.

SHELLFISH

The shallow waters around the coast of Scandinavia are filled with prawns, mussels, crabs and lobsters. These

Fish roe

Scandinavian cooks love to use up all the edible parts of the fish they have caught. The eggs of cod, trout and salmon are eaten fresh and smoked, and are a particular favourite with children for their salty taste. The orange roe of the whitefish lojrom, is as prized in Sweden as caviar is in Russia.

shellfish are becoming more popular as the larger white fish decline in numbers. Crabs and lobsters are sometimes cooked and eaten at the quayside an hour or two after they were swimming, washed down with a glass of beer. Prawns can be found both in the coastal waters and in the more protected fjords, where they are caught while very small; these tiny shellfish are considered to have the best flavour.

RIVER FISH

The salmon that leave the coastal waters to leap upriver in the summer are not the only fish to live at least part of the year away from the sea. Scandinavian rivers are clean and fast-running, and the lakes are deep and cold. These are ideal conditions for large river fish such as pike, trout and carp to grow to maturity. Eels also thrive in these waters; they are usually smoked before being sliced into rings and served with potatoes and a creamy sauce. Crayfish grow to a good size and make an excellent cold dish, poached and marinated in beer and herbs, then served with cheese studded with caraway seeds.

Below: The beautiful orange colour and large eggs of salmon roe make it an ideal garnish for many Swedish dishes.

Using a fish kettle

Poaching is a classic method of cooking whole salmon or trout.

1 Remove the metal insert from the fish kettle and place the salmon on this. Lower the salmon into the kettle. Pour over cold-bouillon, fish stock or water to cover the fish.

2 Add a few fresh herbs, such as parsley, dill or tarragon. Lay slices of lemon on top of the fish, if you like.

3 Cover the fish with buttered baking parchment, place the pan over a medium heat and heat slowly until the water just begins to tremble. Simmer until the fish is opaque.

MEAT, GAME AND POULTRY

The basic daily diet in Scandinavia is beautifully described by a Swedish word, *husmanskost*, meaning hearty home cooking, using whatever ingredients used to be available in the countryside to provide balanced meals for the family. Meat, game and poultry are a central part of *husmanskost*. As in most European countries, in past centuries families supported themselves in the villages by growing vegetables and fruit, hunting and foraging in the forests, raising one or two animals in a small pasture for meat and dairy produce, and keeping some chickens for their eggs in the back yard. Of course, no meat must be wasted, as it was the main source of protein, particularly in the winter. Every part of a carcass was turned into a delicious meal, including the offal and the bones. Scandinavian cooks also have access to the fantastic sources of game that roam the wild acres of northern Sweden and Norway.

FARMED MEAT

Until the 19th century, Scandinavian farms tended to be small peasant holdings, even in the south where the climate is kind. Only when grain began to be imported from North America in the 1800s did the farmers expand their lands and herds of livestock, as they could now feed the animals more cheaply.

Below: An inexpensive cut of meat, pork belly is turned into delicious recipes.

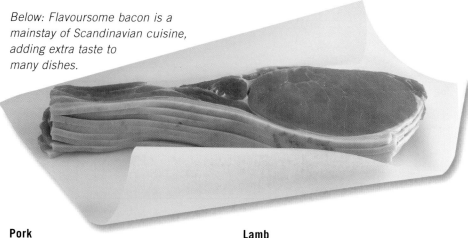

Below: Flavoursome bacon is a mainstay of Scandinavian cuisine, adding extra taste to many dishes.

Pork

This remains the most popular meat in traditional Scandinavian cuisine, although other meats are fast catching up. It is a staple ingredient, particularly in the form of cured ham, bacon and a range of delicious sausages. The Danes are especially fond of thin pork sausages rather like frankfurters, which they tend to eat as a snack bought from a van or stall on the street and served in a white bread roll, with plenty of mustard, ketchup or remoulade sauce. Swedish sausages come in many varieties, from those that resemble salami with large chunks of meat and fat, to the unique sausage known as *isterband*, which contains oatmeal as well as pork. This is usually poached first, then grilled (broiled). Swedish cooks thriftily use all the major pork cuts, from roast joints, through casseroled belly strips, to the delicacies made with pig's cheeks, such as a terrine mixed with foie gras. Minced (ground) pork is very popular, on its own or in combination with minced beef and veal, as part of the vast repertoire of well-seasoned home-made meatballs or meat loaf enjoyed for family meals.

Beef

The southern part of Norway and Sweden contains rich pasture land in the valleys, and this is now home to herds of cattle raised for their milk as well as for beef. The best quality steak may appear raw on an open sandwich, as beef tartare, while lesser cuts are usually minced and made into meatballs or a tasty stuffing mixture for cabbage.

Lamb

While cattle need to be protected from the weather in the lower-lying valleys of Scandinavia, the hardier sheep and goats are free to roam on the moorlands and higher slopes of the hills in the summer, and are brought back down to the villages in the winter. Some are even taken out on to the northern islands for summer grazing, where they can munch the rich green grass and develop meat with an exceptional flavour. Lamb is cooked in all sorts of ways, from prime Danish roasts to time-honoured stews such as the Norwegian classic *farikal* (literally, 'sheep in cabbage'), which is simply lamb on the bone, braised for hours with cabbage and peppercorns to allow the meat to become meltingly tender.

Below: Meatballs, a famous Scandinavian dish, can be made with beef, veal or pork.

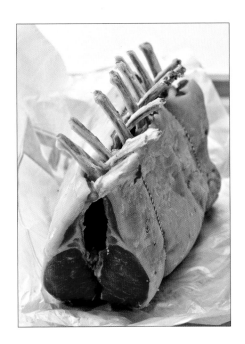

Above: Succulent lamb ribs are roasted by Scandinavian cooks to create dishes such as Easter Rack of Lamb.

POULTRY

Scandinavian cooks tend not to eat much poultry, mainly because they prefer to make egg dishes rather than chicken dishes and it seems a waste to eat the source of eggs. However, duck and goose are popular, especially for celebration dinners at a wedding or a religious festival such as Christmas dinner. Like pheasants and other wild birds, they are often served stuffed with berries and herbs, and accompanied by a tart lingonberry conserve.

GAME

From the elk that wander wild and free over the northern wildernesses to the hare and grouse that hide in the forests, Scandinavia is full of game. This rich source of food has always been used to make warming casseroles in winter. Game meat tends to taste very strong, and is well matched by a dark gravy, often containing tart juniper berries, fruity lingonberries or little red cranberries from the woods to spice up the flavour.

Game birds

Grouse, ptarmigan, quail and pheasant are usually served whole, roasted or poached in a creamy sauce and stuffed with forest fruits and plenty of herbs. These birds have a great flavour in the autumn, after a summer feeding on berries has made them plump.

Reindeer

These small deer are a particular favourite in Scandinavian cuisine. The Sami people of northern Sweden and Norway still keep reindeer in herds and drive them from winter enclosures to summer pastures every year, accompanied by the whole family. This nomadic life is maintained today with the help of powered sledges and computers. Reindeer meat makes a great strong-tasting stew or hearty soup, and a delicious terrine blended with caraway-flavoured aquavit and juniper berries.

Left: Today duck has replaced goose as the traditional Christmas Eve dish in Denmark.

Above: Venison fillets are cured and flavoured with fresh herbs to create top-quality carpaccio.

A taste of wild meat
• Venison is the name given to any deer meat, which can be roe deer, red deer, fallow deer, reindeer or elk (moose). The flesh is dark red and lean, and has a gamey flavour.
• Reindeer is a variety of deer that is usually kept in herds by nomadic Scandinavian farmers. Reindeer flesh can be eaten fresh or dried. It is sometimes also preserved by delicate salting and cold smoking.
• Elk (moose) is another member of the deer family, which roams wild over the moorlands of northern Norway and Sweden. The meat contains very little fat, but has a rich, fine flavour that differs from other types of venison. It is hunted in the autumn months and generally eaten in winter, between November and March.
• The most sought-after wild meat delicacies in Scandinavia are reindeer heart, elk thigh and smoked elk heart.

DAIRY PRODUCE AND EGGS

In a land so plentifully provided with green pastures, rolling hills and fresh, clean air, it is no surprise that dairy produce has always been a natural food resource for the people of Scandinavia. There is little space in these hilly, cold countries to grow cereals such as wheat and barley, which really need wide, flat, sunny fields to be economically viable, but every small farm perched on a hillside is capable of supporting a couple of cows or goats in a small paddock near the house. In days gone by, these animals provided enough milk to make cream, sour cream, butter and cheese for the whole family. Scandinavian dairy products are among the most diverse in the world, with hundreds of varieties of cheese and other milk products to choose from, and the cooks of Scandinavia certainly make the most of this rich resource.

FRESH AND SOURED MILK

In the past, most people relied on preserved dairy produce, and drinking fresh milk was a rare pleasure enjoyed mainly by those living in the countryside. Most of the milk produced for people in the towns would need to be turned into

Below: Skimmed and semi-skimmed milk, and whipped and single cream are used in many sweet and savoury recipes.

sour cream, butter or cheese to extend its keeping qualities. Some was also transformed into delicious sharp-tasting drinks with the addition of bacterial cultures to make a thick, yogurt-type soured milk drink such as Swedish filmjolk or filbunke, or Norwegian blande. These traditional drinks are still popular throughout Scandinavia today.

FRESH CREAM

Although people in Scandinavia are very fond of the taste of soured milk products, fresh cream has its place in many traditional recipes. Savoury dishes use cream as the basis for delicious sauces which seem to blend particularly well with the sharp fishy tang of anchovies, the smoky flavour of strong bacon, or the richness of game. Jansson's Temptation, a favourite Swedish dish consisting of a mound of grated potatoes and onions mixed with chopped anchovies and bound with thick cream, is a tasty example.

Many sweet puddings only reach perfection with the typical Scandinavian pouring sauce, vanilla cream sauce. This is liberally added to apple cake or baked fruit with almond

Above: Sour cream, and the lighter crème fraîche, are used in many recipes, from soups and salads to sauces and desserts.

topping, where its bland flavour complements the sharp, spicy fruit mixture. Whipped thick cream is also found as an integral part of many puddings and cakes, particularly the ones made for special celebrations such as birthdays, christenings or religious festivals.

SOUR CREAM

In common with the cooks of many northern European countries, Scandinavian people use a lot of sour cream in their savoury recipes. A typical Danish potato salad is made with an equal mixture of mayonnaise and sour cream, which lightens the dressing and blends beautifully with dill as the main herb flavouring. Rich game dishes from Norway, such as stuffed roast pheasant, really benefit from the slightly astringent flavour of sour cream in the gravy. And a full-flavoured soup such as the Swedish recipe using chanterelles needs the light touch of sour cream or crème fraîche (a lighter version of sour cream, which is more popular in today's health-conscious world) to lighten the woody flavour of the mushrooms.

BUTTER

Denmark is the country most immediately associated with best quality butter. Here butter is churned from cultured cream, rather than sweet cream, and has a low water content, making it ideal for cooking. Danish butter is made from the milk produced in spring and summer, when the pastures are at their

Above: Mild-tasting Greve is a favourite cheese in Sweden.

Above: Jarlsberg is probably Norway's most famous cheese.

richest, and it has an incredibly fresh flavour. Butter is used throughout Scandinavia every day – spread on bread, melted over a piece of fresh salmon with dill, blended into soup, or forming part of a rich bread or pastry dough.

CHEESE

There is a huge variety of cheeses in Denmark, Sweden and Norway. Many of these originate from times when making cheese was the only way to preserve dairy produce through the winter. They vary from the really fresh, soft white cheese so popular for breakfast in Sweden to the baked, caramelized, strongly flavoured Norwegian Mysost (also known in Sweden as Mesost), made from the heated and stored whey of cow's or goat's milk. Between these extremes of colour and strength lies a range of fantastic traditional cheeses, preserved as local specialities and also exported abroad.

Swedish cheese tends to focus more on the semi-soft varieties, but one favourite hard cheese is known as

Vasterbotten, which is similar to a strong Cheddar and can be used for cooking. Many other cheeses grace the Swedish table, such as Hushallsost, a semi-hard cheese with a slightly sour taste, and Greve, which is sweet and mild. Swedish cheeses also frequently contain spices, such as cloves, caraway or cumin seeds.

Denmark is best known for its strong-flavoured blue cheeses, but there are plenty of others, ranging from soft to firm, including mild, Swiss-style Samsø; firm-textured, buttery tasting Danbo; semi-soft, pungent Esrom; Havarti with its network of tiny holes; and mellow-tasting Tybo, which sometimes contains caraway seeds. In Denmark cheese is seen as worthy of a separate course on its own after dinner, or as an integral part of the open sandwich for lunch, and is rarely used as part of a main course.

Most people associate Norway with Jarlsberg, a mild, creamy cheese similar to Swiss Emmenthal, or with dark brown Mysost, but there are plenty of other local varieties, from blue-veined Gammelost to Graddost, a soft white creamy cheese often used for the famous open sandwiches.

EGGS

Danish farmers proclaim the logic of eating eggs rather than chickens. Why kill and eat the bird if its product can provide them with an income? Both raw and cooked eggs feature in a wealth of Scandinavian recipes. Something of the eastern European fondness for hard-boiled eggs as a garnish in savoury dishes persists in these northern countries – for example, chopped hard-boiled eggs are mixed with butter and prawns to garnish a baked stuffed turbot, or the hard-boiled yolks are mashed with butter to make tasty little butterballs that sit on top of a bowl of steaming nettle soup, melting gently into the dark green liquid. Raw

egg yolks can be balanced precariously on raw beef for a special beef tartare open sandwich, or sit in their carefully broken shells in the centre of a Norwegian salad, ready to be mixed into the cold vegetables as a dressing. It is important to remember that raw eggs should not be served to children, the elderly, pregnant women, convalescents or anyone suffering from an illness. The eggs must be as fresh as possible.

Testing eggs for freshness
Raw eggs feature in some Scandinavian recipes, so these should always be as fresh as possible. You can check how fresh an egg is without breaking it first, by placing the egg in a glass of cold water.

If the egg is fresh, it will sink to the bottom of the glass as it only contains a small air sac and is therefore heavy.

The older the egg, the larger the air sac. An old egg will therefore be lighter and more buoyant at the blunt end of the egg that contains the air sac.

VEGETABLES

A broad array of vegetables are used in Scandinavian cooking. They add vital nutrients to warming soups and are prepared in all sorts of sumptuous ways to accompany roasted meats.

The Scandinavian diet used to contain only a few staple vegetables, as the climate made vegetable farming difficult and the soil was not rich enough to support large-scale production. Foodstuffs that could be harvested for free, such as nettles and mushrooms, were a useful source of vitamin C and made tasty soups, but these ingredients had their limitations and were not always available to everyone in the towns. Also, while mushrooms can be dried for use out of season, nettle soup needs the fresh growing tips for the best flavour.

However, the soil has been vastly improved since the 19th century, particularly in Denmark, where the focus of farming shifted from small local plots to animal husbandry on a grand scale. The resulting manure made excellent fertilizer and helped farmers to grow all kinds of fresh vegetables whenever the weather and day length permitted.

Many traditional Scandinavian recipes contain root crops, which flourish in the naturally cool conditions and provide great sustenance for hungry families. Grated or mashed vegetables are even added to many breads and crispbreads, not only for the extra fibre they provide, but also to lighten the dough. Potato starch is particularly good in bread

Below: Many varieties of potatoes are used in Scandinavian cooking.

Above: Potatoes, carrots and onions are fundamental to many warming winter dishes in Scandinavia.

dough – just a little mashed potato and its cooking liquid makes a wonderfully open loaf – and the typical Norwegian flatbread, lefse, is made simply from mashed potatoes with butter and cream, beaten with flour and cooked like a pancake on a griddle.

POTATOES

The potato did not arrive in Scandinavia until the 18th century, even though it had become established as a common food in other European countries in the 16th and 17th centuries. Its adoption as a main crop was encouraged by the Danish royal family, and it was first planted in the Royal Botanical Garden in 1642, but it was

not grown on a commercial scale until the 1720s. It did not take long for potatoes to be grown on most farms, and their popularity spread quickly throughout all of the Scandinavian countries, to the extent that no evening meal is now considered to be complete without a hearty helping of potatoes somewhere on the plate.

Some of the most well-known dishes from this region focus on potatoes as the base for other ingredients, where their bland taste and soft texture absorb stronger flavours. One famous example – the recipe many people think of when Swedish cooking is mentioned – is Jansson's Temptation. This dish consists of grated potatoes in a milk and cream stock, blended with Swedish anchovies and baked in the oven until meltingly tender. The tiny fish known as Swedish anchovies are in fact sprats, not the salty anchovies produced elsewhere, and their flavour is not overpowering. Jansson's Temptation is served for dinner, as part of a smörgåsbord, or as a late-night supper with a glass of aquavit.

Scandinavian cooks are particular about the variety of potatoes used for each recipe. Small, firm-textured new potatoes are ideal for potato salad, often served with herring on an open sandwich. The best are reckoned to be from Samso, a small island now proudly self-sufficient in energy that sits off the east coast of Denmark in a sheltered part of Kattegat Bay, the sea that surrounds Denmark's eastern shores. Samso is renowned for its early crop of these delicate vegetables. The firm new varieties would not do for mashed potatoes, though – for this the cook needs floury varieties that can be beaten to a smooth purée. Grated potatoes, in contrast, need a certain firmness of texture so that they do not disintegrate when cooked.

One delicious variant on the roast potatoes that often accompany a joint of meat is known as hasselback potatoes. This is made from

Above: Hasselback potatoes are a favourite accompaniment.

medium-sized potatoes that are sliced almost to the base, but not quite cut through. They are then roasted in butter, and topped with breadcrumbs and sometimes also with finely grated cheese for the last few minutes of cooking. The slices open out like a fan and absorb the tasty buttery crumbs.

The Scandinavian potato crop is carefully regulated, with about a third of the total crop going to the shops; about a half being processed into potato flour for baking; and the remainder being preserved as seed potatoes for the next year's harvest.

OTHER ROOT VEGETABLES

The best vegetables for keeping well during the long, dark winter are root vegetables. Before refrigeration, some varieties could be left in the ground until they were needed – the flavour of parsnips, for example, is actually improved by frost – but most would be lifted and stored in a dry, dark place, protected from frost.

Turnips and swede (rutabaga) used to be the mainstay of many a soup and casserole in Scandinavian countries, and they are also cooked as classic accompaniments to meat or fish dishes, often mashed with butter.

Left: Carrots are a staple ingredient in many soups and stews.

Above: Leeks may be served as a side dish, star on a Danish open sandwich, or accompany Norwegian pickled herrings.

Above: Beetroot is perfect with game dishes.

To some extent they were supplanted by potatoes when these became popular in Sweden, Norway and Denmark; however their slightly bitter taste is still valued and their nutritional qualities are prized. Mashed swede is most delicious when mixed with other root vegetables such as potato or parsnip, beaten with fresh Danish butter and sprinkled with a little allspice, salt and pepper to liven it up.

Other root vegetables popular in Scandinavia include carrots, onions, beetroot (beets) and leeks. The rich, sweet flavour and bright colour of beetroot shines through in game dishes, and this vegetable is often preserved in vinegar and eaten cold. The so-called Italian salad that often accompanies cold meat on an open sandwich in Denmark is based on cooked carrots chopped into small chunks, mixed with peas and coated in mayonnaise. Onions are the main flavouring in many stews, but are great served raw, sliced into rings, with pickled herring and a white roll or slice of rye bread and butter.

Below: Swede can form the basis of a casserole, or be served as an accompaniment to a meat dish.

Left: Broccoli can be grown in Denmark and the warmer areas of Norway and Sweden.

Below: Asparagus is celebrated when it comes into season each year.

GREEN VEGETABLES

Once agriculture began to be developed and diversified in Scandinavia, the sturdy potato, swede (rutabaga) and turnip were no longer the only vegetables on the menu. Well-fertilized smallholdings were able to produce good crops of salad vegetables such as lettuce, tomatoes and cucumber, either during the summer or under glass. The southern parts of Sweden and Norway get enough summer sunshine and warm weather for the farmers to grow viable crops of green and red cabbage, broccoli, kale, cauliflower, corn, spinach and peas, while Denmark basks in relative warmth and people's gardens and fields overflow with all kinds of fresh vegetables. The growing season is still short, though – thick snow means

Below: Red cabbage is braised to make a traditional Danish side dish.

that the fields have to be left fallow for several months every year, unlike in warmer countries, where it would be possible to grow winter crops.

Asparagus

The king of early summer vegetables, asparagus is prized as a great delicacy in Scandinavia. It can only be harvested for a few weeks, but during the asparagus season it will appear on every menu. The subtle, unusual taste and juicy texture of asparagus lends itself particularly well to chicken or fish dishes, such as Fish for a Prince, where delicate poached white fish in cream sauce is garnished with the tender green spears, showing their contrasting colour and flavour to best advantage. In its simplest form, and to make the most of its natural taste, asparagus needs only a dressing of melted butter and a squeeze of lemon juice to make a perfect accompaniment to any main course.

Salad vegetables

Lettuce, cucumber and tomatoes are generally grown with some protection in Scandinavia – these days it will be under glass or poly-tunnels, or perhaps just horticultural fleece or a cloche in domestic gardens, except in the height of summer. However, these tender crops are an integral part of many meals, so they are now imported in winter. At

lunchtime, they come into their own as garnishes for open sandwiches. Tomatoes are often eaten raw rather than cooked as part of a stew or casserole, so that the fresh flavour and firm texture can be enjoyed and appreciated fully. Sliced cucumber is usually served in a sharp, fat-free dressing made of vinegar, sugar and dill that is similar to one found in many northern European countries.

MUSHROOMS

These earthy fungi are indigenous to the Scandinavian countryside, and the woods and fields of all three countries are bursting with wild mushrooms in late summer and autumn. Families love to go on foraging parties to harvest mushrooms, berries and nuts, and the best spots for finding them are jealously guarded secrets. If anyone is in doubt about the edibility of what they have found, there are checkpoints where the experts will tell you which ones to eat and which to leave alone.

All the well-known varieties of edible mushroom are found in the Scandinavian forests, from the common

Below: In Denmark, crisp cucumber is simply dressed with distilled white vinegar, sugar and fresh dill.

Left: Wonderfully flavoursome porcini mushrooms are dried to be used all year round in a variety of recipes.

PICKLES, COMPOTES AND DRYING

One way to preserve vegetables and make sure that everyone gets some vitamin C during the winter is to pickle them in vinegar. Classic pickles include beautiful dark red beetroot (beets), which makes a splendid and colourful open sandwich garnish; fermented cabbage, the typical sauerkraut mixture found in many northern countries; pickled cucumber; and pickled red or white onions. Mixed pickles are very popular too, often dressed in a yellow-coloured liquid with turmeric and other spices. The sharp taste of a fresh compote of red onions, berries or apples goes well with a plain meat or game dish, although this kind of mixture would not be stored for the winter, but eaten within a few days.

Drying vegetables and legumes is another way to preserve all the goodness for the cold seasons. Dried peas and beans are often added to

chanterelles and porcini to the most fragrant truffles. People tend to eat them simply sliced and cooked lightly in butter to accompany a really good steak. Mushrooms also make an excellent sandwich with a strong liver pâté, or can be served simply on their own in rich cream and onion sauce. They also match the strong taste of a game stew and add to the dark colour of the cooking liquid. Sweden's woodlands are the source of so many porcini mushrooms that many tons of them are exported all over the world each year.

Below: Pickling vegetables, such as gherkins, is a tasty way of preserving them for the winter months.

Below: Pickled beetroot is a famous Scandinavian classic – its stunning colour makes an attractive side dish.

Using dried mushrooms
A useful stand-by ingredient, dried mushrooms have a rich and intense flavour.

To reconstitute dried mushrooms, soak them in boiling water for 20–30 minutes, depending on the size and variety of the musroom, until they are tender. Drain the mushrooms in a sieve (strainer) or colander, and rinse them thoroughly to remove any trace of grit or dirt. Dried mushrooms often require a longer cooking time than fresh mushrooms.

stews and soups, but really come into their own in a famous yellow pea soup made in all three countries with slight variations, depending on what local ingredients are available. The Danes make theirs with whole dried peas rather than split peas, which makes the cooking process longer, but they maintain that it gives a better result. Yellow pea soup really needs the flavour of a ham bone simmered in the stock, or some bacon added to the mixture, to give it the required meaty flavour. A spoonful of horseradish cream, stirred into the bowl at the last minute, spices the soup. The Swedes might eat it accompanied by a glass of thick, sweet punsch, the liqueur based on Indian spices, as a complete contrast to the uncompromisingly earthy savoury taste.

Dried mushrooms taste different from fresh ones, but no less delicious. They are easy to reconstitute, and can be used just as they are in liquid dishes such as soups and stews.

FRUITS, NUTS AND WILD BERRIES

From the wild uplands of northern Norway to the gently rolling southern fields of Denmark, many different fruits, nuts and berries grow. Orchards of apples, pears and cherries abound in the warmer valleys of Denmark and southern Sweden, while the forests and hills of northern Norway and Sweden are home to many varieties of berry. The climate may be cold near the Arctic Circle, but the extra-long daylight hours of summer serve to ripen these wild berries to perfection, and they are prized ingredients in the Scandinavian diet. There is such a great choice of fruit and nuts that very few are imported, apart from coconut, which has become a favourite since its introduction via the trading links with India.

All kinds of fruit and nuts are used in both sweet and savoury recipes. The tart flavour of a fruity conserve matches either the blandness of white fish or the gamey taste of venison, while the same conserve may be added to creamy desserts such as rice pudding as a complete contrast, to cut through the richness. Fruits such as rhubarb, with its astringent taste, can also be pickled as a semi-sweet mixture that beautifully complements oily fish such as

Below: Apples and prunes are stuffed into a goose or duck, and roasted for a traditional Danish Christmas Eve dinner.

Below: Pears are baked in Sweden for a delicious fruity dessert.

Above: Cherry orchards flourish in the warmer climate of Denmark as well as southern Norway and Sweden.

mackerel, or with sugar added, it forms the basis of a sweet dessert made with fresh cream.

ORCHARD FRUITS

Apples, pears and cherries grow well in the southern parts of Scandinavia. The pear crop is not heavy and the fruits tend to be rather small, but they have a superb flavour and firm texture that is ideal for eating fresh or baking. Scandinavian cooks tend to use sweetish eating apples for their desserts, as these hold their shape well and do not need too much sugar.

In savoury dishes, apples make a wonderfully tart accompaniment. They can be simply sliced and fried with pork, or added to a fruity stuffing for a roast joint or a Christmas ham. Chopped apples are an integral part of a colourful dish of baked red cabbage, which is a favourite side dish to be eaten with meat or fish. A typical Norwegian savoury fruit soup is based mainly on apples as the bulk of the recipe, with cardamom and cinnamon-flavoured stock and juniper berries for a really distinctive taste of Norway.

BERRIES

From the first June raspberries to the wild fruits of the autumn hedgerows, berries are eagerly anticipated and treasured. Cultivated fruits such as raspberries and strawberries have their place in the culinary repertoire, but Scandinavian cuisine really comes into its own with the autumn wild berry harvest. Everyone has a favourite spot

for a berry-picking expedition, and it is a pleasant ritual for families to go off into the fields and woods in late summer and early autumn, returning home laden with baskets of blueberries, cranberries, bilberries, lingonberries and even the elusive and delicate cloudberries if they are lucky enough to find some. The law allows everyone to pick fruits, mushrooms and flowers growing wild, so long as they respect the countryside and other people's property.

Freezing fruit
If there is a glut of berries, you can freeze them for using at other times of the year.

Remove the stalks and leaves, then place the berries on a baking sheet in a single layer. Place in the freezer until the berries are frozen. Once frozen, transfer to a freezer-proof container or bag. Defrost thoroughly before using.

Left: Fresh lingonberries are usually made into a delicious conserve to accompany meat courses.

Right: Blueberries are one of a mixture of fruits used to stuff pheasant in Norway.

but also accompanies more everyday meatballs made of pork or beef. Lingonberries are an important element in Scandinavian cooking, since they are so easy to preserve for the winter and provide an essential source of vitamin C. The conserve also helps to lighten and sharpen dishes that might otherwise come across as rather bland and heavy, such as stuffed cabbage or meat loaf.

Strawberries and raspberries

These fruits can be found growing in the forest, where tiny varieties of both can be gathered. The wild fruits are much smaller in size and their taste is much sharper than the farmed variety. Either wild or cultivated raspberries are ideal for the typical Danish dish of red berries with cream, although wild raspberries will need to be simmered with plenty of sugar. Both strawberries and raspberries are enjoyed during their summer season simply sprinkled with sugar, sometimes on their own, but more often as accompaniments to pancakes or as a luxurious filling for a sponge cake with fresh cream.

Lingonberries

These tiny firm berries grow wild in Norway and Sweden and are imported into Denmark and many other parts of the world. They are usually eaten in the form of lingonberry conserve, a tart and tasty mixture of lingonberries and sugar that goes well as a sauce with savoury dishes or to lighten a creamy dessert. The berries are so full of citric acid that they need no cooking – they are simply stirred with sugar and put straight into jars, where the mixture sets. Lingonberry conserve is served with wild meats such as elk (moose) or venison,

Cloudberries

These rare berries are only found in the north of Sweden and Norway. They resemble amber-coloured, fat raspberries, and grow one to a stalk. Their flavour is quite unique and they are highly prized throughout Scandinavia. When they are used for cooking rather than simply eaten fresh and raw with sugar, the focus tends to be on these precious berries as the main ingredient, for instance in a light and delicate cloudberry soufflé.

Other berries

Wild berries that grow in the countryside include cranberries, blueberries, blackberries, bilberries

Below: Cloudberries are rare, unique in flavour and highly-prized, and they feature in many special local desserts.

Above: Almonds star in a huge number of Scandinavian dishes, including both sweet and savoury recipes.

and rose hips from hedgerow roses. They all feature in Scandinavian dishes, often in savoury recipes as well as in desserts and cakes. These sharp berries can be used either fresh or dried all year round as part of a fruity stuffing for game such as pheasant, or to enliven a chicken or joint of lamb. They also shine in their own right in wild berry tart, where they are piled on top of a soft, buttery pastry base and served with cream, or as a refreshing compote to accompany waffles or pancakes.

NUTS

While nuts such as hazelnuts and walnuts are grown and eaten in Scandinavia, it is almonds that dominate the cuisine. Almonds figure in both sweet and savoury recipes in all their forms, from whole fresh nuts to roasted, blanched, sliced, chopped or ground nuts. They are also made into delicious marzipan paste with sugar and egg white. Marzipan is used both as a topping or filling for sweet cakes such as Danish pastries, and as a sweetmeat in its own right at Christmas and Easter.

HERBS, SPICES AND SEASONINGS

The food of Scandinavia can seem quite plain, dressed only with garden herbs such as parsley and dill, and relying on good quality fresh ingredients – fish, cheese, game and poultry, with seasonal vegetables – for its flavour. In Norway and Sweden, the main flavourings and spices grown locally are caraway seeds, juniper berries and horseradish, all of which thrive in the chilly climate. But in Denmark, there is a tradition of world exploration by sea and consequently trading links were set up many years ago, bringing exotic spices such as cinnamon and ginger, saffron and cardamom, as well as sugar from the Virgin Islands, a former Danish colony. These have spread to the whole of Scandinavia and now form an integral part of the cuisine.

HERBS, ROOTS AND BERRIES

Native plants such as juniper and horseradish are an unmissable part of the flavour of Scandinavia. These strongly flavoured, sometimes fiery condiments are added to many an otherwise bland dish, enlivening the sauce. But garden herbs such as simple parsley and thyme also have their place in the cuisine, and are used in abundance.

Below: Dill, the most classic flavouring of Scandinavian cuisine, is traditionally paired with gravlax.

Dill

This is perhaps the most typical flavouring of Scandinavian food. Dill is a member of the parsley family, and grows long, delicate green fronds that can be chopped and sprinkled on to fish or meat, or stirred into a cream sauce. Even the flowers can be used for marinating fish or shellfish. There are hundreds of recipes using dill, but it is perhaps at its best as a garnish for an open sandwich or in a salad with fish, since the feathery leaves are very decorative as well as having a unique taste.

Juniper berries

As in many northern European countries where game is traditionally on the menu, Scandinavian cooks like to use juniper berries to flavour the sauce for hare, venison, pheasant or other wild animals. They also like to add the young growing tips of the juniper tree to the stock for a well-flavoured soup or stew.

Garden herbs

Parsley, thyme, rosemary, bay leaves and chives all have their place in Scandinavian cuisine. The French tradition of bouquet garni – a bunch of mixed herbs, using whatever is fresh and seasonally available – has been adopted in many a Scandinavian soup or casserole recipe, such as the fragrant winter mushroom soup made with chanterelles from the Swedish woods.

Below: Curly parsley (left), chives (bottom) and bay leaves (right) are all used to add flavour to Scandinavian savoury dishes, such as soups, open sandwiches, casseroles and roasts.

Horseradish

This pretty plant with small white flowers is grown for its long, fleshy white root with its astringent taste. Horseradish root is simply grated, mixed with vinegar to stop it discolouring and turning bitter, and sometimes blended with cream to turn it into a subtler sauce.

SPICES AND SEASONINGS

Back in the days before regular trade with the warmer countries of Asia, cooks in Scandinavia relied mainly on caraway seeds to add zest to their bread and cheese. Nowadays many more fragrant spices have been added to the repertoire and have become firm Scandinavian favourites.

Below: Horseradish adds a strong flavour to sauces and soups.

Above: Caraway seeds (top) are the main flavour in aquavit. Small green and large black cardamom pods (bottom) are widely used in Scandinavian cooking.

Caraway seeds

The caraway plant grows wild in the countryside, wherever it can find a warm spot in the sun. The aniseed-flavoured seeds (actually the tiny fruits of the plant) crop up in many Scandinavian dishes, including rye bread, cheese, cabbage dishes, casseroles, and as the main flavouring for aquavit and other liqueurs.

Cardamom

Of all the imported spices, cardamom has been adopted with most enthusiasm in all three countries. Many recipes would be unthinkable without these little green pods which, when ground, impart their flavour to all kinds of baked goods, particularly cakes, biscuits (cookies) and bread.

Cinnamon

Like cardamom, cinnamon is imported from hotter countries, and helps to give a warm and exotic taste to biscuits and cakes. It has a particular affinity with fruit, and figures in many recipes for apple cake.

Cloves

These tiny dried flowers go well with strongly flavoured sauces such as mustard sauce, and are added to the liquid for Danish vegetable recipes such as pickled beetroot (beets) and cabbage. They can also be ground into powder and used in small quantities in the traditional Christmas ginger biscuits.

Ginger

Like cloves, ginger is used in all sorts of savoury and sweet recipes, such as lobster with tomato sauce, or the more homely baked apples with honey and ginger. It is always a warming and comforting spice, ideally suited to hot food for the long dark winter.

Honey and syrup

These natural ingredients used to be the only sweeteners available in Scandinavia before sugar was imported from the West Indies. Many desserts are flavoured with honey or corn syrup, used sparingly so that they are not over-sweet.

Mustard

This is a real staple of the Scandinavian kitchen. The peppery flavour of ground mustard and mustard seeds enlivens cream sauce for fish, and a mixture of mustard and chopped dill is the ideal condiment accompanying the marinated salmon dish, gravlax, or sliced herrings.

Below: A natural sweetener, honey is used in Scandinavian dessert recipes.

Above: Salt preserves fresh ingredients, such as the famous salted cod.

Peppercorns

Scandinavians tend to prefer white peppercorns to black. They are ground for a mild peppery flavour, or simmered whole in a game casserole, where their sharp taste is softened.

Salt

Although salt is ubiquitous in Scandinavian cooking, it is used more for preserving than for its flavour. Foods such as salted cod need to be soaked to remove much of the salt before cooking.

Vanilla

The long black vanilla pod (bean) with its fragrant taste and tiny black seeds is a vital part of the sweet vanilla sauce made with cream that accompanies many desserts. Vanilla also crops up in rice pudding, where it is used to flavour the milk, and in the vanilla sugar used to make pastries and cakes.

Vinegar

This is a very important condiment in Scandinavia, where fish and vegetables have traditionally been preserved in pickled form for eating in the winter. Vinegar is also used in salad dressings, and as part of the liquid for marinades to soften and flavour fish and meat.

BREADS AND BAKING

Bread is the traditional basis of most meals in Scandinavia, as it is in many other European countries. The daily ration begins at breakfast time, when most people eat a hearty helping of bread and butter with toppings of sweet spreads, cheese, cold meat or fish to start the day. Lunch is based on bread too, with the marvellous tradition of elaborate open sandwiches. At dinner time, while bread takes more of a back seat, it often appears on the table as an accompaniment in the form of a white roll with soup or as breadcrumbs topping a baked dish. Snacks throughout the day might be bread and jam with a cup of coffee, or a white roll with sausage.

CRISPBREAD

Historically, the Norwegians, battling with their rugged climate, had to work hard and plan ahead to provide food for the winter months. When the fresh grain ran out, they needed to invent a kind of bread that would keep right through the coldest season. Typical Norwegian hardbreads or crispbreads, which are now found in Sweden and Denmark too, are made of barley, rye or wheat flour from the autumn grain harvest baked in flat loaves, rusks or thin rectangles until they are firm and solid, with a crunchy

Below: Crispbreads come in many shapes, flavours, colours and textures.

Left: Swedish krisprolls are a type of crispbread often eaten for breakfast.

texture. The loaves are sometimes made into ring shapes with a hole through the centre so that they can be hung on sticks for storage. These Scandinavian crispbreads have now become popular all over the world and they are ideal for a quick snack at any time of the day. There are many varieties – rye, wheat or barley; made of wholewheat or refined flour; with spices or seeds such as cumin or caraway. The spiced versions blend well with the strong flavours of smoked eel and other smoked fish.

FLATBREAD

Norwegians are very fond of a semi-hard flatbread made simply from barley flour, salt and water. This unleavened bread can also be made of rye flour or a mixture of flours, with various ingredients such as grated root vegetables, sour cream or sugar added to the mixture. It is rolled out thinly before being cooked on a griddle or in a hot oven.

Other varieties of flatbread include one known in Norway as lefse. This used to be a favourite with fishermen, as it kept for weeks, and if it dried out on a long voyage it could be softened again by being wrapped in a damp cloth. Lefse is made with wheat flour and/or mashed potatoes as the main starch ingredient; the potato version is beautifully light. It is eaten with soft butter and a dusting of sugar or a spoonful of jam.

WHITE BREAD

Although people in Sweden and Norway eat white bread, it is the Danes who are most fond of light white bread and rolls, particularly for breakfast with jam or thin slices of chocolate, or for open

sandwiches based on fish or shellfish, where the delicate flavour might be swamped by a more gutsy dark rye slice. This mouth-watering white bread is known as franskbrod (French bread) in Denmark, a country where the influence of French cuisine and eating habits has been strong over the last few centuries.

RYE BREAD

The most common bread of the whole Scandinavian region is made from rye, a grain that grows well in the cold climate of these three countries. Rye bread can be made with sourdough (a flour and water mixture that contains wild yeast) as the raising agent, or with cultured yeast. Yeast is a by-product of brewing, and yeasted bread has become more popular since the 19th century with the development of the beer industry. Rye bread comes in many shades of brown, from light rye to the really rich dark wholegrain variety, but all have the distinct strong flavour that blends with savoury or sweet toppings and fresh butter. Rye bread is often sold ready sliced and carefully wrapped so that the moisture does not escape.

It is at lunchtime that really dark, moist rye bread comes into its own. Open sandwiches are a favourite lunch, especially in Denmark, where the range of toppings is staggering. Some involve a mixture of several kinds of meat, cheese or fish, garnished with salad leaves, onion rings, tomatoes and herbs. Other open sandwiches consist of one main element, such as pickled herring or shellfish, hard-boiled or scrambled eggs or cheese, always blending the primary ingredient with its garnish with great skill to appeal to both

Making an open sandwich

The Danes are famous for their open sandwiches. Using the simple starting point of a slice of humble rye bread spread with butter, they make many elaborate creations.

1 Start with a thin slice of firm rye bread and spread right to the edges with fresh salted butter.

2 Pretty green lettuce leaves are often used to separate the buttered bread from the topping.

3 The topping should completely cover the bread. Danish favourites include liver pâté, ham, roast pork, game, prawns (shrimp), pickled herring, potatoes, cheese and eggs.

the eye and the taste buds. A tasty slice of dark rye bread lends its solid flavour as the basis to the dish.

Swedish rye bread comes in a multitude of varieties, often with spices added such as cardamom, caraway, cumin, fennel and anise seeds, as well as dried fruit. One of the best known is called kavring, and contains allspice and caraway, which blends particularly well with flavoursome fish such as smoked salmon or smoked eel. The sweeter breads with dried fruit are known as limpa, or vort limpa for the stronger, darker variety. These are sweetened with molasses or honey, and the final touch is a sprinkling of grated orange rind. Despite their sweetness, these loaves make a splendid base for semi-savoury ingredients, such as soft white cheese, or even strongly savoury toppings, such as salted herring.

EVERYDAY CAKES AND BISCUITS

There are many delightful recipes from Sweden, Denmark and Norway for small cakes and biscuits (cookies), often flavoured with spices, that go well with morning or afternoon coffee. Bakers use a raising agent known as hartshorn or baker's ammonia, which is a by-product of the ground antlers of reindeer. The odour disappears during the baking process, and the resulting biscuits and pastries have a really light, fluffy texture.

Certain cookies and small cakes are favourites at particular times of year, especially Christmas: for example, little twists of sweetened dough blended with the mashed yolks of hard-boiled eggs and dipped in sugar, which are known as Berlin wreath biscuits and are a Danish seasonal classic.

YEAST BAKING

There is a longstanding tradition in Scandinavia of baking sweet goods with yeast, and Danish pastries are the most common cakes made with yeast dough. The basic mixture can be shaped and filled in hundreds of different ways – with fresh fruit, dried fruit, spices, almonds or almond paste, drizzled with icing, dusted with sugar, or filled with sweet cream.

Swedish cooks have their own recipes for yeast buns for special occasions, such as St Lucia buns, light twists of white dough flavoured with saffron, or the delightfully named Fat Tuesday buns, a rich mixture of sweetened dough filled with almond paste and cream to be enjoyed before the religious fasting season of Lent begins in February.

CELEBRATION CAKES

Scandinavian cooks love to make celebration cakes on a grand scale. Princess cake is a favourite for birthdays, and consists of a light sponge filled with cream and jam and completely covered with green-tinted marzipan. Tosca cake from Norway is a light and airy cake topped with an almond, cream and sugar mixture and then flashed under the grill (broiler) to turn the nuts a light brown colour.

Perhaps the most spectacular celebration cake is the one known as ring cake. This is made of a simple mixture of ground almonds and sugar, bound with egg whites and piped into rings of different sizes. When cooked and cooled, the rings are piled up from biggest to smallest to make a cone shape, and then drizzled with white icing in zigzags.

Below: Fresh yeast is used in many sweet baking recipes, such as Danish Pastry.

DRINKS

The dark, cold days of a northern winter need some special drinks, both alcoholic and non-alcoholic, to warm the population and provide good cheer. During the darkest months of the year, Scandinavian people have traditionally experimented with all sorts of warming drinks, from hot mulled wine and beer to the fierce spirit, aquavit, which is served very cold but soon warms the body from the inside. However, the attitude to alcoholic drinks remains ambivalent: Norway brought in complete prohibition at about the same time as the United States, from 1919 to 1927, leading to a vast increase in illegal alcohol production. Nowadays the state still supervises the production and sale of alcohol in Norway, and it tends to be quite expensive, in an attempt to control excessive drinking. Attitudes are more relaxed in Sweden and Denmark, although prices are still high compared to other European countries.

BEER

The tradition of brewing beer, particularly in Denmark, has grown from a local cottage industry to a country-wide operation during the last 200 years, and nowadays well-known brands of Danish beer such as Carlsberg are exported all over the world. But it is known that home-made beer was brewed here in pre-Christian times, and as well as being a thirst-quenching beverage that was safer to drink than water, it was linked with rituals such as harvest festivals and the celebration of the winter equinox. Hops were first grown to make beer in the 13th century, and in Denmark the first large-scale brewery was established in Copenhagen in 1454. The bitter taste of beer complements the flavours of Scandinavian cooking beautifully – a pale lager with a fishy open sandwich for lunch; a darker, thicker brew alongside a rich game casserole. Beer is linked in the minds of many Scandinavians with the fiery spirit, aquavit, and is drunk alternately with it as a soothing chaser during a long smörgåsbord meal.

AQUAVIT

The strong alcoholic spirit known as aquavit (water of life) is found in every Scandinavian country. It is known as akevitt in Norway, and akvavit in Denmark and Sweden. This fiercely alcoholic beverage is a clear or lightly tinted spirit distilled from potatoes or

Above: Aquavit is perhaps the most famous Scandinavian drink, popular in Norway, Denmark and Sweden.

grain, with the addition of herbs and spices such as caraway and cumin seeds to give it a distinctive flavour quite different from the relatively subtle Russian or Polish vodka. Again, as with the local beer, the rather astringent taste matches most Scandinavian food, cutting through the richness of meat and game dishes and highlighting the freshness of smoked fish. It is served in tiny glasses, and kept as cold as possible. In the days before refrigerators, it could be buried in a block of ice before serving. Aquavit is known to stimulate the appetite, and some people still consider it a cure for all ills.

In Norway a special kind of aquavit is made that arose from a lucky accidental discovery. When quantities of the spirit were exported to Australia in old sherry barrels, some were returned unsold. On opening them, the manufacturer discovered that the liquid inside had

Below: From left to right, Red Erik Ceres from Denmark, Spendrup Old Gold from Sweden and Ringnes from Norway.

Above: Coffee is an important part of the food and drink culture of Scandinavia.

turned golden and developed a superior flavour. These days some special Norwegian akevitt travels around the world, crossing the equator twice before being sold at a very high premium.

Aquavit is too highly prized to be drunk without due attention; however on occasion it can be mixed with the main ingredients of a dish to give a subtle kick to the final result, as in the classic recipe for reindeer terrine, which requires a small glass of this intensely flavoured spirit to be added at the initial mixing stage.

Below: A warming drink for cold winters, glögg is a Swedish Christmas classic.

OTHER ALCOHOLIC DRINKS

The climate of these chilly northern countries does not allow for cultivation of grape vines, even on the warmest south-facing slopes. However, in recent years wine has become more and more popular to drink with meals instead of beer, and large amounts are now imported into Scandinavia.

One traditional recipe that uses red wine as a base is the delicious Christmas drink, glögg, which was first made in Sweden and has been enthusiastically adopted by Danes and Norwegians as a winter warmer. It consists of generous quantities of red wine, with a splash or two of aquavit, and plenty of sweet spices such as cinnamon and cardamom. Raisins and sliced almonds are added to the brew. It is simmered on the stove in a large pan and served with small sweet cakes such as Danish doughnuts. It can also make a lovely Swedish dessert when set with gelatine and sugar, and served with cream that has been infused with cloves.

Other drinks have become popular in Scandinavia because of the links with trading partners in warmer parts of the world. One example is punsch, a liqueur that is mainly found in Sweden. This is an aromatic, sweet drink based on the Indian spice arrak. Traditionally punsch is served warm with yellow pea soup – a real case of East meets West.

OTHER SOFT DRINKS

These days bottled water has begun to be a feature of life in all European countries, and Sweden, Norway and Denmark are no exception. Bottled waters from the local fresh springs are delicious.

Fruit drinks, such as lingonberry and elderflower cordials, are a favourite with people of all ages in these nations of berry pickers.

Scandinavians drink very little tea compared with other Europeans – they tend to opt for herbal teas and generally do not add milk to their teas. However, since methods of preserving fresh milk have been developed in modern Scandinavia, many more children drink cold milk on its own throughout the day.

COFFEE

The vast majority of Scandinavians are serious coffee drinkers. It is the first thing they reach for in the morning, and punctuates the day until the last cup after dinner in the evening. It forms a big part of their social life too, with friends meeting for coffee and a pastry mid-morning or mid-afternoon. Coffee is often drunk black and strong by Scandinavians, especially when it accompanies a glass of aquavit or is consumed to settle the stomach after a big meal.

Below: Fruit drinks made from lingonberries or elderflowers are popular in Scandinavia.

SOUPS

Soups are perfect nourishment for the cold, often harsh, climate of Scandinavia. From clear broths that form an appetizer before a main course to hearty stew-like concoctions that constitute a meal in themslves, soups have long provided warmth and nutrition to Scandinavian families. Swedish soups are made with the freshest seasonal vegetables, Norwegian soups with local fish or reindeer and Danish soups may be finished off with a touch of cream — a reminder of Denmark's love of dairy products.

NETTLE SOUP WITH EGG BUTTERBALLS

THIS SWEDISH SOUP, KNOWN AS NÄSSELSOPPA, IS EXTREMELY NUTRITIOUS BUT AS NETTLES CANNOT BE FOUND ALL YEAR ROUND, YOU CAN USE SPINACH, WHICH WORKS EQUALLY WELL. THE USE OF NETTLES IS COMMON IN NORTHERN EUROPE, WHERE THEY GROW MORE PROLIFICALLY THAN IN HOTTER COUNTRIES.

SERVES SIX TO EIGHT

INGREDIENTS
  a knob (pat) of butter
  1 onion, roughly chopped
  225g/8oz nettles (top 4 leaves
    from each plant only) or young
    spinach leaves
  600ml/1 pint/2½ cups chicken stock
  30ml/2 tbsp sherry
  150ml/¼ pint/⅔ cup double
    (heavy) cream
  5ml/½ tsp freshly grated nutmeg
  salt and ground black pepper
For the butterballs
  115g/4oz/½ cup butter
  2 hard-boiled egg yolks
  salt and ground black pepper

1 First make the butterballs. Put the butter and hard-boiled egg yolks in a bowl and mash together. Season the mixture with salt and pepper to taste. Roll into balls approximately 2cm/1in in diameter and chill in the refrigerator until ready to serve.

2 To make the soup, melt the butter in a pan, add the chopped onion and fry until softened.

3 Add the nettles or spinach, stir in the stock and season with salt and pepper. Bring to the boil, then cook over a medium heat for 1 minute.

4 Pour the soup into a food processor and whiz until roughly chopped.

5 Return to the pan, add the sherry, stir in the cream and sprinkle with nutmeg. Heat gently until warm but do not allow the soup to boil. Serve in warmed bowls with the butterballs bobbing on the surface and just beginning to melt.

Per portion Energy 239kcal/982kJ; Protein 2g; Carbohydrate 1.5g, of which sugars 1.3g; Fat 24.5g, of which saturates 14.8g; Cholesterol 109mg; Calcium 68mg; Fibre 0.7g; Sodium 141mg.

JUNIPER AND APPLE SOUP

THIS NORWEGIAN DISH, EPLESUPPE MED ENERBÆR, IS AN EXAMPLE OF THE SAVOURY FRUIT SOUPS THAT ARE POPULAR THROUGHOUT NORTHERN EUROPE. THE APPLE AND JUNIPER FLAVOURS ARE PARTICULARLY NORWEGIAN. HERE IT IS THE BERRIES THAT ARE BEING USED, RATHER THAN THE FRESH YOUNG SHOOTS.

SERVES FOUR

INGREDIENTS
15ml/1 tbsp juniper berries
4 cardamom pods
3 whole allspice
1 small cinnamon stick
bunch of fresh parsley
30ml/2 tbsp olive oil
3 cooking apples, peeled,
  cored and diced
2 celery sticks, finely chopped
2 shallots, chopped
2.5cm/1in piece fresh root ginger,
  finely chopped
1 litre/1¾ pints/4 cups light
  chicken stock
250ml/8fl oz/1 cup (hard) cider
250ml/8fl oz/1 cup double
  (heavy) cream
75ml/5 tbsp Armagnac (optional)
salt and ground black pepper
chopped fresh parsley, to garnish

1 Put the juniper berries, cardamom pods, allspice and cinnamon stick in a piece of muslin (cheesecloth) and tie together with string. Tie the bunch of parsley together with string by the stalks.

2 Heat the olive oil in a pan with a lid, then add the prepared apples, celery, shallots and ginger, and season with salt and pepper.

3 Place a piece of dampened baking parchment on top, cover the pan with a lid and cook gently for 10 minutes. Discard the baking parchment.

4 Add the stock and cider and stir well. Add the bunches of spices and parsley. Bring slowly to the boil, then lower the heat and simmer for 40 minutes.

5 Remove and discard the bunches of mixed spices and parsley, then pour the soup into a blender or food processor and blend or process until it is smooth.

6 Pass the blended soup through a sieve (strainer) into a clean pan.

7 Bring the soup to the boil and add the double cream and Armagnac, if using. Season with salt and pepper to taste, if necessary, then serve the soup hot, garnished with chopped fresh parsley.

Per portion Energy 406kcal/1677kJ; Protein 1.4g; Carbohydrate 8.5g, of which sugars 8.1g; Fat 39.2g, of which saturates 21.7g; Cholesterol 86mg; Calcium 48mg; Fibre 1.2g; Sodium 29mg.

CURRY SOUP

INDIAN SPICES HAVE BEEN ENJOYED IN NORWAY FOR MANY CENTURIES, PARTICULARLY IN THE SOUTH OF THE COUNTRY, AND CURRY POWDER HAS BEEN USED TO ENLIVEN MANY DISHES. MORE RECENTLY, SOUTH-EAST ASIAN FOOD HAS BECOME POPULAR IN NORWAY AND THE COCONUT MILK IN THIS NORWEGIAN RECIPE, KARRISUPPE, REPLACES THE MORE FAMILIAR AND TRADITIONAL CREAM.

2 Stir the curry paste and flour into the pan and cook over a low heat for 1–2 minutes, without colouring.

3 Remove the pan from the heat and gradually pour in the stock, stirring constantly, to form a smooth sauce.

4 Return the pan to the heat and, stirring constantly, cook until the soup boils and thickens. Lower the heat and simmer the soup gently for about 10 minutes.

5 Add the coconut milk to the soup and stir well. Taste to check the seasoning, and add salt and pepper if necessary.

6 Pour the soup into individual serving bowls and serve with a swirl of cream or coconut milk on top of each, as well as a sprinkling of chopped parsley, to garnish.

COOK'S TIP
For a smooth soup, blend the soup in a blender or food processor before reheating and serving.

SERVES FOUR

INGREDIENTS
  50g/2oz/4 tbsp butter
  2 shallots, finely chopped
  1 cooking apple, peeled, cored
    and chopped
  10ml/2 tsp curry paste
  30ml/2 tbsp plain (all-purpose) flour
  1.25 litres/2¼ pints/5½ cups
    chicken or beef stock
  400ml/14fl oz can unsweetened
    coconut milk
  salt and ground black pepper
To garnish
  60ml/4 tbsp double (heavy) cream
    or 4 tbsp of the coconut milk
  chopped fresh parsley

1 Melt the butter in a pan, add the shallots and cook gently for about 5 minutes until softened but not coloured. Add the chopped apple, season with salt and pepper and cook for a further 2 minutes, until the apple is slightly softened.

Per portion Energy 195kcal/812kJ; Protein 1.7g; Carbohydrate 14.3g, of which sugars 7.6g; Fat 15g, of which saturates 9.2g; Cholesterol 37mg; Calcium 66mg; Fibre 1.3g; Sodium 200mg.

YELLOW PEA SOUP <u>WITH</u> HORSERADISH CREAM

YELLOW PEA SOUP IS A WINTERTIME FAVOURITE SERVED THROUGHOUT SCANDINAVIA, WITH EVERY COUNTRY CLAIMING OWNERSHIP. A TRADITIONAL COUNTRY DISH FULL OF RIB-STICKING GOODNESS, THERE ARE MANY VARIATIONS DEPENDING ON WHAT VEGETABLES ARE INCLUDED. SPLIT PEAS SPEED UP THE PROCESS, BUT THIS TRADITIONAL DANISH VERSION, GULE ÆRTE MED PEBERROD CRÈME FRAÎCHE, USES WHOLE PEAS.

SERVES EIGHT

INGREDIENTS
  450g/1lb dried yellow peas,
    picked over
  500g/1¼lb meaty ham bone
    or boneless pork shoulder
  1 onion, chopped
  3 carrots, sliced
  3 medium leeks, sliced
  10ml/2 tsp dried thyme
  175ml/6fl oz/¾ cup crème
    fraîche mixed with 15ml/1 tbsp
    creamed horseradish
  salt and ground white pepper
  75ml/5 tbsp chopped fresh parsley,
    to garnish

1 Put the dried peas in a large, heavy pan and add cold water to cover. Leave to soak overnight.

2 Rinse the peas under cold running water. Return the peas to the pan and add 1.75 litres/3 pints/7½ cups water and the ham bone or pork shoulder.

3 Bring to the boil and skim off any foam from the surface, then lower the heat, cover the pan with a lid and simmer for about 1 hour until the peas are almost tender.

4 Add the chopped onion, sliced carrots and leeks, and dried thyme. Season to taste with salt and pepper.

5 Cook for about 1 hour more, until the vegetables are tender.

6 Remove the ham bone, slice off any meat and return it to the soup.

7 Correct the seasoning and serve sprinkled with parsley and a dollop of horseradish cream.

COOK'S TIP
If whole yellow peas are not available, this soup is equally delicious made with split yellow peas, or green peas, either whole or split.

Per portion Energy 248kcal/1051kJ; Protein 21.6g; Carbohydrate 32.8g, of which sugars 5.3g; Fat 4.3g, of which saturates 1.2g; Cholesterol 9mg; Calcium 69mg; Fibre 7.4g; Sodium 348mg.

POTATO SOUP

POTATOES, INTRODUCED FROM FRANCE IN 1720, HAVE LONG BEEN A STAPLE IN DANISH COOKING. THE DANES ADOPTED THE HUMBLE TUBER AFTER SOME HESITATION, BUT TODAY, NO MAIN MEAL IN DENMARK WOULD BE COMPLETE WITHOUT THEM, AND EVERY DANISH KITCHEN GARDEN HAS A LUXURIANT POTATO PATCH. POTATOES STAR IN THIS CREAMY LEEK AND POTATO SOUP, WHICH ALTHOUGH SERVED HOT, IS SIMILAR TO THE CLASSIC FRENCH VICHYSSOISE.

SERVES SIX TO EIGHT

INGREDIENTS
25g/1oz/2 tbsp butter
6 leeks, chopped
1 large onion, chopped
1kg/2¼lb potatoes, peeled
  and thinly sliced
1 celery stalk, chopped
1.2 litres/2 pints/5 cups good
  beef stock
5ml/1 tsp salt, or to taste
2.5ml/½ tsp ground white pepper
475ml/16fl oz/2 cups single
  (light) cream
120ml/4fl oz/½ cup crème fraîche,
  to garnish
60ml/4 tbsp chopped fresh chives,
  to garnish

1 Melt the butter in a large heavy pan over medium heat. Stir in the leeks and onion, tossing to coat with the butter. Cook, stirring, until the leeks have wilted and the onion is transparent.

2 Add the potatoes, celery and stock, with sufficient water to cover the vegetables.

3 Cover the pan with a lid and simmer for about 30 minutes, or until the potatoes are tender.

4 Using a blender or food processor, blend or process the soup, in batches, to a purée. Return the soup to the pan, then season with salt and pepper and heat gently.

5 Stir in the cream, then heat the soup gently, but do not let it boil. Taste to check the seasoning, and add salt and pepper if needed.

6 Pour the soup into individual warmed soup bowls, then swirl 15ml/1 tbsp crème fraîche on to each portion. Garnish with a sprinkling of chives before serving.

COOK'S TIP
If available, a cordless, hand-held stick blender is useful for puréeing the soup as it can be done in the pan.

Per portion Energy 265kcal/1107kJ; Protein 6g; Carbohydrate 28.2g, of which sugars 8.2g; Fat 15g, of which saturates 9g; Cholesterol 40mg; Calcium 100mg; Fibre 4.4g; Sodium 72mg.

ASPARAGUS SOUP

After long dark winters, Danes crave any sign of spring. Snowdrops, crocuses and the first stems of asparagus coming up in the garden are all cause for celebration. Although widely available now, asparagus used to be a rare delicacy. Serving the tender green shoots in a vegetable stock-based soup was one way thrifty Danish cooks could extend the pleasure of this beloved harbinger of the warmer months.

SERVES FOUR

INGREDIENTS

2 carrots, chopped
1 parsnip, chopped
3 celery sticks, chopped
1 large onion, chopped
2 bay leaves
450g/1lb fresh asparagus,
  cut into 2.5cm/1in pieces
25g/1oz/2 tbsp butter
35g/1¼oz/¼ cup plain
  (all-purpose) flour
250ml/8fl oz/1 cup whipping cream
1 egg yolk
salt and ground white pepper

1 Bring 1.5 litres/2½ pints/6¼ cups water, or enough to cover the vegetables, to the boil in a large pan and add the carrots, parsnip, celery, onion and bay leaves. Cook, uncovered, over medium heat for 15–20 minutes, until tender. Strain the stock through a sieve (strainer). Discard the vegetables.

2 Meanwhile, pour 250ml/8fl oz/1 cup water into another pan, add the asparagus and bring to the boil over a medium-high heat. Cook the asparagus for 3–4 minutes until it is bright green and tender.

3 Drain the cooking water into the reserved vegetable stock, and refresh the asparagus under cold water.

4 Melt the butter in a separate pan over a medium heat, and stir in the flour. Cook for 3–5 minutes, stirring, then slowly stir in the cream.

5 Remove from the heat and stir in the egg yolk. Return to a low heat and stir in 250ml/8fl oz/1 cup of the reserved vegetable stock.

6 Gently reheat the mixture, stirring until it thickens, but do not let it boil. Stir the cream mixture into the remaining stock, add the asparagus and warm gently.

7 Season to taste and serve immediately.

COOK'S TIP
Shorten the boiling time for very thin asparagus. It will need approximately 2 minutes to become crisp-tender.

Per portion Energy 353kcal/1457kJ; Protein 6.1g; Carbohydrate 11g, of which sugars 4.2g; Fat 31.8g, of which saturates 19.3g; Cholesterol 130mg; Calcium 88mg; Fibre 2.2g; Sodium 76mg.

WILD MUSHROOM SOUP

A LARGE PROPORTION OF NORWAY IS COVERED IN FORESTS AND WILD MUSHROOMS ARE PLENTIFUL. NORWEGIANS ARE GENERALLY SKILLED AT KNOWING WHICH ONES ARE EDIBLE AND WHICH ONES SHOULD BE AVOIDED. LATE SUMMER AND AUTUMN ARE THE BEST TIMES TO GO MUSHROOM HUNTING IN NORWAY. ONE WAY OF USING THE PRECIOUS HARVEST IS IN THIS SOUP, KNOWN AS SOPPSUPPE.

3 Put the sliced mushrooms in a pan, cover with the stock and simmer for 10 minutes. Strain the stock and reserve.

4 Melt the butter in a large pan and add the sliced mushrooms and the soaked mushrooms. Fry gently for 2–3 minutes. Season with salt and pepper.

5 Stir the flour into the pan and cook over a low heat for 1–2 minutes, without colouring.

6 Remove from the heat and gradually stir in the reserved stock and the dried mushroom soaking liquid to form a smooth sauce. Return to the heat and, stirring all the time, cook until the sauce boils and thickens. Lower the heat and simmer gently for 5–10 minutes.

7 Add the cream to the soup and lemon juice to taste. Add the sherry, if using.

8 Pour the soup into individual serving bowls and top with a little cream swirled on top of each and a final garnish of chopped parsley.

SERVES FOUR

INGREDIENTS
    10g/¼oz/1 tbsp dried mushrooms,
      such as ceps, if using cultivated
      fresh mushrooms
    400g/14oz mushrooms, preferably
      wild, sliced
    1.25 litres/2¼ pints/5½ cups light
      stock, vegetable or chicken
    50g/2oz/4 tbsp butter
    30–45ml/2–3 tbsp plain
      (all-purpose) flour
    60ml/4 tbsp double (heavy) cream,
      plus extra to garnish
    a squeeze of fresh lemon juice
    15–30ml/1–2 tbsp medium
      sherry (optional)
    salt and ground black pepper
    chopped fresh parsley, to garnish

1 If using dried mushrooms, put in a small bowl and pour over boiling water to cover. Leave to soak for at least 20 minutes, until soft.

2 Using a slotted spoon, remove the mushrooms from the bowl then strain the soaking liquid and reserve. Chop the soaked mushrooms.

Per portion Energy 154kcal/638kJ; Protein 3.2g; Carbohydrate 9.3g, of which sugars 0.5g; Fat 11.8g, of which saturates 7.2g; Cholesterol 29mg; Calcium 26mg; Fibre 1.6g; Sodium 82mg.

CREAMY WINTER CHANTERELLE SOUP

THIS SOUP IS MADE FROM WINTER CHANTERELLE MUSHROOMS, WHICH ARE DIFFERENT TO THOSE CHANTERELLE MUSHROOMS THAT ARE ALSO KNOWN AS GIROLLES. HOWEVER, THEY MAY BE DIFFICULT TO GET HOLD OF OUTSIDE OF SWEDEN, SO YOU CAN USE SEASONAL CHANTERELLES IN THIS RECIPE, IF YOU LIKE. LIKE OTHER SWEDISH RECIPES, THIS SOUP IS THOUGHT TO HAVE JEWISH ORIGINS.

SERVES SIX

INGREDIENTS
  40g/1½ oz/3 tbsp butter
  400g/14oz chanterelle
    mushrooms, chopped
  4 shallots, finely chopped
  45ml/3 tbsp plain (all-purpose) flour
  1.5 litres/2½ pints/6¼ cups
    vegetable stock
  bouquet garni (see Cook's tip)
  150ml/¼ pint/⅔ cup crème fraîche
  15ml/1 tbsp lemon juice
  rye bread, to serve

2 Sprinkle over the flour and cook for a further 1 minute, stirring all the time, then gradually stir in the vegetable stock.

3 Add the bouquet garni to the pan and simmer the soup over a low-medium heat for 30 minutes.

COOK'S TIP
To make a bouquet garni, tie together a few sprigs of thyme, some parsley stalks and a bay leaf. Alternatively, tie them in a small piece of muslin (cheesecloth).

4 Remove the bouquet garni, add the crème fraîche and lemon juice and season to taste. Serve hot, with rye bread.

1 Melt the butter in a pan, add the chanterelle mushrooms and shallots and fry over medium heat until the shallots are transparent.

Per portion Energy 196kcal/812kJ; Protein 3.1g; Carbohydrate 10.7g, of which sugars 3.6g; Fat 16g, of which saturates 10.5g; Cholesterol 44mg; Calcium 43mg; Fibre 1.7g; Sodium 61mg.

CAULIFLOWER SOUP <u>WITH</u> PRAWNS

CONSIDERED THE MOST ELEGANT MEMBER OF THE CABBAGE FAMILY, CAULIFLOWER IS MUCH APPRECIATED IN DENMARK. ALONG WITH ITS OTHER CABBAGE COUSINS, IT IS A FAVOURITE IN DANISH KITCHEN GARDENS. IN THIS SIMPLE OLD-FASHIONED RECIPE, BLOMKÅLSUPPE MED REJER, CAULIFLOWER IS ELEVATED INTO A SOPHISTICATED, CREAMY SOUP PRETTILY GARNISHED WITH SWEET, PINK PRAWNS.

SERVES SIX

INGREDIENTS

    1 large cauliflower (about 800g/1¾ lb
      trimmed and chopped)
    5ml/1 tsp salt, or to taste
    25g/1oz/2 tbsp butter
    35g/1¼oz/⅓ cup plain
      (all-purpose) flour
    250ml/8fl oz/1 cup whipping cream
    1 egg yolk, beaten
    salt and ground white pepper
    225g/8oz cooked small prawns
      (shrimp), to garnish

1 Put the cauliflower into a large pan and add 1.5 litres/2½ pints/6¼ cups water and the salt. Bring to the boil and cook over a medium heat for 12–15 minutes until tender. Remove 475ml/16fl oz/2 cups of the cooking liquid and reserve. Cover the pan and keep it warm.

VARIATIONS
• Season the cream mixture with 5ml/1 tsp curry powder.
• Purée the cauliflower before adding the cream mixture for a smooth soup.

2 Melt the butter in a separate pan over a medium heat, and stir in the flour to make a smooth paste. Cook, stirring constantly, for 3–5 minutes until the roux is pale beige. Slowly stir in the cream. Remove from the heat and stir in the egg yolk.

3 Stir the reserved cauliflower water into the roux and cook over a low heat, stirring constantly, until the mixture thickens. Do not allow it to boil.

4 Add the cream mixture to the cauliflower, then season. Divide the soup among six warm soup plates and garnish with a few prawns. Serve immediately.

Per portion Energy 294kcal/1217kJ; Protein 13.3g; Carbohydrate 9.7g, of which sugars 4.6g; Fat 22.6g, of which saturates 13.3g; Cholesterol 159mg; Calcium 95mg; Fibre 2.6g; Sodium 121mg.

LOBSTER AND TOMATO SOUP

THIS LUXURIOUS NORWEGIAN SOUP, HUMMERSUPPE MED TOMAT, IS FOR SPECIAL OCCASIONS. NORWEGIAN LOBSTERS ARE SMALLER THAN THOSE CAUGHT IN THE US, BUT THEIR FLESH IS JUST AS DELICIOUS. THE SOUP CAN ALSO BE MADE WITH PRAWNS, IF YOU ARE FEELING LESS EXTRAVAGANT. IT IS IMPORTANT TO KEEP THE SHELLS BECAUSE THEY ARE USED TO PROVIDE ADDITIONAL FLAVOUR TO THE SOUP.

SERVES FOUR

INGREDIENTS

1 large cooked lobster or
  500g/1¼lb/3 cups cooked
  prawns (shrimp)
25g/1oz/2 tbsp butter
30ml/2 tbsp finely chopped shallot
2 red (bell) peppers, seeded
  and chopped
2.5cm/1in root ginger,
  finely chopped
1 clove garlic, finely chopped
60ml/4 tbsp brandy
30ml/2 tbsp tomato purée (paste)
1.25 litres/2¼ pints/5½ cups water
15ml/1 tbsp sherry vinegar
15ml/1 tbsp sugar
4 ripe tomatoes, skinned,
  seeded and chopped, or
  400g/14oz can tomatoes
juice of 1 lime
salt and ground black pepper
chopped fresh dill, to garnish

1 Remove the cooked lobster or prawn meat from their shells, reserving the shells. Set the meat and shells aside in separate bowls.

2 Melt the butter in a pan over a medium heat, then add the chopped shallot, peppers, ginger and garlic and cook, stirring often, for about 5 minutes.

3 Add the lobster or prawn shells to the pan and cook gently for a further 10 minutes.

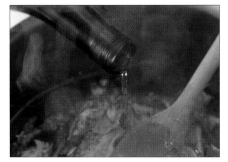

4 Add the brandy to the pan and set alight. Stir in the tomato purée.

5 Add the water, season lightly with salt and pepper, and bring slowly to the boil. Lower the heat and simmer very gently for 40 minutes.

6 Strain the mixture into a clean pan.

7 Add the vinegar, sugar, tomatoes and lime juice to taste. Taste to check the seasonings, adding salt and pepper only if necessary.

8 Divide the lobster or prawn meat between four individual serving bowls. Bring the soup to the boil, then pour over the shellfish. Garnish with chopped dill.

Per portion Energy 275kcal/1155kJ; Protein 29.6g; Carbohydrate 14.1g, of which sugars 13.5g; Fat 7.8g, of which saturates 3.7g; Cholesterol 151mg; Calcium 99mg; Fibre 2.6g; Sodium 479mg.

NORWEGIAN FISH SOUP

THERE ARE AS MANY NORWEGIAN FISH SOUPS AS THERE ARE COOKS. THEY ARE SERVED THROUGHOUT NORWAY, PARTICULARLY ALONG THE COAST, AND ON THE LOFOTEN ISLANDS. THE CLASSIC FISH SOUP BELONGS TO BERGEN AND THIS RECIPE IS A DELICIOUS VERSION OF IT. MONKFISH GIVES A NICE, SOLID TEXTURE BUT COD OR OTHER WHITE FISH CAN BE USED INSTEAD.

SERVES FOUR

INGREDIENTS
  55g/2oz/3½ tbsp butter
  60ml/4 tbsp plain (all-purpose) flour
  800ml/1 pint 7fl oz/3⅓ cups
    fish stock
  120ml/4fl oz/½ cup double
    (heavy) cream
  1 small carrot
  1 leek, white part only
  225g/8oz/½ cup cooked fish,
    such as monkfish, diced
  12 cooked mussels
  12 cooked, peeled prawns (shrimp)
  30ml/2 tbsp sour cream
  10ml/2 tsp lumpfish caviar
  salt and ground black pepper

1 Melt 40g/1½oz/2½ tbsp of the butter in a pan, stir in the flour and cook over a low heat for 1–2 minutes, without colouring.

2 Remove the pan from the heat and gradually stir in the fish stock to form a smooth sauce.

3 Return the pan to the heat and, stirring constantly, cook until the sauce boils and thickens.

4 Lower the heat, then simmer the sauce gently for 5–10 minutes until all taste of flour has been cooked out and the sauce is thick, smooth and coats the back of a spoon.

5 Season the sauce with salt and pepper to taste, then stir in the double cream.

6 Finely dice the carrot and leek.

7 Melt the remaining 15g/½oz/1 tbsp butter in a frying pan, add the carrot and leek and sauté for about 5–7 minutes until softened.

8 Add the vegetables and cooked fish to the soup and heat gently until the fish is heated through.

9 Add the mussels to the pan and heat the soup for a further 1 minute, stirring occasionally.

10 Finally, add the cooked prawns to the soup and taste to check the seasonings, adding salt and pepper only if necessary.

11 Distribute the fish soup into four warmed individual serving bowls and serve them immediately, with a little sour cream topped with lumpfish caviar on the surface of each serving.

COOK'S TIP
The success of this recipe depends mainly on the quality of the fish stock that is used. On the Lofoten Islands in Norway, the recommendation is to make fish stock from an entire fish, including the head. Poach the fish gently, with sufficient water to cover, plus 100ml/4fl oz/½ cup of medium dry white wine, a small bunch of parsley, a small onion, a slice of lemon, a pinch of salt and 4 peppercorns. When the fish is cooked through (this takes approximately 20 minutes, but the cooking time should be adjusted according to the size of the fish), remove the flesh from the bones. Put the bones back into the liquid and continue simmering the bones for a further 20 minutes. Pour the stock and bones through a sieve (strainer), discarding the bones and retaining the stock.

Per portion Energy 382kcal/1588kJ; Protein 20.2g; Carbohydrate 15.3g, of which sugars 3g; Fat 28.7g, of which saturates 16.7g; Cholesterol 156mg; Calcium 83mg; Fibre 1.5g; Sodium 274mg.

CHICKEN SOUP

A FAVOURITE APPETIZER FOR A SPECIAL GATHERING IN DENMARK, HØNSEKODSSUPPE IS AN ESSENTIAL PART OF EVERY DANISH COOK'S REPERTOIRE. A RICH STOCK IS PREPARED USING A WHOLE CHICKEN. THE MEAT CAN THEN BE REMOVED AND SERVED SEPARATELY, AND THE SOUP EATEN WITH DUMPLINGS. ALTERNATIVELY, IT CAN BE PULLED FROM THE BONES AND ADDED TO THE SOUP.

3 To make the dumplings, place the flour in a mixing bowl. Bring 250ml/8fl oz/ 1 cup water to the boil in a pan, add the butter and return to the boil. Stir it into the flour, beating to blend it smoothly. The dough should pull away from the sides of the bowl. Leave to cool.

4 Beat in the eggs, one at a time, to make a soft dough. Stir in the sugar and salt to taste. Leave the dough to rest for 20 minutes to thicken slightly.

5 Bring a large pan of lightly salted water to the boil. Use a teaspoon to form 5mm/¼in balls of dough, and drop them one at a time into the simmering water. They will sink to the bottom, then rise to the top when cooked, in 3–5 minutes. Lift them out with a slotted spoon and set aside.

SERVES EIGHT TO TEN

INGREDIENTS
   1 chicken, about 2kg/4½lb
   350g/12oz beef bone
   2 bay leaves
   3 large leeks, sliced
   1 parsnip, thinly sliced
   4 carrots, thinly sliced
   6 celery sticks, sliced
   salt
   75ml/5 tbsp chopped fresh
      parsley, to garnish
For the dumplings
   350g/12oz/3 cups plain
      (all-purpose) flour
   125g/4oz/½ cup butter
   4 eggs
   5ml/1 tsp sugar
   salt

1 Bring 3 litres/5 pints/12½ cups water to the boil in a pan. Add the chicken, beef bone and bay leaves. Return to the boil. Skim. Lower the heat. Simmer for 1 hour.

2 Add the leeks, parsnip, carrots and celery to the chicken stock and season with salt. Simmer for about 20 minutes, until the vegetables are tender.

6 Remove and discard the beef bone from the soup. Lift out the chicken and carve in slices to serve separately, or pull the meat from the bones and return to the soup. Add the dumplings to the soup to warm through, and serve.

Per portion Energy 266kcal/1115kJ; Protein 25.7g; Carbohydrate 24g, of which sugars 6.6g; Fat 7.5g, of which saturates 1.2g; Cholesterol 109mg; Calcium 48mg; Fibre 2.7g; Sodium 86mg.

REINDEER SOUP

THIS NORWEGIAN RECIPE, KNOWN AS BIDOS, IS CALLED A SOUP BUT MANY WOULD CLASS IT AS A STEW. IT COMES FROM THE SAMI PEOPLE, THE LAPLANDERS, WHO HAVE LIVED IN THE FAR NORTH OF SCANDINAVIA FOR OVER A THOUSAND YEARS. THEIR ECONOMY IS CENTRED AROUND REINDEER, WHICH PROVIDES THE BASIS FOR THIS RECIPE. THIS IS A HEARTY AND WARMING DISH.

SERVES FOUR

INGREDIENTS
25–40g/1–1½oz/2–3 tbsp butter
   plus 15g/½oz/1 tbsp for frying
   the mushrooms (see below)
450g/1lb reindeer or venison,
   finely diced
1 onion, chopped
3 potatoes, diced
3 carrots, diced
6 juniper berries, crushed
115g/4oz/1⅔ cups mushrooms, diced
60ml/4 tbsp sour cream, to garnish
salt and ground black pepper

1 Heat 25g/1oz/2 tbsp butter in a large pan, add the meat and fry until browned on all sides, adding a little extra butter if necessary. Transfer the meat to a plate.

2 Add the onion to the pan and fry gently for about 5 minutes until softened. Add a little water, stirring to lift any sediment left on the bottom of the pan.

3 Return the meat to the pan. Add the potatoes, carrots, juniper berries, 5ml/1 tsp salt, pepper and water to cover the meat. Bring to the boil, lower the heat and simmer for 15 minutes until the meat is tender.

COOK'S TIP
Cooking the mushrooms separately, instead of adding them with the onion, produces a fresher result.

4 Meanwhile, heat 15g/½ oz/1 tbsp butter in a pan. Add the mushrooms and sauté until browned. Add to the soup and simmer for a further 5 minutes.

5 Spoon the soup into four individual warmed serving bowls and serve hot, with a swirl of sour cream on top of each portion.

Per portion Energy 289kcal/1214kJ; Protein 27.6g; Carbohydrate 15.5g, of which sugars 3.9g; Fat 14.1g, of which saturates 8.1g; Cholesterol 87mg; Calcium 36mg; Fibre 1.7g; Sodium 144mg.

MELDAL SOUP

THIS IS A DISH THAT IS BOTH A SOUP AND A MAIN COURSE. IT IS THE NORWEGIAN EQUIVALENT OF THE FRENCH POT-AU-FEU, WHICH IS MEAT POACHED IN A BROTH THAT IS SERVED AS A SOUP, WITH THE MEAT SLICED AND SERVED AS A MAIN COURSE. IT IS CALLED MELDALSSODD IN NORWAY.

SERVES EIGHT TO TEN

INGREDIENTS
  500g/1¼ lb boneless beef,
    such as brisket
  500g/1¼ lb boneless pork,
    such as leg or lean belly
  500g/1¼ lb boneless mutton
    or lamb, such as shoulder
  3 litres/5 pints/12½ cups water
  20ml/4 tsp salt
  5ml/1 tsp peppercorns
  2.5cm/1in piece fresh root ginger
  1 bay leaf
  250g/9oz sausage meat
    (bulk sausage)
  15ml/1 tbsp chopped onion
  4 carrots
  1 turnip or swede (rutabaga)
  ½ small white cabbage
  boiled potatoes, to serve
For the flour dumplings
  200ml/7fl oz/scant 1 cup single
    (light) cream
  25ml/1½ tbsp sugar
  130g/4½ oz plain (all-purpose) flour
  2 eggs
  pinch of freshly grated nutmeg
  pinch of salt

1 Put the three pieces of meat in a large pan. Add the water, salt, peppercorns, ginger and bay leaf and bring to simmering point. Simmer gently for 1–1½ hours until the pieces of meat are tender.

2 Make the meatballs by rolling the sausage meat into small balls. Set the meatballs aside.

3 To make the flour dumplings, put the cream and sugar in a pan and bring to the boil. Immediately add the flour and beat well with a wooden spoon until the mixture comes away from the sides of the pan.

4 Remove the pan from the heat and add the eggs, one at a time, beating well together until incorporated.

5 Season the dumpling mixture with the nutmeg and salt. Wet your hands and roll the dumpling mixture into 16–20 small balls (best done when the dumplings can be put into the soup immediately, otherwise place them on a sheet of baking parchment or a wet plate).

6 When they are cooked, remove the three pieces of meat from the stock and allow them to cool.

7 Slice the cooled meat and arrange it on a serving dish. Drizzle over a little of the cooking liquid to prevent the meat slices from drying out and cover the dish.

8 Cut the carrots into thin sticks. Dice the turnip or swede and cut the cabbage into small pieces.

9 Skim the stock of any fat, then add the chopped onion, carrots, turnip or swede and cabbage. Bring to the boil, lower the heat and simmer for 10 minutes until the vegetables are just tender.

10 Add the meatballs and simmer for 5 minutes. Add the dumplings and continue to simmer for a further 5 minutes.

11 Ladle the soup, meatballs and dumplings into serving bowls and serve hot. Serve the sliced meat as a main course, accompanied by boiled potatoes.

Per portion Energy 453kcal/1892kJ; Protein 38.4g; Carbohydrate 22.9g, of which sugars 10.2g; Fat 23.7g, of which saturates 10.5g; Cholesterol 158mg; Calcium 111mg; Fibre 2.9g; Sodium 351mg.

APPETIZERS AND
SIDE DISHES

Serving many types of food in small portions is popular in

Scandinavian food culture. The Swedish smörgåsbord and the

Norwegian and Danish koldt bord (cold table) are very

similar, with everyone helping themselves to a selection of

small, light dishes. These can include gravlax in Sweden,

pickled herrings in Denmark and cured elk in Norway, as well

as a variety of cheeses, breads, crispbreads, pâtés and salads,

followed by a choice of traditional desserts.

LACY POTATO PANCAKES

THESE PRETTY, LACY PANCAKES ARE GOOD SERVED AS AN APPETIZER, TOPPED WITH SMOKED SALMON, CRÈME FRAÎCHE OR SOUR CREAM, AND CHOPPED RED ONION. THEY CAN ALSO BE SERVED AS AN ACCOMPANIMENT TO A FISH DISH OR SMOKED SALMON. IN SWEDEN, WHERE THEY ARE CALLED RÅRAKOR, SMALL ONES ARE OFTEN SERVED AS DELICATE AND ATTRACTIVE CANAPÉS AT PARTIES.

SERVES SIX

INGREDIENTS
    6 large potatoes
    1 leek
    1 carrot (optional)
    15g/½oz butter
    15ml/1 tbsp vegetable oil
    salt and ground black pepper
    strips of smoked salmon,
        crème fraîche or sour cream,
        and chopped red onion,
        to serve

1 Peel and grate the potatoes. Finely slice the leek and grate the carrot, if using.

2 Put the potatoes, carrot and leek into a bowl, and mix them all together.

3 Heat the butter and oil in a frying pan and when smoking, add spoonfuls of the potato mixture to make 7.5cm/3in pancakes. Fry the pancakes, turning once, until golden brown on both sides.

4 Season the pancakes with salt and pepper, and serve hot, topped with smoked salmon, crème fraîche or sour cream, and chopped red onion.

COOK'S TIP
To stop grated potatoes turning brown, put them in a bowl of water.

Per portion Energy 182kcal/767kJ; Protein 3.9g; Carbohydrate 33.1g, of which sugars 3.3g; Fat 4.6g, of which saturates 1.8g; Cholesterol 5mg; Calcium 20mg; Fibre 2.7g; Sodium 38mg.

VÄSTERBOTTEN CHEESE FLAN

THIS MELT-IN-THE-MOUTH LIGHT CHEESE FLAN IS GUARANTEED TO WIN NEW FANS EVERY TIME IT IS SERVED. KNOWN IN SWEDEN AS VÄSTERBOTTENOST FLAN, IT IS EASY TO MAKE AND DELICIOUS SERVED SLIGHTLY WARM. VÄSTERBOTTEN IS THE BEST CHEESE TO USE, BUT IF YOU CANNOT GET HOLD OF THIS KING OF SWEDISH CHEESES, THEN MATURE CHEDDAR CHEESE IS AN EFFECTIVE SUBSTITUTE.

SERVES SIX TO EIGHT

INGREDIENTS
  90g/3oz/¾ cup plain (all-purpose) flour
  20g/¾oz/1½ tbsp butter
  20g/¾oz/1½ tbsp lard or
    white cooking fat
  about 15ml/1 tbsp water
  225g/½lb Västerbotten or mature
    (sharp) Cheddar cheese, grated
  200ml/7fl oz/¾ cup double
    (heavy) cream
  4 egg yolks
  salt and ground black pepper
For the onion marmalade
  300g/11oz onions, finely sliced
  100ml/4fl oz/½ cup water
  15g/½oz/1 tbsp butter
  15ml/1 tbsp sugar
  15ml/1 tbsp sherry vinegar

1 To prepare the onion marmalade, put the onions in a frying pan with the water, butter and a pinch of salt and simmer for 30 minutes until translucent.

2 Add the sugar to the pan and boil until reduced, golden brown and syrupy.

3 Finally add the sherry vinegar and reduce again.

4 To make the shortcrust pastry, put the flour and salt in a food processor. Cut the butter and lard or white cooking fat into small pieces, add to the flour, then mix together, using a pulsating action, until the mixture resembles fine breadcrumbs.

5 Gradually add the water until the mixture forms a smooth dough. Wrap and store in the refrigerator for 30 minutes or up to 24 hours.

6 Preheat the oven to 200°C/400°F/Gas 6. Roll out the pastry on a lightly floured surface and line a deep 20cm/8in flan tin (pan).

7 Line the pastry with a sheet of baking parchment and fill the pastry case with baking beans. Bake blind in the oven for 10–15 minutes until the pastry has set.

8 Remove the flan from the oven and carefully remove the paper and beans, then return to the oven for a further 5 minutes until the base is dry.

9 Reduce the oven temperature to 180°C/350°F/Gas 4. Put the cheese, cream, egg yolks and salt and pepper in a bowl and mix them together.

10 Fill the pastry case with the mixture. Bake in the oven for 45 minutes until golden. Allow to cool, then serve the flan with the warm onion marmalade.

Per portion Energy 386kcal/1598kJ; Protein 10.5g; Carbohydrate 14.1g, of which sugars 4.7g; Fat 31.7g, of which saturates 18.5g; Cholesterol 174mg; Calcium 259mg; Fibre 0.9g; Sodium 242mg.

PICKLED HERRING

DESPITE THE DANISH FONDNESS FOR MEAT, NO KOLDT BORD OR 'COLD TABLE' – DENMARK'S VERSION OF THE SWEDISH SMÖRGÅSBORD – WOULD BE COMPLETE WITHOUT PICKLED HERRINGS, OR SPEGESILD.

SERVES FOUR

INGREDIENTS
  400g/14oz salted herring fillets
  250ml/8fl oz/1 cup wine vinegar
  250ml/8fl oz/1 cup water
  115g/4oz/½ cup sugar
  1 carrot, thinly sliced
  2 bay leaves
  6cm/2½in fresh root ginger,
    peeled and finely chopped
  4cm/1½in fresh horseradish,
    peeled and finely chopped
  10ml/2 tsp mustard seeds
  6 allspice berries
  1.5ml/¼ tsp ground coriander
  1 red onion, thinly sliced

1 Rinse the herring fillets several times in cold water. Place in a bowl of cold water, cover and refrigerate overnight.

2 Combine the vinegar, water and sugar in a pan and bring to the boil over medium heat. Boil, uncovered, for 10 minutes.

3 Add the carrot, bay leaves, ginger, horseradish, mustard seeds, allspice and coriander; cook for 10 minutes more. Remove from the heat and cool.

4 Taste the herring; if too salty, rinse the fillets again. Drain, cut into 2.5cm/1in pieces and place in a non-metallic bowl, layering them with onions. Pour the vinegar mixture over the herring and onions. Cover and refrigerate overnight or for up to four days before serving.

HERRING MARINATED IN SHERRY

ONCE CONSIDERED THE FOOD OF THE POOR, SALTED HERRING IS NOW POPULAR THROUGHOUT SCANDINAVIA AND THERE ARE MANY PREPARATIONS. THIS ONE, MATJES SILD, IS A DANISH RECIPE.

SERVES EIGHT TO TEN

INGREDIENTS
  400g/14oz (about 4 or 5) salted
    herring fillets
  1 onion, thinly sliced
  150ml/¼ pint/⅔ cup distilled
    white vinegar
  150ml/¼ pint/⅔ cup water
  25g/1oz/2 tbsp white sugar
  12 allspice berries
  12 whole cloves
  1 bay leaf
  250ml/8fl oz/1 cup medium-sweet
    sherry or Madeira

1 Rinse the herring fillets several times in cold water, then place them in a bowl of fresh cold water, cover and refrigerate overnight.

2 Taste the herring for saltiness. If it is still too salty, rinse the fillets again.

3 Drain and cut the herring fillets into 2.5cm/1in pieces.

4 Place the herring pieces in a non-metallic bowl and scatter the onion slices over the fish.

5 Combine the vinegar, water, sugar, allspice, cloves, bay leaf and sherry or Madeira in a bowl and pour the mixture over the herring and onions. Cover and refrigerate overnight or for up to four days before serving.

Per portion Energy 231kcal/963kJ; Protein 12.5g; Carbohydrate 7.5g, of which sugars 7.5g; Fat 16.6g, of which saturates 1.2g; Cholesterol 32mg; Calcium 10mg; Fibre 0g; Sodium 623mg.
Per portion Energy 228kcal/960kJ; Protein 12.8g; Carbohydrate 20.7g, of which sugars 20.4g; Fat 8.4g, of which saturates 0g; Cholesterol 32mg; Calcium 21mg; Fibre 0.2g; Sodium 626mg.

HERRINGS WITH CARROT AND LEEK

THIS NORWEGIAN DISH, SPEKESILD MED GULRÖTTER, COMBINES MARINATED HERRINGS WITH THE FRESH TASTE OF CARROT AND LEEK FOR A TASTY APPETIZER.

SERVES FOUR

INGREDIENTS
    2 salted herring fillets or 2 jars
        (150g–200g/5–7oz) herring fillets
        in brine, drained (no need to soak)
    200ml/7fl oz/3/4 cup water
    400ml/14fl oz/1 2/3 cups wine vinegar
    150g/5oz/3/4 cup sugar
    1 onion, sliced
    1 bay leaf
    6 allspice berries
    6 black peppercorns
    1 small carrot, finely sliced
    1/2 small leek, white part only,
        finely sliced
    2 shallots, quartered

1 Soak the herring fillets in cold water for 8–12 hours. Drain, rinse under cold water and place in a glass jar.

2 To make the marinade, put the water, vinegar and sugar in a large bowl and stir until the sugar has dissolved.

3 Add the sliced onion, bay leaf, allspice and peppercorns.

4 Pour the marinade over the herring fillets. Leave in a cold place for 6–7 hours.

5 Cut the herring fillets into 2.5cm/1in thick pieces, then arrange the fish pieces on a serving dish as if they were still whole.

6 Add a little of the marinade to the fillets and then the sliced carrot and leek. Place the quartered shallots around the edge of the dish and serve.

HERRINGS WITH ONION AND TOMATO

THIS WAY OF DRESSING MARINATED HERRINGS, SPEKESILD MED LÖK OG TOMAT, USES A CLASSIC COMBINATION OF SLICES OF ONION AND TOMATO, WHCH IS ALWAYS POPULAR IN NORWAY.

SERVES FOUR

INGREDIENTS
    2 salt herring fillets or 2 jars
        (150–200g/5–7oz) herring fillets in
        brine, drained (no need to soak)
    200ml/7fl oz/3/4 cup water
    400ml/14fl oz/1 2/3 cups wine vinegar
    150g/5oz/3/4 cup sugar
    2 onions, finely sliced
    1 bay leaf
    6 allspice berries
    6 black peppercorns
    1 large tomato, skinned and sliced
    fresh dill fronds, to garnish

1 Soak the herring fillets in cold water for 8–12 hours. Drain, rinse under cold water and place in a glass jar.

2 To make the marinade, put the water, vinegar and sugar in a large bowl and stir until the sugar has dissolved.

3 Add 1 sliced onion, the bay leaf, allspice and peppercorns. Pour over the herring. Leave in a cold place for 6–7 hours.

4 Cut the herring fillets into 2.5cm/1in thick pieces.

5 Arrange the fish pieces on a serving dish as if they were still whole. Add a little of the marinade to the fillets and then arrange the onion and tomato slices, overlapping, on top. Serve garnished with dill fronds.

Per portion Energy 174kcal/731kJ; Protein 13.2g; Carbohydrate 10.9g, of which sugars 10.3g; Fat 8.5g, of which saturates 0.1g; Cholesterol 32mg; Calcium 24mg; Fibre 1.2g; Sodium 628mg.
Per portion Energy 165kcal/694kJ; Protein 12.8g; Carbohydrate 9.3g, of which sugars 8.9g; Fat 8.4g, of which saturates 0g; Cholesterol 32mg; Calcium 15mg; Fibre 0.4g; Sodium 625mg.

MUSTARD HERRINGS

IN SWEDEN, HERRINGS FORM AN ESSENTIAL PART OF THE DIET AND, AS AN OILY FISH RICH IN VITAMIN D, THEY HAVE GREAT HEALTH BENEFITS. THIS DISH IS KNOWN AS SENAPSILL IN SWEDISH.

SERVES FOUR

INGREDIENTS
    750g/1lb 10oz fresh small herrings
    350ml/12fl oz/1½ cups water
    75ml/5 tbsp white vinegar
    fresh dill fronds, to garnish
    boiled new potatoes, to serve
For the mustard sauce
    75ml/5 tbsp mayonnaise
    25ml/1½ tbsp French
        wholegrain mustard
    7.5ml/1½ tsp caster (superfine) sugar
    60ml/4 tbsp chopped fresh dill

1 To prepare the herrings, cut off the heads and fins. Make a slit down the belly and remove the guts. Rinse under cold water and pat dry on kitchen paper.

2 Put the fish, skin side up, on a board and with the heel of your hand press down firmly to loosen the backbone. Turn the fish over, then cut the backbone near the head and remove it.

3 Finally, pull off the skin down towards the tail, being careful not to break the flesh.

4 In a large, shallow dish, mix the water and vinegar together and place the fish fillets in the mixture. Leave to marinate in the refrigerator for 10–12 hours.

5 Drain the marinade and dry the fish on kitchen paper. Mix the mayonnaise, mustard, sugar and dill together in the cleaned shallow dish. Add the fish and leave in the refrigerator for a further day.

6 Garnish with dill fronds and serve with boiled new potatoes.

CURRIED HERRINGS

THIS TASTY SWEDISH WAY TO SERVE HERRINGS, KNOWN AS CURRYSILL, CAN BE PREPARED MUCH MORE QUICKLY THAN MUSTARD HERRINGS, MAKING THEM IDEAL FOR ENTERTAINING UNEXPECTED GUESTS.

SERVES FOUR

INGREDIENTS
    150g/5oz jar matjes herrings
    3–4 cold, boiled new potatoes
    2 hard-boiled eggs
    5ml/1 tsp curry powder
    105ml/7 tbsp mayonnaise
    small bunch fresh parsley and dill
        fronds, to garnish
    crispbread, to serve

1 Start by cutting the herrings into 1cm/½in pieces. Cube the cold boiled potatoes and chop the hard-boiled eggs.

2 Stir the curry powder into the mayonnaise. Then add the fish, potatoes and hard-boiled eggs, and mix together.

3 Leave in the refrigerator for 15 minutes to chill. Garnish with parsley and dill and serve with crispbread.

COOK'S NOTE
Herrings have a high nutritional value. They contain protein and provide the essential amino acids that the body needs. They also provide the vitamins A, B, D and E, as well as minerals including iron and phosphorus. They are rich in Omega-3 fatty acids, which are thought to reduce the risk of blood clots, strokes and even cancer. They contain polyunsaturated fats and overall are low in calories.

SUNNY-EYE ANCHOVIES

THE SMALLEST MEMBER OF THE HERRING FAMILY, ANCHOVIES HAVE EXCELLENT HEALTH BENEFITS LIKE ALL OILY FISH. THIS SWEDISH RECIPE, SOLÖGA, USES RAW EGG YOLKS, SO BE SURE TO USE FRESH EGGS.

SERVES FOUR

INGREDIENTS
    100g/3½oz can Swedish anchovies
        (see Cook's tip)
    1 red onion, finely chopped
    15ml/1 tbsp small capers
    15ml/1 tbsp chopped pickled
        beetroot (beet)
    2 egg yolks
    crispbread, to serve

1 Chop the anchovies and put them in the centre of a serving dish. Arrange the onion in a ring around the anchovies, followed by a ring of capers and then a ring of chopped beetroot.

2 Cut a nick in the shell of each egg and open up the lid you have created. Pour away the white and return the yolk to the shell. Place the raw egg yolks in their shell in the middle of the dish.

3 Alternatively, mix all the ingredients together in a bowl, season with ground black pepper, and serve the anchovies on crispbread.

COOK'S TIP
If you do not have Swedish anchovies, soak normal, salted anchovies in milk for 2–3 hours before you use them, adding a final sprinkling of ground cinnamon and cloves.

Per portion Energy 381kcal/1582kJ; Protein 26.7g; Carbohydrate 3.2g, of which sugars 3g; Fat 29.1g, of which saturates 5.7g; Cholesterol 68mg; Calcium 133mg; Fibre 0.6g; Sodium 479mg.
Per portion Energy 370kcal/1537kJ; Protein 12.7g; Carbohydrate 16.5g, of which sugars 5.2g; Fat 28.5g, of which saturates 4.2g; Cholesterol 178mg; Calcium 45mg; Fibre 1.1g; Sodium 492mg.
Per portion Energy 86kcal/357kJ; Protein 8g; Carbohydrate 1.6g, of which sugars 1.3g; Fat 5.3g, of which saturates 1.2g; Cholesterol 117mg; Calcium 92mg; Fibre 0.4g; Sodium 997mg.

GRAVAD LAX WITH HORSERADISH

FOR A CELEBRATORY MEAL THERE'S NO FINER FISH THAN SALMON. CURING IT YOURSELF IN A BLANKET OF SALT AND SUGAR — THE PREPARATION KNOWN AS GRAVAD LAX IN DENMARK — IS SIMPLE AND AUTHENTICALLY SCANDINAVIAN, AND YOU'LL REVEL IN THE APPLAUSE WHEN YOU SERVE THE TENDER, ROSY FILLET IN PAPER-THIN SLICES. CHOOSE FRESH WILD PACIFIC SALMON AND FREEZE THE SALMON FILLET FOR UP TO FOUR HOURS BEFORE PREPARING IT. THIS IS A DANISH RECIPE.

6 Drizzle with lemon juice, rub with half the salt mixture and sprinkle with half the dill. Arrange the lemon slices on top.

7 Place the second fillet on a board and rub the flesh evenly with the remaining salt mixture, then sprinkle with the remaining dill.

8 Carefully lift the second fillet and place it over the fillet in the dish, turning it skin side up to make a 'sandwich'.

9 Wrap tightly in the foil or film and weight with a heavy pot or board. Chill for 48 hours, turning the fish twice daily. It is cured when it turns a deep, bright red and the edges are slightly white.

10 Cut the salmon into very thin slices to serve; discard the skin.

11 To make the dressing, stir together the sour cream, double cream, horseradish, dill, salt and pepper, and chill until ready to serve. Garnish both the horseradish cream and the salmon with dill sprigs.

SERVES EIGHT TO TEN

INGREDIENTS
1kg/2¼lb fresh salmon fillet, skin on
75g/3oz/⅓ cup coarse salt
25g/1oz/2 tbsp sugar
10ml/2 tsp ground white pepper
30ml/2 tbsp fresh lemon juice
105ml/7 tbsp chopped fresh dill
½ lemon, thinly sliced, plus extra
   to garnish
For the dressing
250ml/8fl oz/1 cup sour cream
30ml/2 tbsp double (heavy) cream
45ml/3 tbsp prepared creamed
   horseradish sauce, or to taste
45ml/3 tbsp chopped fresh dill
salt and ground white pepper
fresh dill sprigs, to garnish

1 Line a baking tin (pan) with a large piece of foil or clear film (plastic wrap) that is slightly larger than the baking tin, leaving the ends overlapping the sides of the dish.

2 Carefully remove any small pin bones from the salmon fillet using a pair of tweezers.

3 Cut small nicks in the skin to allow the salt and seasonings to penetrate, then cut the fillet in half.

4 Stir together the salt, sugar and pepper in a small bowl.

5 Place one piece of salmon skin side down in the lined dish.

Per portion Energy 479kcal/1981kJ; Protein 26.2g; Carbohydrate 0.4g, of which sugars 0.3g; Fat 40.4g, of which saturates 6.4g; Cholesterol 113mg; Calcium 35mg; Fibre 0g; Sodium 169mg.

GRAVLAX WITH MUSTARD AND DILL SAUCE

In Sweden, salmon cured in salt and sugar is known as gravlax (spellings vary between countries) and this is the most famous Swedish dish. The name, with grav meaning 'hole in the ground' and lax meaning 'salmon', derives from the fact that it used to be prepared by burying it underground to cure, so that it would remain cool. The key to successful authentic Swedish gravlax is the mustard and dill sauce with which it is served.

SERVES SIX TO EIGHT

INGREDIENTS
  1kg/2¼lb fresh salmon, filleted
    and boned, with skin on
  50g/2oz/½ cup coarse salt
  50g/2oz/½ cup caster (superfine) sugar
  10ml/2 tsp crushed white
    peppercorns
  200g/7oz/2 cups chopped fresh
    dill with stalks
  fresh dill fronds, to garnish
For the mustard and dill sauce
  100g/4oz Swedish mustard
  100g/4oz/½ cup sugar
  15ml/1 tbsp vinegar
  5ml/1 tsp salt
  ground black pepper
  300ml/½ pint/1¼ cups vegetable oil
  100g/4oz/2 cups chopped fresh
    dill fronds

1 Using tweezers, remove any pinbones from the salmon. Then mix the salt and sugar together.

2 Sprinkle a little of the mixture on to the centre of a sheet of foil and place half the salmon fillet, skin side down, on the mixture. Sprinkle the salmon with a little more salt mixture.

3 Sprinkle the white pepper on the flesh side of both salmon fillets and then add the chopped dill to both fillets. Place the second salmon fillet, skin side up, on top of the first fillet and finally sprinkle over the remaining salt mixture.

4 Wrap the foil around the salmon fillets and leave in the refrigerator for 48 hours, turning the salmon fillets every 12 hours. (The foil will contain all the juices which will help to marinate the salmon.)

5 To make the mustard and dill sauce, put the mustard, sugar, vinegar and salt and pepper into a bowl and mix them all together.

6 Very slowly drizzle the oil into the mixture, whisking it all the time until you end up with a thick, shiny sauce. Finally add the chopped dill to the sauce mixture.

7 When the salmon has marinated slice it thinly, from one end, at an angle of 45 degrees. Either serve the gravlax on individual serving plates or on one large dish with the dill and mustard sauce. Garnish with dill fronds.

Per portion Energy 543kcal/2258kJ; Protein 26.4g; Carbohydrate 21g, of which sugars 20.7g; Fat 39.8g, of which saturates 5.4g; Cholesterol 63mg; Calcium 58mg; Fibre 0.3g; Sodium 428mg.

SMOKED EEL WITH SCRAMBLED EGGS

SMOKED EEL IS A DELICACY IN SWEDEN WHERE IT IS SMOKED IN A SPECIAL WAY REFERRED TO AS 'FLAT SMOKED EEL', AND IS CUT IN A SIMILAR WAY TO GRAVLAX, SLICED THINLY AT A 45 DEGREE ANGLE. IN THIS DISH, CALLED RÖKT ÅL MED ÄGGRÖRA, IT IS SERVED WITH CREAMY SCRAMBLED EGGS.

SERVES EIGHT

INGREDIENTS
10 eggs
a little freshly grated nutmeg
50ml/2fl oz/¼ cup double
   (heavy) cream
25g/1oz/2 tbsp butter
15ml/1 tbsp chopped fresh chives
16 slices smoked eel or 8 slices
   flat smoked eel
salt and ground black pepper
knobs (pats) of butter and dill
   fronds, to garnish

1 Break the eggs into a large bowl and whisk together with the grated nutmeg, cream, salt and pepper.

2 Melt half the butter in a heavy pan over a low heat. Add the egg mixture and stir carefully with a wooden spoon until the mixture starts to set.

3 Add the remaining butter and the chopped chives to the scrambled eggs and stir through.

4 Arrange the smoked eel on individual serving plates.

5 Serve the scrambled eggs immediately with the smoked eel, garnished with a knob of butter to make the scrambled eggs shiny, dill fronds and an extra sprinkling of black pepper.

Per portion Energy 188kcal/781kJ; Protein 12.1g; Carbohydrate 0.1g, of which sugars 0.1g; Fat 15.7g, of which saturates 6.4g; Cholesterol 291mg; Calcium 44mg; Fibre 0g; Sodium 130mg.

ANCHOVY TERRINE

THIS DISH, GUBBRÖRA, IS BASED ON A TRADITIONAL SWEDISH RECIPE CALLED OLD MAN'S MIX. SIMILAR TO THE ENGLISH SPECIALITY, GENTLEMAN'S RELISH, IT USES ANCHOVIES AS THE MAIN INGREDIENT, IN THIS CASE THE SWEET, SWEDISH VARIETY THAT ARE FLAVOURED WITH CINNAMON, CLOVES AND ALLSPICE.

SERVES SIX TO EIGHT

INGREDIENTS

    5 hard-boiled eggs
    100g/3½oz can Swedish or
      matjes anchovies
    2 gelatine leaves
    200ml/7fl oz/scant 1 cup
      sour cream
    ½ red onion, chopped
    1 bunch fresh dill, chopped
    15ml/1 tbsp Swedish or
      German mustard
    salt and ground black pepper
    peeled prawns (shrimp) or
      lumpfish roe and dill fronds,
      to garnish
    Melba toast or rye bread, to serve

1 Line a 20cm/8in terrine with clear film (plastic wrap).

2 Mash the hard-boiled eggs in a bowl. Drain the liquid from the anchovy can and add to the eggs.

3 In a large, separate bowl, mash the anchovies. Melt the gelatine as directed on the packet.

4 Add the gelatine to the eggs with the sour cream, mashed anchovies, chopped onion, dill and Swedish or German mustard.

5 Season the mixture with salt and pepper to taste and stir all the ingredients together thoroughly.

6 Pour the mixture into the prepared terrine and chill in the refrigerator for 2 hours.

7 To serve, turn out the terrine on to a serving platter or plate and garnish it with peeled prawns or lumpfish roe, and dill fronds.

8 Serve the terrine with Melba toast or rye bread.

Per portion Energy 127kcal/529kJ; Protein 8.1g; Carbohydrate 1.8g, of which sugars 1.6g; Fat 9.9g, of which saturates 4.3g; Cholesterol 142mg; Calcium 88mg; Fibre 0.3g; Sodium 602mg.

WEST COAST SALAD

AFTER ITS FASHIONABLE POPULARITY IN THE 1960S, THIS CRUSTACEAN SALAD, VÄSTKUST SALAD, HAS NOW BECOME A STYLISH CLASSIC IN SWEDEN. THE WEST COAST, FROM WHERE IT ORIGINATES, ABOUNDS WITH FRESH SEAFOOD FROM THE PICTURESQUE FISHING VILLAGES SUCH AS SMÖGEN AND GREBBESTAD. THE DISH IS DELICIOUS SERVED WITH COLD BEER.

SERVES SIX TO EIGHT

INGREDIENTS
    200g/7oz fresh asparagus spears
    1kg/2¼lb shell-on cooked
        prawns (shrimp)
    200g/7oz can mussels in brine
    100g/3½oz can crab meat in
        brine or the meat from 2 large
        cooked crabs
    200g/7oz small mushrooms, sliced
    1 cos or romaine lettuce
For the dressing
    105ml/7 tbsp mayonnaise
    5ml/1 tsp tomato purée (paste)
    pinch of salt
    1 garlic clove, crushed
    15ml/1 tbsp chopped fresh dill
For the garnish
    1 potato
    vegetable oil, for deep-frying
    4 baby tomatoes, quartered
    2 lemons, cut into wedges
    1 bunch fresh dill

1 Stand the asparagus spears upright in a deep pan or put them in an asparagus pan. Pour in enough boiling water to come three-quarters of the way up the stalks. Simmer for about 10 minutes until tender.

2 Drain and, when cool enough to handle, cut into 5cm/2in lengths.

3 Carefully remove the shells from the prawns, keeping them intact. Drain the brine from the mussels, and the crab, if using canned crab.

4 Carefully mix the peeled prawns with the mussels, crab meat, asparagus and mushrooms.

5 To make the potato garnish, finely grate the potato and rinse under cold running water to wash off the starch. Put the potato on a clean dish towel and pat dry.

6 Heat the oil in a deep-fryer or pan to 180–190°C/350–375°F or until a cube of bread browns in 30 seconds. Add the grated potato and fry until golden brown, then remove from the pan with a slotted spoon. Drain on kitchen paper and leave to cool.

7 To make the dressing, mix together the mayonnaise, tomato purée, salt, garlic and dill.

8 Add the dressing to the fish mixture and carefully mix all the ingredients together so that the prawns and mussels remain whole.

9 Chop the lettuce very finely and place on individual plates.

10 To serve, place the salad on the chopped lettuce and garnish with the fried potato, tomatoes, lemon wedges and dill.

VARIATION
For a luxurious touch to this dish, try adding some lobster.

Per portion Energy 594kcal/2531kJ; Protein 113.3g; Carbohydrate 2.8g, of which sugars 1.2g; Fat 14.6g, of which saturates 2.9g; Cholesterol 1337mg; Calcium 565mg; Fibre 0.9g; Sodium 7723mg.

BIRD'S NEST SALAD

FUGLEREDE IS A PARTICULARLY ATTRACTIVE DISH ON THE NORWEGIAN COLD TABLE. THE INGREDIENTS ARE ARRANGED, AS THE NAME SUGGESTS, IN THE SHAPE OF A BIRD'S NEST ENCIRCLING A RAW EGG YOLK. ALL THE INGREDIENTS, INCLUDING THE YOLK, SHOULD BE STIRRED TOGETHER BY THE FIRST PERSON TO HELP THEMSELVES TO THE DISH. USE ONLY THE FRESHEST EGGS WHEN CONSUMING THE YOLK RAW.

SERVES FOUR

INGREDIENTS

    8 anchovy fillets, roughly chopped
    30ml/2 tbsp capers
    2 potatoes, cooked, cooled and
      diced, total quantity 45ml/3 tbsp
    45ml/3 tbsp chopped pickled
      beetroot (beet)
    15–30ml/1–2 tbsp finely diced onion
    1 very fresh egg

COOK'S TIP
Raw egg yolk should not be served to children, the elderly, pregnant women, convalescents or anyone suffering from an illness. The egg must be very fresh.

1 Place an egg cup in a medium, round serving dish, upside down.

2 In successive circles around the cup, arrange the chopped anchovies, capers and chopped potatoes.

3 Next arrange the chopped beetroot and diced onions around the edge of the dish.

4 Carefully remove the egg cup. Break the egg, separating the yolk from the white, and carefully put the whole egg yolk where the egg cup was positioned. Alternatively, use an egg shell half to hold the yolk.

Per portion Energy 93kcal/390kJ; Protein 5.9g; Carbohydrate 10.1g, of which sugars 2.3g; Fat 3.6g, of which saturates 0.9g; Cholesterol 99mg; Calcium 41mg; Fibre 0.9g; Sodium 284mg.

CRAB SALAD WITH CORIANDER

CRAB, LIKE OTHER SHELLFISH FROM THE NORTH SEA AROUND NORWAY, IS FULL OF FLAVOUR. NORWEGIANS LOVE CRAB WHEN IT IS SIMPLY DRESSED OR SERVED IN A MIXED SALAD SUCH AS THIS ONE. THE CRAB'S RICHNESS IS BLENDED WITH TWO TYPES OF CREAM, CONTRASTING WITH THE FRESHNESS OF THE APPLES AND SPRING ONIONS. CORIANDER GIVES AN EXTRA PUNCH TO THE FLAVOUR.

SERVES 4

INGREDIENTS
1 head romaine lettuce
2 eating apples
juice of 1 lemon
1 bunch spring onions
  (scallions), chopped
150ml/¼ pint/⅔ cup
  whipping cream
135ml/4½ fl oz/generous ½ cup
  crème fraîche
30ml/2 tbsp chopped fresh coriander
  (cilantro), plus extra to garnish
brown and white meat of 2 crabs
salt

1 Separate the lettuce leaves and arrange on a shallow serving bowl. Peel, core and finely dice the apples.

2 Put the apples in a bowl, add the lemon juice and toss together. Add the spring onions and mix together.

3 Whisk the whipping cream in a large bowl until it stands in soft peaks, then fold in the crème fraîche. Add the chopped apple mixture and the chopped coriander.

4 Mix together the brown and white crab meat and season with salt to taste.

5 Fold the crab meat mixture into the cream mixture. Taste to check the seasoning, adding more salt if necessary.

6 Spoon on to the lettuce and serve garnished with chopped coriander.

Per portion Energy 382kcal/1585kJ; Protein 20.6g; Carbohydrate 6.4g, of which sugars 6.2g; Fat 30.6g, of which saturates 19.3g; Cholesterol 151mg; Calcium 188mg; Fibre 1.4g; Sodium 571mg.

TARTLETS

Danes love these light, buttery tartlets, with all kinds of creamy fillings. They also often buy pre-baked cases to fill at home, which in Denmark are widely available made with a yeast-based pastry, wienerbrød. If you can find these prepared shells, you could use them instead to save time.

MAKES 18

INGREDIENTS
For the pastry:
    200g/7oz/1¾ cups plain (all
      purpose) flour, sifted
    125g/4½oz/9 tbsp butter, softened
    150ml/¼ pint/⅔ cup cold water
For the prawn (shrimp) filling:
    45g/1½oz/scant ¼ cup butter
    20g/¾oz/scant ¼ cup plain
      (all-purpose) flour
    475ml/16fl oz/2 cups single
      (light) cream
    275g/10oz cooked prawns (shrimp)
    salt and ground white pepper
    25ml/1½ tbsp chopped fresh dill sprigs
For the chicken and asparagus filling:
    65g/2½oz/5 tbsp butter
    225g/8oz fresh asparagus,
      cut into 2cm/¾in pieces
    15ml/1 tbsp vegetable oil
    225g/8oz skinless, boneless chicken
      breasts, cut into 2cm/¾in cubes
    20g/¾oz/scant ¼ cup plain
      (all-purpose) flour
    475ml/16fl oz/2 cups single
      (light) cream
    salt and ground white pepper
    45ml/3 tbsp chopped fresh parsley,
      to garnish

1 Preheat the oven to 200°C/400°F/Gas 6. In a bowl, rub the butter into the flour. Mix in sufficient water to form a dough. Roll out the pastry on a floured surface.

2 Cut circles to fit 7cm/2¾in fluted tart tins (muffin pans). Prick the bases.

3 Line each pastry shell with baking parchment or foil and fill with a handful of dried peas or beans to help the pastry keep its shape. Chill for at least 30 minutes to rest the pastry.

4 Bake for 10–15 minutes until crisp and golden. Remove the beans and paper or foil for the final 5 minutes.

5 To make the creamed prawn filling, melt the butter in a pan over a medium heat, and stir in the flour. Cook the roux for 3–5 minutes until pale beige. Slowly stir in the cream and cook, stirring, for about 5 minutes, until thickened.

6 Stir the prawns into the sauce and heat gently for 3–4 minutes. Season well with salt and pepper.

7 To make the chicken and asparagus filling, melt 25g/1oz/2 tbsp of the butter in a frying pan over a medium heat. Add the asparagus, toss to coat evenly with butter and cook, stirring, for about 4 minutes, until tender. Remove and set aside on a plate.

8 In the same pan, heat the oil over a medium heat. Add the chicken. Cook for 5 minutes, until cooked. Set aside.

9 Melt the remaining butter in a pan over a medium heat and stir in the flour. Cook the roux for 3–5 minutes until pale beige-coloured. Slowly stir in the cream and cook, stirring constantly, for about 5 minutes until the sauce has thickened. Add the asparagus and chicken and heat for 3–4 minutes. Season well.

10 Fill half the tart cases with creamed prawns, and sprinkle with fresh dill. Fill the rest with chicken and asparagus, and sprinkle with fresh parsley. Serve.

Per tartlet Energy 274kcal/1138kJ; Protein 9g; Carbohydrate 11g, of which sugars 1.7g; Fat 21.9g, of which saturates 13.4g; Cholesterol 95mg; Calcium 83mg; Fibre 0.6g; Sodium 131mg.

HARE PÂTÉ

WILD HARE ARE A COMMON SIGHT IN RURAL SWEDEN. THEY ARE OFTEN HUNTED AT THE SAME TIME AS DEER AND FEATURE PROMINENTLY ALONGSIDE VENISON IN THE SWEDISH DIET. THE MEAT IS OFTEN COMPARED TO VENISON AS IT IS DARK WITH A SWEET FLAVOUR.

SERVES SIX TO EIGHT

INGREDIENTS

40g/1½oz/3 tbsp butter
3 bay leaves
250g/9oz chicken livers, trimmed
15ml/1 tbsp fresh thyme
120ml/4fl oz/½ cup port
1 oven-ready hare (jackrabbit)
500g/1¼lb unsmoked bacon, cubed
200ml/7fl oz/scant 1 cup double
  (heavy) cream
2 eggs
15ml/1 tbsp plain (all-purpose) flour
1 garlic clove, crushed
15ml/1 tbsp brandy
pinch of freshly grated nutmeg
ground black pepper
brown bread, toasted, to serve

1 Preheat the oven to 140ºC/275ºF/Gas 1. Butter a 20cm/8in loaf tin (pan) with 15g/½oz/1 tbsp of the butter and put 2 bay leaves in the bottom. Melt the remaining butter in a frying pan, add the chicken livers, thyme and remaining bay leaf and, stirring constantly, fry for about 4 minutes until browned.

2 Transfer the livers and their cooking juices to a bowl. Pour over the port and leave to cool.

3 Meanwhile, cut the hare into small cubes. Using a food processor or mincer, mince (grind) half of the cubes of meat.

4 Put all the meat in a bowl, and add the cubed bacon, cream, eggs, flour, crushed garlic, brandy, grated nutmeg and black pepper. Mix the ingredients together well.

5 When the chicken livers have cooled, put the livers and port in a pan and boil until the port has reduced by half to make a sauce.

6 Add the chicken livers and port sauce to the meat mixture and mix it all together. Put the mixture into the prepared loaf tin and cook in the oven for 2 hours.

7 Leave the pâté to cool in the tin before turning out and serving with toasted brown bread.

Per portion Energy 470kcal/1950kJ; Protein 34.5g; Carbohydrate 3.7g, of which sugars 2.3g; Fat 33g, of which saturates 16.6g; Cholesterol 298mg; Calcium 46mg; Fibre 0.1g; Sodium 1091mg.

HERB-CURED FILLET OF ELK

THE ROOTS OF THIS NORWEGIAN RECIPE, URTEMARINET DYRESTEK MED RØMMESAUS, CAN BE FOUND IN THE TRADITIONAL PRACTICE OF FINDING WAYS OF PRESERVING FOOD THROUGH THE LONG WINTERS. THE SAME METHOD OF CURING CAN BE APPLIED TO FILLET OF VENISON OR BEEF.

SERVES EIGHT TO TEN

INGREDIENTS
    30ml/2 tbsp salt
    60ml/4 tbsp sugar
    90ml/6 tbsp chopped mixed fresh
      herbs, such as basil, marjoram,
      thyme, parsley, rosemary and
      juniper sprigs
    100ml/3½fl oz/scant ½ cup
      red wine
    60ml/4 tbsp virgin olive oil
    500g/1¼lb fillet of elk or red or fallow
      deer (or alternatively venison or beef)
    ground black pepper
For the sour cream sauce
    150g/5oz cranberry jam, or
      lingonberry jam or berries
    135ml/4½fl oz/generous ½ cup
      sour cream
    15–30ml/1–2 tbsp sugar (if fresh
      berries are being used)

1 Put the salt, sugar, chopped herbs, wine and olive oil in a bowl. Season generously with pepper and then stir together until well mixed.

2 Put the fillet of meat in a strong plastic bag, add the marinade and ensure that it covers the meat. Place the bag in the refrigerator and leave the meat to marinate for 3 days, turning over the bag at least twice a day.

COOK'S TIP
Juniper sprigs are the new shoots at the end of branches. You can use 2–3 crushed juniper berries instead – the flavour will be slightly different, but still delicious.

3 To make the sour cream sauce with cranberry or lingonberry jam, put the jam in a bowl, add the sour cream and mix well together. If using fresh cranberries or lingonberries, put them in a bowl, add sugar to taste, crush together with a fork, and stir in the sour cream, mixing well.

4 To serve, slice the meat very thinly. It is easier to do this if the meat has been partially frozen after marinating. Accompany with the sour cream sauce. Alternatively, you could serve the cured fillet as a main course, accompanied by roast vegetables and boiled potatoes.

Per portion Energy 187kcal/780kJ; Protein 11.3g; Carbohydrate 11.1g, of which sugars 11.1g; Fat 10.4g, of which saturates 3.8g; Cholesterol 39mg; Calcium 29mg; Fibre 0.3g; Sodium 37mg.

STUFFED CABBAGE ROLLS

AFTER KARL XII'S INVASION OF TURKEY IN 1713 HIS SOLDIERS BROUGHT THIS DISH BACK TO SWEDEN AND REPLACED THE VINE LEAVES WITH CABBAGE LEAVES. KÅLDOLMAR ARE OFTEN SERVED WITH A BROWN SAUCE AS PART OF THE CHRISTMAS TABLE IN SWEDEN. A DELICIOUS VEGETARIAN VERSION OF THE SAME DISH IS ALSO GIVEN HERE.

SERVES SIX TO EIGHT

INGREDIENTS
1 Savoy cabbage
100g/4oz/½ cup long grain rice
100ml/4fl oz/½ cup water
15g/½oz/1 tbsp butter
1 large Spanish (Bermuda)
  onion, chopped
250g/9oz minced (ground) beef
1 egg, beaten
2.5ml/½ tsp chopped fresh thyme
5ml/1 tsp salt
ground black pepper
melted butter for brushing
boiled new potatoes and lingonberry
  conserve, to serve
For the vegetarian version
2 pointed cabbages
100g/4oz/½ cup risotto rice
500ml/18fl oz/2½ cups vegetable
  stock, boiling
50g/2oz dried ceps
1 Spanish (Bermuda) onion, chopped
2 shallots, chopped
30g/1oz/2 tbsp butter
400g/14oz chanterelle or girolle
  mushrooms
100g/4oz mature (sharp) Cheddar
  or Västerbotten cheese, grated
20g/¾oz chopped fresh parsley
salt and ground black pepper
melted butter for brushing
lingonberry conserve, to serve

1 Cut the base off the cabbage and separate the leaves. Cook in boiling salted water for 1 minute, drain and remove the hard centre of each leaf.

2 Put the rice and water in a pan, bring to the boil, then simmer for 10–12 minutes until the rice is tender. Drain and leave to cool.

3 Preheat the oven to 200°C/400°F/ Gas 6. Melt the butter in a pan, add the chopped onion and fry over a medium heat until softened.

4 Put the minced beef into a large bowl and add the softened onion, cooled rice, beaten egg, thyme, and salt and pepper to season.

5 Put 30ml/2 tbsp of the meat mixture into each cabbage leaf and wrap them into parcels. Brush the parcels with melted butter and place them in an ovenproof dish.

6 Bake the stuffed parcels in the preheated oven for about 40 minutes until they are golden brown.

7 Serve them immediately, accompanied by boiled new potatoes and lingonberry conserve.

For the vegetarian version

1 Follow step 1 (as the meat version). Put the rice in a pan with a little stock and simmer for 20 minutes, gradually adding the remaining stock and stirring until the rice is tender.

2 Soak the ceps in boiling water. Fry the onion and shallots in 15g/½oz/1 tbsp of the butter until golden brown, then set aside.

3 Fry the chanterelles or girolles in the remaining butter until tender. Drain the ceps and add them to the rice with the fried onion, chanterelles, cheese, parsley, salt and pepper.

4 Put 30ml/2 tbsp of the vegetable and rice mixture into each cabbage leaf and wrap them into parcels.

5 Brush the parcels with melted butter and place them in an ovenproof dish. Bake in the oven at 200°C/400°F/Gas 6 for about 30 minutes until they are golden brown.

Per portion Meat version, Energy 169kcal/702kJ; Protein 9.2g; Carbohydrate 16.1g, of which sugars 5.2g; Fat 7.6g, of which saturates 3.3g; Cholesterol 47mg; Calcium 49mg; Fibre 1.8g; Sodium 51mg.
Vegetarian version, Energy 174kcal/724kJ; Protein 7.1g; Carbohydrate 18.4g, of which sugars 7.1g; Fat 7.8g, of which saturates 4.7g; Cholesterol 20mg; Calcium 157mg; Fibre 3.2g; Sodium 125mg.

BAKED HAM OMELETTE

THE NORWEGIANS HAVE A GIFT FOR TURNING LEFTOVERS INTO SOMETHING SPECIAL, AND THIS BAKED OMELETTE IS A PERFECT EXAMPLE. IT IS EQUALLY GOOD HOT OR COLD. CUT INTO SMALL SQUARES, IT CAN BE SERVED WITH DRINKS, OR IT CAN BE PLACED ON A COLD TABLE. WITH A SALAD IT PROVIDES A LIGHT LUNCH OR SUPPER DISH. IN NORWAY IT MIGHT BE SERVED AS ONE OF THE 'AFTONS' OR LATE EVENING SNACKS THAT COMPENSATE FOR THE MAIN MEAL OF THE DAY BEING SERVED SO EARLY.

SERVES FOUR

INGREDIENTS

15g/½oz/1 tbsp butter, plus extra
  for greasing
1 leek, white and pale green parts only,
  thinly sliced, or 1 shallot, chopped
4 eggs
300ml/½ pint/1¼ cups single
  (light) cream
115g/4oz cooked ham, preferably
  smoked, diced
salt and ground black pepper
chopped fresh parsley,
  to garnish (optional)

VARIATIONS
Cooked chicken or smoked sausage can be used instead of cooked ham, and the omelette can be topped with grated cheese.

1 Preheat the oven to 180°C/350°F/Gas 4. Butter a 20cm/8in ovenproof dish. Melt the butter in a pan, add the leek or shallot and fry for 2–3 minutes.

2 Break the eggs into a bowl and beat lightly together. Add the cream, season with salt and pepper, and beat until well combined. Add the chopped ham.

3 Pour the omelette mixture into the prepared ovenproof dish and bake in the preheated oven for about 25 minutes, until set and golden brown in colour.

4 Serve the baked omelette immediately, garnished with chopped fresh parsley, if you like.

Per portion Energy 287kcal/1190kJ; Protein 14.8g; Carbohydrate 3.2g, of which sugars 2.9g; Fat 24.1g, of which saturates 13g; Cholesterol 256mg; Calcium 109mg; Fibre 1g; Sodium 460mg.

JERUSALEM ARTICHOKES <u>AU</u> GRATIN

THE DANES MAKE GOOD USE OF THESE SOMEWHAT OVERLOOKED VEGETABLES. JERUSALEM ARTICHOKES ARE NOT RELATED TO GLOBE ARTICHOKES, BUT TO THE SUNFLOWER, WHICH IS WHY THEY'RE SOMETIMES SOLD AS 'SUNCHOKES'. THEY HAVE A DELIGHTFUL, NUTTY FLAVOUR AND APPEALING CRUNCH, BUT CHOOSE TUBERS THAT ARE FIRM AND FRESH LOOKING, WITHOUT WRINKLES. PEEL THEM BEFORE COOKING OR JUST WASH THEM WELL. THIS IS A LOVELY ACCOMPANIMENT TO ROAST MEAT OR FRIED FISH.

SERVES FOUR

INGREDIENTS

675g/1½lb Jerusalem artichokes,
  coarsely chopped
250ml/8fl oz/1 cup sour cream
50ml/2fl oz/¼ cup single (light) cream
40g/1½ oz/½ cup grated
  Danbo cheese
60ml/4 tbsp fresh breadcrumbs
salt

1 Preheat the oven to 190°C/375°F/ Gas 5. Lightly grease an ovenproof dish. Place the Jerusalem artichokes in a large bowl.

2 Add the sour cream and single cream, and a pinch of salt. Toss to coat the artichokes evenly with the mixture. Spread the artichokes over the bottom of the prepared dish.

3 Sprinkle the artichokes evenly with the cheese, then the breadcrumbs. Bake for about 30 minutes, until the cheese melts and the top is brown and bubbling.

Per portion Energy 296kcal/1230kJ; Protein 6.9g; Carbohydrate 27.6g, of which sugars 15.5g; Fat 18.1g, of which saturates 11.1g; Cholesterol 52mg; Calcium 186mg; Fibre 4.4g; Sodium 240mg.

BRAISED RED CABBAGE

Sweet, tangy red cabbage is a wintertime favourite everywhere in Scandinavia, but nowhere more so than in Denmark. Outstanding paired with roast pork, rød kål is also the traditional accompaniment for the Christmas goose or duck. If the sweet, sour and fruity flavours weren't enticing enough, the vivid violet colour would captivate anyone.

3 Meanwhile, melt the butter in a large frying pan over a medium heat. Stir in the onion and apples and cook for 5–7 minutes until soft.

4 Stir the apples and onions into the cabbage with the sugar, blackcurrant juice or jam, allspice and cloves, and season with salt. Simmer gently for a further 1½ hours. Adjust the seasoning to taste before serving.

SERVES SIX

INGREDIENTS
1.3kg/3lb red cabbage
50ml/2fl oz/¼ cup distilled
  white vinegar
25g/1oz/2 tbsp butter
1 medium onion, finely chopped
2 tart apples, peeled, cored and
  thinly sliced
50g/2oz/¼ cup sugar
120ml/4fl oz/½ cup blackcurrant
  juice or jam
1.5ml/¼ tsp ground allspice
6 whole cloves
salt

VARIATION
If using blackcurrant jam, you will need less sugar than if using juice. You could also use apple juice or redcurrant jelly.

1 Remove the outer leaves and core of the cabbage and cut into quarters. Thinly chop or shred the cabbage, and place in a large pan. Add 120ml/ 4fl oz/½ cup water and the vinegar and bring to the boil.

2 Reduce the heat, cover and simmer for 1 hour, stirring occasionally to prevent scorching.

Per portion Energy 90kcal/381kJ; Protein 3.1g; Carbohydrate 19.4g, of which sugars 18g; Fat 0.5g, of which saturates 0g; Cholesterol 0mg; Calcium 98mg; Fibre 5g; Sodium 14mg.

PICKLED BEETROOT

DARK PURPLE BEETROOT ARE BELOVED IN DENMARK AND THE REST OF SCANDINAVIA, SINCE THEY THRIVE EVEN IN SHORT NORTHERN SUMMERS AND ARE HIGHLY NUTRITIOUS. TO EXTEND THEIR VERSATILITY IN THE KITCHEN, THEY ARE PICKLED FOR USE IN EVERYTHING FROM SALADS TO SOUPS, TO SERVE AS SIDE DISHES AND TO GARNISH OPEN SANDWICHES. THIS DISH IS CALLED SYLTEDE RØDBEDER.

SERVES SIX

INGREDIENTS
    1.2kg/2½ lb fresh beetroot (beets),
      preferably with stems attached
    45ml/3 tbsp distilled white vinegar
For the marinade
    120ml/4fl oz/½ cup water
    60ml/4 tbsp distilled white vinegar
    90g/3½ oz/½ cup sugar
    1 bay leaf
    2.5ml/½ tsp caraway seeds
    3 whole cloves
    salt and ground black pepper

1 Trim the beetroot stems to 2.5cm/ 1in, but do not peel the skins or cut the roots.

2 Place 2 litres/3½ pints/8¾ cups of water and the white vinegar in a deep pan and bring to the boil.

3 Add the beetroot, adding more water if necessary to cover them, and simmer for about 45 minutes until the beetroot are tender.

COOK'S TIP
Leaving the stems and peel on the beetroot until after they are cooked helps to prevent the vivid red colour draining out.

4 Remove the pan from the heat and drain the beetroot, reserving 250ml/ 8fl oz/1 cup of the cooking liquid. Set the cooked beetroot aside and allow them to cool.

5 To prepare the marinade, combine all the marinade ingredients in a pan and bring to the boil.

6 Immediately remove the pan from the heat, pour the marinade into a large bowl and leave until cool.

7 Peel the cooled beetroot and cut them into 5mm/¼in slices.

8 Add the beetroot slices to the bowl with the marinade and toss gently to coat the beetroot in the marinade. Cover the bowl and refrigerate for 8 hours or overnight.

Per portion Energy 115kcal/490kJ; Protein 2.7g; Carbohydrate 27.4g, of which sugars 26.5g; Fat 0.2g, of which saturates 0g; Cholesterol 0mg; Calcium 39mg; Fibre 2.9g; Sodium 430mg.

CUCUMBER SALAD

HOTHOUSE CUCUMBERS GROW LUXURIANTLY UNDER ARTIFICIAL LIGHT AND CAN THEREFORE BE GROWN SUCCESSFULLY DURING THE LONG SCANDINAVIAN WINTERS. AS A RESULT, THIS DISH, AGURKESALAT, IS A SURPRISING FAVOURITE IN DENMARK. THE DRESSING SHOULD BE PERFECTLY BALANCED BETWEEN SWEET AND SOUR, WITH ACCENTS OF FRESH DILL. IT IS IMPORTANT TO MAKE THIS SALAD SHORTLY BEFORE YOU INTEND TO SERVE IT, SO THE CUCUMBER RETAINS ITS CRISPNESS AND DOESN'T BECOME SOGGY.

SERVES SIX

INGREDIENTS
1 large English cucumber,
   about 35cm/14in long
75ml/5 tbsp distilled white vinegar
25g/1oz/2 tbsp white sugar
45ml/3 tbsp chopped fresh dill
salt and ground white pepper

COOK'S TIP
This salad is served with poached fish, such as salmon. The vinegar and sugar can also be mixed into 250ml/8fl oz/1 cup sour cream for a rich, creamy dressing that goes well with fish cakes and fried fish.

1 Cut the cucumber into 3mm/⅛in slices and place the slices in a serving bowl. (If you want to achieve a pretty edge, first stand the cucumber on its end and, using a peeler, remove 4 strips of peel.)

2 Combine the vinegar, sugar and dill in a small bowl and season with salt and pepper. Pour the dressing over the cucumber slices and toss to coat evenly. Chill until ready to serve.

Per portion Energy 30kcal/125kJ; Protein 0.7g; Carbohydrate 1.1g, of which sugars 1g; Fat 2.6g, of which saturates 1.6g; Cholesterol 8mg; Calcium 26mg; Fibre 0.4g; Sodium 8mg.

POTATO SALAD

WHILE THE POTATO IS NOW A STAPLE ON DANISH TABLES, IT WASN'T ALWAYS THAT WAY. THOUGH IT REACHED EUROPE IN 1570, THE HARDY TUBER DIDN'T ARRIVE IN DENMARK UNTIL ALMOST TWO CENTURIES LATER. EVEN THEN THERE WAS GREAT RESISTANCE TO EATING IT AND IT TOOK PARISH PRIESTS TO LEAD THE WAY, DEMONSTRATING THE POTATO'S VIRTUE AS A WHOLESOME FOOD. TODAY, THIS COLD POTATO SALAD, KARTOFFELSALAT, IS A YEAR-ROUND FAVOURITE.

SERVES SIX TO EIGHT

INGREDIENTS
1.8kg/4lb potatoes
45ml/3 tbsp finely chopped onion
2 celery stalks, finely chopped
250ml/8fl oz/1 cup sour cream
250ml/8fl oz/1 cup mayonnaise
5ml/1 tsp mustard powder
4ml/¾ tsp celery seed
75ml/5 tbsp chopped fresh dill
salt and ground white pepper

VARIATION
If you like, you could add chopped cucumber, crumbled bacon rashers, or chopped hard-boiled eggs to the potato salad.

1 Boil the potatoes in lightly salted water for 20–25 minutes, until tender, then drain and allow to cool.

2 Peel and coarsely chop the potatoes and place them in a large mixing bowl. Add the onion and celery.

3 In a separate bowl, stir together the sour cream, mayonnaise, mustard, celery seed, dill, salt and pepper.

4 Add the dressing to the potatoes and toss gently. Adjust the seasoning, cover and chill until ready to serve.

Per portion Energy 440kcal/1834kJ; Protein 5.2g; Carbohydrate 38.5g, of which sugars 4.9g; Fat 30.5g, of which saturates 7.7g; Cholesterol 42mg; Calcium 50mg; Fibre 2.4g; Sodium 183mg.

OPEN SANDWICHES

The open sandwich, or smørrebrød, has been celebrated for over three centuries as one of Denmark's most popular culinary icons, which is why it deserves a special chapter. Although the name translates simply as 'buttered bread', these Danish creations are sophisticated in taste and appearance. Often humble ingredients are artistically arranged to please the eye as well as the palate. Although of Danish origin, they are also enjoyed in Sweden and Norway, where they put their own stamp on this classic dish.

GRILLED GOAT'S CHEESE WITH BABY BEETROOT

BEETROOT ARE CONSIDERED A DELICACY WHEN THEY ARE FRESHLY DUG OUT OF THE GROUND IN EARLY SUMMER. IN SWEDEN THESE EARLY VEGETABLES ARE CALLED 'PRIMÖR', AND ARE USUALLY SERVED WITH WHIPPED BUTTER. HERE, GOAT'S CHEESE MARRIES WELL WITH THE SWEETNESS OF THE BEETROOT.

SERVES SIX

INGREDIENTS
  6 small raw beetroot (beets)
  6 slices French bread
  6 slices (250g/9oz) goat's cheese
  30ml/2 tbsp walnut oil
  salt and ground black pepper

1 Cook the raw beetroot in a large pan of salted boiling water (leaving the skin on) for about 40 minutes until tender.

2 Leave to cool slightly, then remove the skin and slice the beetroot.

3 Toast the slices of French bread on both sides.

4 Arrange the slices of beetroot in a fan on top of each of the toasted French bread slices, then place a slice of the goat's cheese on top of each portion.

5 Place the slices on a grill (broiler) pan and grill (broil) until the goat's cheese has melted and has turned golden brown in colour.

6 Serve immediately, drizzled with a little walnut oil and with some black pepper ground on top.

Per portion Energy 290kcal/1215kJ; Protein 13.3g; Carbohydrate 26.7g, of which sugars 5g; Fat 15.2g, of which saturates 7.9g; Cholesterol 39mg; Calcium 114mg; Fibre 1.9g; Sodium 530mg.

MARINATED HERRING IN SOUR CREAM

FISHERMEN HAVE FISHED THE SEAS AROUND DENMARK FOR CENTURIES. COD, PLAICE, MACKEREL AND OF COURSE HERRING WERE PLENTIFUL IN THE COLD WATERS. SILVERY HERRING BECAME A STAPLE IN THE DANISH DIET, AND THE FAT, YOUNG, REDDISH-COLOURED MATJES WERE ESPECIALLY PRIZED.

SERVES FOUR

INGREDIENTS
150ml/¼ pint/½ cup sour cream
2.5ml/½ tsp creamed horseradish
15ml/1 tbsp Pickled Beetroot
(beet) juice (see page 89)
3 matjes herring, about 150g/5oz,
cut into 2.5cm/1in squares
115g/4oz/½ cup Pickled Beetroot
(beets), diced
250g/9oz/1 cup Cucumber
Salad, drained and chopped
(see page 90)
25g/1oz/2 tbsp salted butter, softened
2 slices rye bread
2 round (butterhead) lettuce leaves
2 hard-boiled eggs, cut into wedges
4 parsley sprigs
salt and ground black pepper

1 Combine the sour cream, horseradish and beetroot juice in a mixing bowl.

2 Stir in the herring, beetroot and cucumber salad; toss to coat evenly with the sour cream mixture. Season with salt and pepper, then chill in the refrigerator until needed.

3 To make the open sandwiches, butter each slice of bread to the edges, then top with the lettuce leaves.

4 Cut each slice of bread in half.

5 Leaving a curl of lettuce visible on each slice, spoon on the herring salad. Arrange three egg wedges on top of each sandwich. Season with salt and pepper. Tuck a parsley sprig under the egg.

Per portion Energy 346kcal/1437kJ; Protein 13.5g; Carbohydrate 15.4g, of which sugars 9.7g; Fat 25.9g, of which saturates 12.5g; Cholesterol 165mg; Calcium 114mg; Fibre 1.6g; Sodium 506mg.

POTATOES WITH LEEKS AND HERRING

SOME MIGHT CALL THIS SMØRREBRØD A POOR PEASANT'S SANDWICH GIVEN ITS HUMBLE INGREDIENTS, BUT THE OPPOSITE IS TRUE. THE FIRST NEW POTATOES ARE CELEBRATED WITH GUSTO THROUGHOUT SCANDINAVIA, GENERALLY WITH HEAPS OF CREAMY BUTTER. ALTHOUGH UNKNOWN IN THE FAR NORTH BEFORE THE 18TH CENTURY, POTATOES ARE NOW AN ESSENTIAL PART OF THE TRADITIONAL DANISH DIET. SELECT THE BEST QUALITY POTATOES YOU CAN FIND FOR THIS SANDWICH.

4 Spread the slices of bread to the edges with the remaining butter, top with the lettuce leaves and cut each slice in half to make the bases for four open sandwiches.

5 Layer 4–6 slices of potato on top of the lettuce on each sandwich.

6 Arrange 3–4 herring pieces down the centre of the potatoes and spoon 30ml/2 tbsp leeks over the herring on each sandwich.

7 Sprinkle the sandwiches with chopped chives and serve.

COOK'S TIP
After the bread has been sliced, move the slices to a serving plate or individual plates before arranging the toppings and garnish.

MAKES FOUR

INGREDIENTS
  40g/1½oz/3 tbsp salted
    butter, softened
  90g/3½oz leeks, sliced
  2 slices rye bread
  2 round (butterhead) lettuce leaves
  4–5 small new potatoes, peeled,
    boiled and thinly sliced
  12–16 pieces Pickled Herring (see
    page 68), about 2.5cm/1in square
  10ml/2 tsp chopped chives

1 Melt 15g/½oz/1 tbsp of the butter in a frying pan.

2 Stir in the leeks and cook over a medium heat for 5 minutes, until wilted.

3 Remove from the heat and set aside to cool.

Per portion Energy 196kcal/819kJ; Protein 6.6g; Carbohydrate 17.2g, of which sugars 4.2g; Fat 11.5g, of which saturates 5.3g; Cholesterol 32mg; Calcium 27mg; Fibre 1.7g; Sodium 347mg.

SMOKED SALMON WITH DILL AND LEMON

SMOKED SALMON IS A DELICACY IN DENMARK. NOW PRIMARILY FARM-RAISED IN NORWAY OR SCOTLAND, THIN SLICES OF THE SUCCULENT PINK FISH ARE A FAVOURITE SMØRREBRØD TOPPING. SO AS NOT TO COMPETE WITH THE SALMON'S RICH FLAVOUR, CRUSTY WHITE BREAD, OR WHAT DANES CALL FRANSKBRØD, IS THE PREFERRED CHOICE FOR THIS SMØRREBRØD. THE CRUSTS ARE LEFT ON THE BREAD, AND A DRIZZLE OF MUSTARD SAUCE WITH DILL AND LEMON SLICES ARE THE TRADITIONAL GARNISHES.

SERVES FOUR

INGREDIENTS
- 25g/1oz/2 tbsp salted butter, softened
- 2 slices crusty white bread
- 2 round (butterhead) lettuce leaves
- 4 slices smoked salmon
- 4 lemon slices
- 4 dill sprigs

For the mustard sauce
- 15ml/1 tbsp distilled white vinegar
- 25g/1oz/2 tbsp sugar
- 90ml/6 tbsp Dijon mustard
- 1 egg yolk (optional)
- 50ml/2fl oz/¼ cup vegetable oil
- 7.5ml/1½ tsp chopped fresh dill
- salt and ground black pepper

1 To make the mustard sauce, mix the vinegar, sugar, mustard, egg yolk (if using) and oil in a small bowl. Stir in the chopped dill, and season.

2 Butter the slices of bread to the edges, top with the lettuce leaves and cut each slice in half. Spoon 5ml/1 tsp mustard sauce down the middle of each sandwich.

3 Leaving one curl of lettuce visible on each slice of bread, arrange a slice of smoked salmon on top of each sandwich, folding or rolling the edges to fit on top of the lettuce.

4 Cut each lemon slice from the outside to the centre, then twist it and place in the middle of the salmon. Tuck a sprig of dill under each lemon twist to garnish, and serve immediately.

VARIATION
A layer of thinly sliced cucumber can be substituted for the lettuce leaves.

Per portion Energy 249kcal/1037kJ; Protein 9.3g; Carbohydrate 15.7g, of which sugars 8.9g; Fat 17g, of which saturates 6.2g; Cholesterol 30mg; Calcium 44mg; Fibre 0.3g; Sodium 1265mg.

FRIED PLAICE FILLET WITH REMOULADE

DANES ADORE REMOULADE. A TANGY, CREAMY MAYONNAISE-BASED RELISH WITH PICKLES, SIMILAR TO TARTARE SAUCE, THIS VERSATILE CONDIMENT IS EATEN WITH SEAFOOD AND FRIKADELLER (DANISH MEATBALLS), AND USED HERE AS A GARNISH FOR AN OPEN FRIED PLAICE SANDWICH.

MAKES FOUR

INGREDIENTS
1 egg
50g/2oz/½ cup fine breadcrumbs
225g/8oz plaice fillet
40g/1½oz/3 tbsp salted
   butter, softened
2 slices crusty white bread
2 round (butterhead) lettuce leaves
4 lemon slices
4 fresh dill sprigs
For the remoulade
250ml/8fl oz/1 cup mayonnaise
120ml/4fl oz/½ cup chopped sweet
   dill pickles or relish
15ml/1 tbsp mustard powder
15ml/1 tbsp finely chopped
   fresh dill
30ml/2 tbsp finely chopped parsley
30ml/2 tbsp diced onion
2.5ml/½ tsp lemon juice
15ml/1 tbsp capers (optional)

1 First make the remoulade. Put the mayonnaise in a bowl and stir in lemon juice, mustard powder, the dill pickles or relish, dill, parsley, onion and capers (if using) until blended. Cover and chill.

2 Briefly whisk the egg with 5ml/1 tsp water in a dish. Place the breadcrumbs in another shallow dish. Cut the fillet into four 10–15cm/4–6in pieces. Dip the plaice fillet into the egg, then the breadcrumbs, coating both sides.

3 Melt 15g/½oz/1 tbsp of the butter in a pan over a medium heat, and cook the fillet for about 6 minutes, turning once, until golden brown on each side. Drain on kitchen paper and leave to cool.

4 Spread the slices of bread to the edges with the remaining butter. Place a lettuce leaf on each slice and cut in half. Leaving a curl of lettuce visible on each sandwich, arrange the fish on the lettuce. Add some remoulade, a lemon slice and dill sprig.

Per portion Energy 667kcal/2762kJ; Protein 15.6g; Carbohydrate 19.1g, of which sugars 2.3g; Fat 59.9g, of which saturates 12.9g; Cholesterol 140mg; Calcium 89mg; Fibre 0.7g; Sodium 593mg.

DANISH CAVIAR WITH TOAST AND CRÈME FRAÎCHE

TRUST THE THRIFTY DANES TO DEVISE INEXPENSIVE 'CAVIAR' FROM THE PLENTIFUL LUMPFISH OF NORTH ATLANTIC WATERS. THE LIGHTLY SALTED BLACK ROE IS A TASTY SUBSTITUTE FOR THE REAL THING. THE MIX OF FLAVOURS AND TEXTURES IN THIS SIMPLE CLASSIC IS EXCEPTIONAL.

SERVES FOUR

INGREDIENTS
    6 slices good white bread,
      crusts removed
    100g/3¾oz lumpfish caviar
    100ml/3½fl oz/scant ½ cup
      crème fraîche
    ½ red onion, thinly sliced
    60ml/4 tbsp chopped fresh dill

VARIATIONS
• Substitute red lumpfish caviar for the black variety.
• You could use sour cream instead of crème fraîche.
• Try substituting chopped fresh basil leaves in place of the chopped dill.

1 Lightly toast the bread and cut each slice into four triangles. Spread each toast triangle with lumpfish caviar.

2 Top with a teaspoon of crème fraîche and a slice of red onion, and sprinkle with dill.

3 Alternatively, arrange the toast on a serving plate. Spoon the lumpfish caviar, crème fraîche and dill into separate small bowls, and place on the serving plate. Arrange the red onion on one corner of the plate.

Per portion Energy 208kcal/869kJ; Protein 6.5g; Carbohydrate 19.5g, of which sugars 1.8g; Fat 12.1g, of which saturates 7g; Cholesterol 99mg; Calcium 60mg; Fibre 0.6g; Sodium 731mg.

TOAST SKAGEN

THIS DISH IS FROM THE WEST COAST OF SWEDEN, BETWEEN SWEDEN AND DENMARK. SKAGENRÖRA, WHICH TRANSLATES AS 'A MIXTURE FROM THE SKAGERRAK SEA', IS OFTEN SERVED IN RESTAURANTS AS A SNACK. YOU CAN USE PEELED PRAWNS, BUT THOSE WITH THEIR SHELL ON TASTE AND LOOK BETTER.

2 Put the sour cream, mayonnaise, chopped dill, chives and lemon juice in a large bowl. Season the mixture with salt and pepper to taste, then stir in the peeled prawns.

3 Melt the butter in a large frying pan, add the bread slices and fry until golden brown on both sides.

4 Serve the prawn mixture piled on top of the fried bread and garnish with a small amount of the salmon roe and a frond of dill.

COOK'S TIPS
Salmon roe is ideal to use as a garnish, as its orange colour and large eggs make the dish look rather special. Grated horseradish is another good accompaniment.

SERVES SIX TO EIGHT

INGREDIENTS
 1kg/2¼lb shell-on cooked
  prawns (shrimp)
 250ml/8fl oz/1 cup sour cream
 250ml/8fl oz/1 cup thick mayonnaise
 30ml/2 tbsp chopped fresh dill
  plus fronds, to garnish
 30ml/2 tbsp chopped fresh chives
 a squeeze of lemon juice
 25–50g/1–2oz/2–4 tbsp butter
 8 slices bread, halved
 5ml/1 tsp red salmon roe
 salt and ground black pepper

1 Carefully remove the shells from the cooked prawns, keeping them intact. Set the peeled prawns aside while you make the dressing.

Per portion Energy 415kcal/1726kJ; Protein 14.5g; Carbohydrate 15.2g, of which sugars 2.5g; Fat 33.4g, of which saturates 9.2g; Cholesterol 180mg; Calcium 128mg; Fibre 0.7g; Sodium 1065mg.

PRAWNS WITH EGG AND CUCUMBER

THE ICY WATERS AROUND GREENLAND, A DANISH PROVINCE SINCE THE VIKING ERA, ARE THE PREFERRED SOURCE FOR THE SWEET, WILD PRAWNS IN THIS CLASSIC OPEN SANDWICH. HEAP THE PRAWNS OVER THE LETTUCE OR ARRANGE THEM IN ORDERLY ROWS ACCORDING TO YOUR STYLE.

SERVES FOUR

INGREDIENTS
25g/1oz/2 tbsp salted butter, softened
2 slices crusty white bread
2 round (butterhead) lettuce leaves
2 hard-boiled eggs, sliced
300g/11oz/2 cups small cooked
  prawns (shrimp)
mayonnaise
4 dill sprigs
8 cucumber slices
4 lemon slices

1 Butter the slices of bread to the edges, top with the lettuce leaves and cut each slice in half.

2 Place three slices of egg toward the top of each lettuce leaf, leaving one curl visible.

VARIATION
Tomato could be used as a garnish instead of cucumber, if you like. If using tomato slices, substitute the lemon slices for lemon wedges for extra eye appeal. The egg slices can be placed on top of the prawns, instead of underneath them, topped with mayonnaise.

3 Divide the prawns among the sandwiches and arrange them over the rest of the lettuce, leaving some of the egg slices showing.

4 To garnish, top the prawns with a spoonful of mayonnaise, then place a sprig of dill in the centre of the mayonnaise on each sandwich.

5 Stack two cucumber slices with one lemon slice between them; cut the stack halfway across, then twist to form a curl. Repeat with the remaining cucumber and lemon.

6 Place a decorative twist of cucumber and lemon either on or beside each sandwich to garnish.

Per portion Energy 256kcal/1066kJ; Protein 17.6g; Carbohydrate 6.4g, of which sugars 0.5g; Fat 18.1g, of which saturates 5.5g; Cholesterol 264mg; Calcium 90mg; Fibre 0.2g; Sodium 337mg.

HAM WITH ITALIAN SALAD

*THE DANES LOVE ALL PORK PRODUCTS AND A WIDE VARIETY OF HAM IS SOLD READY-COOKED IN
STORES. GARNISHED WITH ANOTHER FAVOURITE, A SIMPLE PEA AND CARROT COMBINATION KNOWN
IN DENMARK AS ITALIAN SALAD, THIS HAM SANDWICH IS FRESH AND SATISFYING. YOU CAN MAKE THE
SALAD IN ADVANCE AND CHILL IT IN THE REFRIGERATOR UNTIL YOU ASSEMBLE THE SANDWICHES.*

SERVES FOUR

INGREDIENTS
    25g/1oz/2 tbsp salted butter, softened
    2 slices rye bread
    4 leaves cos (romaine) lettuce
    8 thin slices (125g/4¼oz) cooked ham
    12 slices cucumber
    4 parsley sprigs
For the Italian salad
    115g/4oz/1 cup chopped carrots
    115/4oz/1 cup fresh or frozen peas
    50ml/2fl oz/¼ cup mayonnaise
    5ml/1 tsp lemon juice
    10ml/2 tsp chopped fresh dill
    salt and ground white pepper

1 To make the Italian salad, place the
carrots in a pan with 50ml/2fl oz/
¼ cup water. Bring to the boil and
cook the carrots for 4–5 minutes until
nearly tender.

2 Stir in the peas and cook for a
further 2 minutes.

3 Drain the cooked carrots and peas,
refresh them under cold running water,
then drain again and transfer them
to a bowl.

4 Set the cooked peas and carrots aside
to cool completely.

5 Stir the mayonnaise, lemon juice and
dill into the peas and carrots, and season
with salt and pepper. Chill until needed.

6 To make the sandwiches, butter the
slices of bread to the edges, top with
the lettuce leaves and cut each slice
in half.

7 Leaving one curl of lettuce visible on
each piece, pleat or fan two slices of
ham over the lettuce.

8 Top the ham on each sandwich
with 15ml/1 tbsp Italian salad.
Garnish with cucumber slices and
parsley sprigs.

Per portion Energy 231kcal/959kJ; Protein 9.4g; Carbohydrate 12.3g, of which sugars 3.8g; Fat 16.4g, of which saturates 5.2g; Cholesterol 41mg; Calcium 30mg; Fibre 2.8g; Sodium 550mg.

LIVER PÂTÉ WITH BACON AND MUSHROOMS

ONE OF THE MOST POPULAR SMØRREBRØD TOPPINGS OF ALL IN DENMARK, LIVER PÂTÉ DEMONSTRATES ITS FLAVOURSOME VERSATILITY PAIRED WITH CRISP BACON RASHERS AND SAUTÉED MUSHROOMS. TRADITIONALLY, THE RYE BREAD WOULD HAVE BEEN SPREAD WITH BACON FAT OR LARD TO ENHANCE THE RICH, EARTHY TASTE OF THE LIVER PÂTÉ.

SERVES FOUR

INGREDIENTS

40g/1½oz/3 tbsp salted
  butter, softened
4 brown cap (cremini) mushrooms or
  button (white) mushrooms, sliced
4 unsmoked streaky (fatty) bacon
  rashers (strips)
300g/11oz block of Liver Pâté
2 slices rye bread
2 leaves round (butterhead) lettuce
2 slices Pickled Beetroot (beet) (see
  page 89), cut into matchsticks
chopped fresh parsley, to garnish

1 Melt 15g/½oz/1 tbsp of the butter in a frying pan over a medium heat. Stir in the mushrooms and cook for 4–5 minutes, until lightly browned.

2 Remove the mushrooms from the pan and set them aside to cool.

3 Place the bacon in the frying pan over a medium heat. Cook until browned and crisp. Remove the bacon from the frying pan and drain on kitchen paper.

4 Cut the liver pâté into slices with a sharp knife. How thick you cut the slices depends on how much you want, but, as a guide, aim for a thickness of around 5mm/¼in.

5 Spread the slices of bread to the edges with the remaining butter. Place a lettuce leaf on each slice and cut the slices in half. Leaving one curl of lettuce visible, arrange two slices of liver pâté on the lettuce on each sandwich.

6 Place a slice of bacon over the pâté. Garnish each sandwich with two or three sticks of beetroot and some chopped parsley.

VARIATIONS
Garnish with small pickled gherkins to accent the sandwich's textures and flavours. Small, whole beetroot slices can also be used as a garnish.

Per portion Energy 418kcal/1731kJ; Protein 15g; Carbohydrate 7.8g, of which sugars 1.7g; Fat 36.6g, of which saturates 13.5g; Cholesterol 157mg; Calcium 35mg; Fibre 2.2g; Sodium 868mg.

THE VETERINARIAN'S EVENING SANDWICH

THE TALE BEHIND THIS CLASSIC DISH, DYRLÆGENS NATMAD, DATES FROM THE 1880S AND INVOLVES A COPENHAGEN VETERINARIAN WHO VISITED THE OSKAR DAVIDSEN SMØRREBRØD RESTAURANT EVERY DAY FOR A BREAKFAST SANDWICH, AND EACH EVENING FOR ANOTHER. FOR BOTH MEALS, HIS FAVOURITE COMBINATION INCLUDED LIVER PÂTÉ AND BOILED BEEF, GARNISHED WITH BEEF ASPIC AND SWEET ONIONS.

SERVES FOUR

INGREDIENTS

25g/1oz/2 tbsp salted butter,
  softened
2 slices rye bread
small bunch watercress or
  rocket (arugula), thick
  stalks removed
4 slices Liver Pâté, 5mm/¼in thick
  (about 300g/11oz total weight)
4 thin slices deli pastrami
  (about 115g/4oz total weight)
16 small sweet onion rings
4 tomato slices, seeded
For the beef aspic
250ml/8fl oz/1 cup boiling water
1 beef stock (bouillon) cube
1 sachet (15ml/1 tbsp)
  powdered gelatine
15ml/1 tbsp dry sherry

1 Make the beef aspic at least 2 hours before you need it. Pour the boiling water into a small bowl. Add the stock cube and gelatine, and stir until dissolved. Add the sherry. Pour into a small, rectangular shallow dish. Chill for 2 hours, until set.

2 Butter the bread and cut the slices in half (to give 4 pieces). Arrange about 10 watercress or rocket leaves on each.

3 Place two slices of liver pâté on one half of a slice, and two slices of pastrami on the other half, cutting or folding them to fit. Do the same with the other slice.

4 Chop the beef aspic into 5mm/¼in cubes and place 4–5 cubes on top of the meats on each sandwich. Arrange four onion rings over the aspic cubes and garnish with a slice of tomato.

Per portion Energy 373kcal/1545kJ; Protein 16.1g; Carbohydrate 8.1g, of which sugars 1.9g; Fat 30.9g, of which saturates 10.8g; Cholesterol 158mg; Calcium 33mg; Fibre 0.9g; Sodium 1019mg.

BACON <u>WITH</u> APPLES

APPLES APPEAR IN MANY SAVOURY DISHES IN DENMARK, FROM THE CLASSIC PORK LOIN STUFFED WITH PRUNES AND APPLES, TO POACHED APPLE HALVES FILLED WITH CURRANT JELLY SERVED AS A SIDE DISH WITH ROAST PORK. IN THIS SANDWICH, THE SWEET COMBINATION OF APPLES AND ONIONS MIXED TOGETHER WITH CRISP, SALTY BACON IS RICH AND SATISFYING. SERVE THE SANDWICH WARM.

SERVES FOUR

INGREDIENTS

    8 unsmoked streaky (fatty) bacon
      rashers (strips)
    75g/3oz/1 cup finely chopped onion
    2 firm apples, peeled and chopped
    25g/1oz/2 tbsp salted butter, softened
    2 slices rye bread
    2 leaves round (butterhead) lettuce
    4 parsley sprigs

1 Fry the bacon over a medium-high heat until crisp; drain on kitchen paper, leaving the fat in the pan.

2 Cook the onion in the reserved bacon fat for 5–7 minutes, until transparent but not browned.

3 Add the apples, and continue cooking for about 5 minutes, until tender. Crumble half the bacon into the apple mixture.

4 Butter the slices of bread to the edges, top with the lettuce leaves and cut each slice in half.

5 Leaving one curl of lettuce visible on each piece, spoon the apple and bacon mixture on to the lettuce, dividing it evenly among the sandwiches.

6 Break the four reserved bacon rashers in half, and place two pieces on each sandwich. Garnish with parsley sprigs.

Per portion Energy 215kcal/895kJ; Protein 9.8g; Carbohydrate 13.9g, of which sugars 8g; Fat 13.7g, of which saturates 6.4g; Cholesterol 40mg; Calcium 21mg; Fibre 2g; Sodium 883mg.

BEEF TARTARE WITH EGG YOLK, ONION AND BEETROOT

RAW MEAT MAY NOT BE TO EVERYONE'S TASTE, BUT BEEF TARTARE IS A LUXURY FOR CONNOISSEURS. CONTRASTING TEXTURES AND FLAVOURS, PLUS THE DRAMA OF A RAW EGG YOLK BALANCED ON THE VIVID PURPLE BEETROOT, GIVE THIS DANISH SMØRREBRØD EXTRA FLAMBOYANCE.

SERVES FOUR

INGREDIENTS

350g/12oz fillet steak (beef tenderloin)
25g/1oz/2 tbsp salted butter, softened
2 slices rye bread
32–40 watercress or rocket
  (arugula) leaves
8 slices Pickled Beetroot (beet)
  (see page 89)
16 thin slices sweet onion
4 egg yolks
25ml/1½ tbsp capers

1 Cut the fillet steak into thin slices. It is easier if you freeze it for 5–8 minutes first.

2 Butter the slices of bread to the edges, and cut the slices in half. Arrange 8–10 watercress or rocket leaves in a fan shape on each slice.

3 Place the beef slices on the bread, overlapping the watercress, layering or folding the slices as needed and extending over the bread.

4 Arrange two slices of beetroot on each sandwich, then four onion rings over the beetroot. Carefully place an egg yolk on each sandwich (put it in an onion ring to secure it). Sprinkle with capers.

COOK'S TIPS

• Buy the best-quality well hung fillet steak (beef tenderloin) you can find.
• Separate the egg yolk when you need it. So there is less chance of it breaking, simply transfer the yolk from the eggshell on to the sandwich.
• Use very fresh eggs. Do not serve raw egg to children, the elderly, pregnant women or convalescents. You can use hollandaise sauce instead of egg yolk.

Per portion Energy 291kcal/1215kJ; Protein 22.1g; Carbohydrate 11g, of which sugars 4.8g; Fat 18g, of which saturates 7.7g; Cholesterol 258mg; Calcium 56mg; Fibre 1.8g; Sodium 201mg.

ROAST BEEF, REMOULADE, CRISPY ONIONS AND HORSERADISH

THINLY SLICED ROAST BEEF WITH HORSERADISH IS A DELICIOUS COMBINATION. IN THIS DANISH OPEN SANDWICH, REMOULADE AND CRISPY ONIONS GIVE ADDED TEXTURE AND FLAVOUR. USE COLD CUTS FROM YOUR OWN BEEF JOINT, OR BUY THE MEAT READY CUT.

SERVES FOUR

INGREDIENTS
  25g/1oz/2 tbsp salted butter, softened
  2 slices rye bread
  2 leaves round (butterhead) lettuce
  8–12 thin slices roast beef, about
    115g–185g/4oz–6½oz
  8 small slices Pickled Beetroot (beet)
    (see page 89)
  20ml/4 tsp Remoulade (see page 98)
  20ml/4 tsp creamed horseradish
For the crispy onion rings
  250ml/8fl oz/1 cup buttermilk
  1 small onion, thinly sliced,
    rings separated
  175g/6oz/1½ cups plain
    (all-purpose) flour
  250ml/8fl oz/1 cup vegetable oil,
    for frying
  salt and ground white pepper

1 First make the crispy onion rings. Pour the buttermilk into a bowl and season with salt and pepper. Add the onion rings and toss well to coat them evenly. Leave to soak for about 10 minutes, then drain, discarding the buttermilk.

2 Place the flour in a shallow bowl. Dip the onion rings in the flour to coat them evenly on all sides. Shake off any excess flour.

3 Heat the oil in a frying pan, then fry the onion rings, in batches, over a medium-high heat until golden brown. Drain on kitchen paper and set aside.

4 Butter the slices of bread to the edges, top with the lettuce leaves and cut each slice in half.

5 Leaving one curl of lettuce visible on each piece, pleat or fan 2–3 slices of beef over the lettuce.

6 Top each sandwich with two slices of beetroot, 5ml/1 tsp remoulade, a few crispy onion rings and 5ml/1 tsp creamed horseradish.

Per portion Energy 171kcal/711kJ; Protein 8g; Carbohydrate 7.7g, of which sugars 2g; Fat 12.2g, of which saturates 5g; Cholesterol 34mg; Calcium 18mg; Fibre 0.9g; Sodium 205mg.

FISH AND
SHELLFISH

With long coastlines as well as fjords, rivers and lakes, fish and shellfish have always been an important part of Scandinavian cuisine and economy. From the Vikings who travelled on dried cod, or stockfish, to today's luxury exports of cured salmon, fish and fishing is intrinsic to Scandinavian culture. Herring, cod, salmon, plaice, halibut and trout, and shellfish such as crab, crayfish, lobster and prawns all appear in a wonderful variety of local dishes.

POACHED TURBOT WITH EGG AND PRAWNS

TURBOT, KNOWN AS THE KING OF FLAT FISH BECAUSE OF ITS FIRM, WHITE FLESH AND DELICATE FLAVOUR, IS FOUND IN THE NORTH SEA ON THE WEST COAST OF SWEDEN, AS WELL AS THE SOUTH-WEST OF THE BALTIC SEA. IN SWEDEN, TURBOT IS IRREVERENTLY CALLED 'DASSLOCK', MEANING TOILET SEAT, WHICH IS A REFERENCE TO ITS EXPANSIVE FLAT SHAPE.

SERVES SIX TO EIGHT

INGREDIENTS

1kg/2¼lb whole turbot, gutted
1 leek, finely chopped
1 bunch fresh parsley, chopped
1 lemon, sliced
salt and ground black pepper
For the sauce
1 egg
250g/9oz/1 cup plus 2 tbsp butter
175g/6oz shell-on cooked
  prawns (shrimp)
15ml/1 tbsp grated fresh horseradish

COOK'S TIPS
• Ask your fishmonger to gut the turbot.
• Turbot is a flat fish and it is advisable to prepare it when it is a couple of days old so that the meat becomes firmer and develops more flavour. This is quite different to round fish, which should always be eaten freshly caught.
• If turbot is unavailable, halibut, sole or flounder are good substitutes.

1 Preheat the oven to 180°C/350°F/Gas 4. Lay the gutted turbot on a large sheet of foil.

2 Mix together the chopped leek and parsley, and season with salt and pepper.

3 Use the leek and parsley mixture to stuff the body cavity of the turbot, then add the lemon slices. Wrap the turbot in the foil and bake for 45 minutes.

4 To make the sauce, hard boil the egg and leave to cool. Mash the egg.

5 Melt the butter and set aside. Peel the prawns, then add the prawns, butter and horseradish to the egg.

6 Serve the turbot on a large serving dish, accompanied by the sauce.

Per portion Energy 350kcal/1448kJ; Protein 20.8g; Carbohydrate 0.8g, of which sugars 0.7g; Fat 29.2g, of which saturates 17.1g; Cholesterol 113mg; Calcium 71mg; Fibre 0.5g; Sodium 337mg.

FISH FOR A PRINCE

THIS CLASSIC NORWEGIAN FISH DISH, PRINSEFISK, IS A SPECIALITY OF BERGEN AND IS PERFECT TO SERVE ON A SPECIAL OCCASION. EACH OF THE INGREDIENTS SHOULD BE OF PRIME QUALITY WITH EXCELLENT FLAVOUR, BUT IT IS THE COLOURS OF THE WHITE FISH, GREEN ASPARAGUS AND SEAFOOD GARNISH THAT MAKE THE DISH PARTICULARLY ATTRACTIVE AND FIT FOR A ROYAL TABLE.

SERVES FOUR

INGREDIENTS

    600g/1⅓lb piece boneless, skinned
        cod or halibut fillet
    about 475ml/16fl oz/2 cups fish stock
    about 24 asparagus spears
    40g/1½oz/3 tbsp butter
    40g/1½oz/3 tbsp plain
        (all-purpose) flour
    120ml/4fl oz/½ cup double
        (heavy) cream
    a squeeze of lemon juice
    45ml/3 tbsp medium dry sherry
    150g/5oz/½ cup peeled cooked
        prawns (shrimp), with tails on,
        or 4 large crayfish tails
    salt and ground black pepper
    chopped fresh parsley, to garnish

1 Preheat the oven to 190°C/375°F/Gas 5. Cut the fish into four portions. Put in an ovenproof dish and pour over enough stock to cover. Bake in the oven for 10–15 minutes, until just tender.

2 Meanwhile, steam the asparagus spears for 6–8 minutes, until tender.

3 Transfer the cooked fish to a serving dish, reserving the stock, and keep warm. Pour the stock through a sieve (strainer).

4 Melt the butter in a pan, stir in the flour and cook over a low heat for 1–2 minutes, without colouring. Remove from the heat and gradually stir in the fish stock to form a smooth sauce. Add the cream.

5 Return the pan to the heat and, stirring all the time, cook until the sauce boils and thickens. Simmer over a low heat for 2–3 minutes. Add a squeeze of lemon juice and the sherry and season to taste with salt and pepper.

6 Pour a little of the sauce over each piece of fish. Garnish the dish with the prawns or crayfish tails and the asparagus spears and sprinkle each fish with a little chopped parsley. Serve hot, accompanied by the remaining sauce.

COOK'S TIP
Serving on individual plates controls the size of each portion but, if you prefer, all the ingredients can be arranged on an attractive large dish.

Per portion Energy 425kcal/1769kJ; Protein 36.3g; Carbohydrate 9.5g, of which sugars 1.9g; Fat 25.9g, of which saturates 15.5g; Cholesterol 205mg; Calcium 81mg; Fibre 0.7g; Sodium 232mg.

SMOKED PIKE WITH CRÈME FRAÎCHE AND CHIVES

SWEDEN IS A LAND OF FORESTS AND LAKES, HOME TO A WEALTH OF NATURAL PRODUCE. THIS RECIPE WAS INSPIRED BY A TRADITIONAL COOKING METHOD WHERE FRESHLY CAUGHT FISH IS WRAPPED IN WET NEWSPAPERS AND COOKED ON A SMALL BONFIRE. THIS WAY OF PREPARING FISH IS UNEXPECTEDLY DELICIOUS AND SATISFYINGLY SIMPLE. THE DISH CAN BE COOKED ON A BARBECUE.

3 Use the herb mixture and lemon quarters to stuff the body cavity of the pike or eel.

4 Hold about five layers of newspaper under cold running water so that they become completely wet through (they need to be saturated otherwise the fish will burn) and then use the wet newspaper to wrap up the pike or eel completely.

5 Either place the newspaper parcel on a grill (broiler) rack on top of a smouldering bonfire, or lay it on damp leaves placed over burning logs, and leave to smoke for 25–30 minutes until cooked through. Alternatively, you can cook the fish on a barbecue, if you like.

6 Once the fish is cooked, take it off the fire or barbecue and carefully unwrap the newspaper. Transfer the fish to a serving plate, being careful that the stuffing does not fall out. Sprinkle the fish with chopped chives to garnish.

7 Serve the fish hot, accompanied by spoonfuls of crème fraîche.

SERVES SIX TO EIGHT

INGREDIENTS
300g/11oz/3 cups coarse salt
2kg/4½lb pike or eel, gutted
15ml/1 tbsp juniper berries
2–3 sprigs fresh thyme
15ml/1 tbsp olive oil
1 red onion, finely chopped
1 lemon, quartered
newspaper
chopped fresh chives, to garnish
crème fraîche, to serve

1 Sprinkle the salt all over the pike or eel and leave for about 1 hour.

2 Using a mortar and pestle, grind the juniper berries, fresh thyme and olive oil together. Add the chopped onion and stir the mixture together thoroughly using a fork.

COOK'S TIP
To cook the fish more quickly, turn the newspaper package on the bonfire or barbecue every 2–3 minutes and continue to wet down the newspaper. This way, the fish will take only about 15 minutes to cook.

Per portion Energy 195kcal/818kJ; Protein 28.5g; Carbohydrate 0.8g, of which sugars 0.6g; Fat 8.7g, of which saturates 0.2g; Cholesterol 0mg; Calcium 124mg; Fibre 0.4g; Sodium 80mg.

BAKED COD WITH CREAM

ALWAYS VERSATILE, COD IS ENJOYED THROUGHOUT THE YEAR, BUT BAKED OR POACHED WHOLE FRESH COD IS TRADITIONALLY SERVED IN DENMARK FOR DINNER ON NEW YEAR'S EVE. THIS SIMPLE PREPARATION SHOWS OFF THE LEAN, FIRM TEXTURE OF THE FLAVOURSOME WHITE FISH. SERVE BAGT TORSK MED FLØDE WITH BOILED POTATOES, REMOULADE OR MUSTARD SAUCE AND PEAS.

SERVES FOUR TO SIX

INGREDIENTS

   1.3kg/3lb cod steaks
   15ml/1 tbsp salt
   1 egg, beaten
   50g/2oz/½ cup fine breadcrumbs
   40g/1½oz/3 tbsp butter, cut into
     small pieces
   300ml/½ pint/1¼ cups single
     (light) cream
   45ml/3 tbsp chopped fresh parsley,
     to garnish
   8 lemon wedges, to garnish

2 Sprinkle with breadcrumbs and dot with butter. Pour the cream around the steaks.

3 Bake the fish for about 15–20 minutes, depending on thickness, until the topping is browned and the flesh flakes easily with a fork.

4 Serve the fish sprinkled with chopped fresh parsley and garnished with lemon wedges.

COOK'S TIP
If you can find a whole cod, bake it in the oven for around 1 hour, adding the cream 20 minutes before the end of the cooking time.

1 Preheat the oven to 190°C/375°F/ Gas 5. Pat the fish steaks dry and rub the salt over the skin. Place in a lightly greased baking dish, then brush with the egg.

Per portion Energy 355kcal/1484kJ; Protein 42.5g; Carbohydrate 8.9g, of which sugars 1.4g; Fat 16.7g, of which saturates 9.8g; Cholesterol 141mg; Calcium 78mg; Fibre 0.2g; Sodium 261mg.

SALT COD <u>WITH</u> MUSTARD SAUCE

MUSTARD SAUCE IS THE TRADITIONAL ACCOMPANIMENT FOR SALMON, BUT DANES ALSO ENJOY IT WITH OTHER FISH. SOAK THE SALT COD IN COLD WATER FOR 48 HOURS, CHANGING THE WATER SEVERAL TIMES. AFTER SOAKING, TASTE A SMALL PIECE OF THE FISH TO TEST ITS SALT CONTENT — THICKER PARTS MAY NEED TO BE SOAKED LONGER. SERVE WITH BOILED NEW POTATOES AND PICKLED BEETROOT.

SERVES FOUR

INGREDIENTS
800g/1¾lb salt cod
1 litre/1¾ pints/4 cups water
30ml/2 tbsp salt
1 onion, sliced
1 bay leaf
10 whole black peppercorns
4 whole cloves
4 lemon slices
60ml/4 tbsp butter
2 hard-boiled eggs, chopped, and
  chopped parsley to garnish
For the mustard sauce
15ml/1 tbsp distilled white vinegar
25g/1oz/2 tbsp sugar
90ml/6 tbsp Dijon mustard
1 egg yolk (optional)
50ml/2fl oz/¼ cup vegetable oil
7.5ml/1½ tsp chopped fresh dill
salt and ground black pepper

1 Soak the cod in cold water for two days, changing the water at least three times a day. Drain. Remove the skin and bones.

2 After the cod has been sufficiently soaked, cut it into 4 serving-size pieces, and set aside.

3 Fill a large pan with enough water to cover the fish and add the salt, onion, bay leaf, peppercorns, cloves and lemon slices.

4 Bring the water to the boil, then add the soaked salt cod pieces. Lower the heat, cover the pan with a lid and simmer over a low-medium heat until the fish turns opaque and flakes easily with a fork; this will take about 10 minutes.

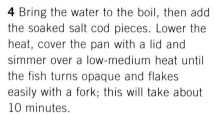

5 Meanwhile, make the mustard sauce. Mix together the vinegar, sugar, mustard, egg yolk (if using) and oil. Stir in the chopped fresh dill and season the sauce to taste with salt and black pepper.

6 When the salt cod is cooked through, remove the fish from the broth using a slotted spoon and divide the pieces among four individual warmed serving plates.

7 Top each serving with 15ml/1 tbsp butter, and generously sprinkle with the chopped hard-boiled egg and chopped parsley. Serve the salt cod with the mustard sauce, as well as boiled new potatoes and pickled beetroot, if you like.

Per portion Energy 570kcal/2387kJ; Protein 70.6g; Carbohydrate 8.8g, of which sugars 8.4g; Fat 28.4g, of which saturates 10.5g; Cholesterol 296mg; Calcium 86mg; Fibre 0g; Sodium 1592mg.

CHEF'S-STYLE KLIPFISH

KLIPFISH IS ANOTHER NAME FOR SALT COD. NOWADAYS, THERE IS NO NEED TO SALT COD TO PRESERVE IT, BUT THE TASTE FOR CLASSIC DISHES WITH THIS INGREDIENT REMAINS. THE FOLLOWING RECIPE, KOKKENS KLIPPFISK, IS A TASTY CASSEROLE, WHICH DRAWS ON THE SALTED COD TRADITION, AND IS A NEW INTERPRETATION OF A CLASSIC IDEA BY THE NORWEGIAN CHEF, HAROLD OSA.

SERVES FOUR

INGREDIENTS

   1kg/2¼lb salt cod
   450g/1lb leeks, white and pale green
     parts only, thinly sliced
   150g/5oz carrots, thinly sliced
   45ml/3 tbsp double (heavy) cream
   250g/9oz rindless, unsmoked,
     thick cut streaky (fatty) bacon,
     cut into small pieces
   salt and ground black pepper
   boiled potatoes, to serve

1 Soak the cod in cold water for two days, changing the water at least three times a day. Drain, remove the skin and bones, then cut the fish into thin slices.

2 Put the leeks and carrots in a pan and add enough water to just cover. Add the cream and season with salt and pepper. Bring to the boil, then lower the heat and simmer for about 10 minutes, until tender.

3 Bring back to the boil and boil hard for a further 2–3 minutes, then remove the pan from the heat, drain the vegetables and set aside to cool.

4 Put the bacon in a frying pan and fry until the fat starts to melt. Remove the frying pan from the heat and set aside.

5 Preheat the oven to 200°C/400°F/Gas 6. Grease an ovenproof dish.

6 Layer the vegetables with the cod slices in the dish, starting and ending with the vegetables.

7 Sprinkle the bacon over the top. Bake in the oven for about 15 minutes. Serve hot, with boiled potatoes.

COOK'S TIP
If possible, use bacon dry-cured in the old fashioned way, as bacon cured by modern methods may produce too much liquid during frying.

Per portion Energy 609kcal/2556kJ; Protein 93.1g; Carbohydrate 6.1g, of which sugars 5.2g; Fat 23.7g, of which saturates 9.5g; Cholesterol 204mg; Calcium 98mg; Fibre 3.1g; Sodium 1801mg.

SALTED COD CASSEROLE

THIS DISH FROM NORWAY, CALLED BACALAO, IS A CASSEROLE MADE FROM SALT COD, TOMATOES, POTATOES AND OIL. THE TOMATOES AND OLIVE OIL GIVE IT A BIT OF A MEDITERRANEAN FEEL, BUT IT IS A TRADITIONAL FAVOURITE IN THE SALT-FISH PORTS OF KRISTIANSUND AND ALESUND.

3 Layer the salt cod, then the potatoes and finally the onion in a medium flameproof casserole.

4 Put the water, oil, passata and chilli in a pan and bring to the boil. Pour into the casserole.

5 Return the liquid to the boil, reduce the heat, cover with a lid and simmer for 1½–2 hours, until the potatoes are tender. Serve hot.

SERVES FOUR

INGREDIENTS
  1kg/2¼lb salt cod
  500g/1¼lb potatoes, sliced
  1 onion, sliced
  100ml/3½fl oz/scant ½ cup water
  100ml/3½fl oz/scant ½ cup olive oil
  75ml/2½fl oz/⅓ cup passata
    (bottled strained tomatoes)
  a little chopped red chilli

COOK'S TIP
It helps to have two sharp knives for preparing the cod; a small one to cut away the flesh from the bones, and a larger, flexible-bladed one to slide, in a sawing motion, between the flesh and skin. Some salt on the fingers will help grip the skin.

1 Soak the salt cod in cold water for two days, changing the water at least three times a day. Drain, then remove the skin and bones.

2 Using a sharp knife, cut the soaked salt cod into pieces measuring about 5cm/2in square.

Per portion Energy 590kcal/2484kJ; Protein 83.7g; Carbohydrate 21.9g, of which sugars 3.1g; Fat 19.2g, of which saturates 3g; Cholesterol 148mg; Calcium 68mg; Fibre 1.7g; Sodium 1016mg.

SAUTÉED PERCH WITH GIROLLES

PERCH AND GIROLLE MUSHROOMS ARE A CLASSIC COMBINATION IN THIS SWEDISH RECIPE — THE EARTHY TASTE OF THE PERCH COMPLEMENTS THE APRICOT PERFUME OF THE MUSHROOMS BEAUTIFULLY. DON'T REMOVE THE SKIN BECAUSE THAT IS WHERE MOST OF THEIR DELICIOUS FLAVOUR IS.

SERVES SIX

INGREDIENTS
  300g/11oz girolle or chanterelle
    mushrooms
  50g/2oz/¼ cup butter
  1 onion, chopped
  75g/3oz/⅔ cup plain
    (all-purpose) flour
  6 perch, about 500g/1¼lb,
    scaled and filleted (cod is
    a good alternative)
  1 bunch fresh parsley, about
    25g/1oz, finely chopped
  salt and ground black pepper
  boiled new potatoes, to serve

1 Slice the mushrooms if large, otherwise leave them whole.

2 Melt 25g/1oz/2 tbsp of the butter in a large frying pan, add the mushrooms and onion and fry until golden.

3 Season the flour with salt and pepper and use to dust the fish fillets.

4 In a separate large frying pan, melt the remaining butter, add the fish fillets and fry over a medium heat for 2–3 minutes on each side, until cooked through.

5 Add the chopped parsley to the mushroom and onion mixture and serve with the perch. Accompany with boiled new potatoes.

COOK'S TIPS
• Perch have a spiky fin, so take care in the initial stages of preparation.
• You can ask your fishmonger to scale and fillet the fish, but if you need to scale the perch yourself do so with a knife, and work in a bowl of water so that the scales don't go everywhere.
• To fillet the fish, cut along the backbone from head to tail, to expose the backbone. Then, with smooth cutting strokes, separate the flesh from the bones. Repeat on the other side of the fish.

Per portion Energy 181kcal/760kJ; Protein 17.5g; Carbohydrate 10.8g, of which sugars 0.9g; Fat 7.9g, of which saturates 4.5g; Cholesterol 56mg; Calcium 32mg; Fibre 1.1g; Sodium 104mg.

FISH CAKES

BAKED IN THE OVEN, FISH CAKES ARE A STEADFAST FAVOURITE THROUGHOUT SCANDINAVIA, AND DENMARK IS NO EXCEPTION. SERVE THESE FISH CAKES, CALLED FISKEFRIKADELLER IN DANISH, WITH REMOULADE, BUTTERED POTATOES AND PICKLED CUCUMBER SALAD TO MAKE A COMPLETE SUPPER.

SERVES FOUR

INGREDIENTS
    450g/1lb cod or plaice fillet
    225g/8oz salmon fillet
    175g/6oz smoked salmon
    30ml/2 tbsp finely chopped onion
    40g/1½oz/3 tbsp melted butter
    3 eggs
    25g/1oz/¼ cup plain (all-purpose) flour
    salt and ground white pepper
    Remoulade (see page 98), boiled
        potatoes and Cucumber Salad
        (see page 90), to serve

COOK'S TIP
You can fry or grill (broil) the fish instead.

1 Place the cod and salmon fillets in a shallow dish, and sprinkle with 15ml/1 tbsp salt to draw some of the moisture out. Leave the fish to rest for 10 minutes, then pat dry with kitchen paper.

2 Place the cod and salmon, with the smoked salmon, in a food processor or blender. Add the onion, butter, eggs and flour and pulse until smooth; season with pepper and a little salt, and spoon into a bowl.

3 Preheat the oven to 190°C/375°F/ Gas 5. Lightly grease a 23 x 33cm/ 9 x 13in baking tray. With damp hands, form the fish mixture into 16 slightly flattened, round patties, and place them on the prepared tray.

4 Bake in the preheated oven for 30–35 minutes, until they are cooked through. Serve with remoulade, boiled potatoes and pickled cucumber salad.

Per portion Energy 407kcal/1700kJ; Protein 48.5g; Carbohydrate 5.5g, of which sugars 0.6g; Fat 21.4g, of which saturates 7.9g; Cholesterol 259mg; Calcium 64mg; Fibre 0.3g; Sodium 1029mg.

POLLOCK WITH ONIONS

A POPULAR, LESS EXPENSIVE ALTERNATIVE TO COD, POLLOCK IS OFTEN SERVED ALONG THE NORWEGIAN COAST. THE FLESH IS FIRMER THAN COD AND HAS A SLIGHTLY PEARLY HUE. IT IS FULL OF FLAVOUR AND A PERFECT PARTNER FOR THE FRIED ONIONS THAT FEATURE IN THIS DISH, LYR MED LØK.

SERVES FOUR

INGREDIENTS
    50g/2oz/½ cup plain
      (all-purpose) flour
    675g/1½lb pollock fillet, skinned
      and cut into 4 serving portions
    50g/2oz/4 tbsp butter
    15ml/1 tbsp vegetable oil
    2 large onions, sliced
    5ml/1 tsp sugar
    200ml/7fl oz/scant 1 cup water
    salt and ground black pepper
To serve
    boiled potatoes
    a green vegetable, such as cabbage

1 Preheat the oven to 180°C/350°F/ Gas 4. Put the flour on a large plate and season with salt and pepper. Dip the fish portions in the flour to coat on both sides.

2 Put a knob (pat) of the butter and the oil in a large frying pan and heat until the butter has melted. Add the floured fish and fry it quickly on both sides until browned. Place the fish in an ovenproof dish.

3 Melt the remaining butter in the same pan, add the onions, season with salt and pepper and fry gently for 10 minutes until softened and golden brown.

4 Add the sugar to the pan, increase the heat and allow the onions to caramelize slightly. Spread the onions over the fish.

5 Add the water to the frying pan, stirring to lift any sediment on the bottom of the pan, bring to the boil then pour over the fish and onions.

6 Bake in the oven for about 20 minutes, until the fish is tender.

7 Serve with boiled potatoes and a green vegetable.

Per portion Energy 298kcal/1247kJ; Protein 32.9g; Carbohydrate 16g, of which sugars 5g; Fat 11.8g, of which saturates 6.7g; Cholesterol 104mg; Calcium 52mg; Fibre 1.3g; Sodium 180mg.

FRIED SALT HERRING <u>WITH</u> ONION COMPOTE

BY THE 12TH CENTURY, SALT HERRING WAS A STAPLE FOOD THROUGHOUT SCANDINAVIA. ALTHOUGH SALT WAS RARE AND COSTLY IN MEDIEVAL DENMARK, IT WAS WORTH THE EXPENSE TO PRESERVE THE SEASONAL SHOALS OF HERRING, WHICH ARRIVED ALONG THE DANISH COAST ONLY IN LATE SUMMER.

3 To make the red onion compote, place the chopped onions in a pan and add the vinegar and red wine. Bring to the boil and cook, uncovered, over a medium heat for about 30 minutes, stirring occasionally, until the liquid has evaporated.

4 Stir in the water, honey, brown sugar and butter, and season with salt and pepper. Cook for 15 minutes more, stirring occasionally, until reduced and thick. Cover and keep warm.

5 Place the breadcrumbs in a shallow dish. Dip the herring into the crumbs to coat both sides. Sprinkle with pepper.

SERVES FOUR

INGREDIENTS
    8 salted herring fillets (about
        675g/1½lb total weight)
    15g/3oz/1½ cups fine breadcrumbs
    40g/1½oz/3 tbsp butter
    2.5ml/½ tsp ground white pepper
For the red onion compote
    675g/1½lb red onions, diced
    75ml/2½fl oz/⅓ cup cider vinegar
    350ml/12fl oz/1½ cups red wine
    250ml/8fl oz/1 cup water
    50ml/2fl oz/¼ cup honey
    15ml/1 tbsp soft light brown sugar
    10ml/2 tsp butter
    salt and ground black pepper

VARIATION
Add 250ml/8fl oz/1 cup single (light) cream to the pan after removing the fish. Cook for 3 minutes over a medium heat, stirring. Pour the sauce over the fish.

1 Rinse the salted herring fillets several times in cold water, then place them in a bowl of cold water, cover and leave them to soak overnight in the refrigerator.

2 Taste the herring fillets for saltiness. If the fish is too salty, rinse the fillets once again in more cold water. Otherwise, drain the fillets, pat them dry with kitchen paper and place them on a plate.

6 Melt the butter in a large frying pan over a medium-high heat. Fry the fillets, in batches if necessary, turning once, for 4 minutes on each side, until the coating is golden brown and the fish flakes easily with a fork. Remove the fish from the pan, drain on kitchen paper, and keep warm until all the fillets are cooked.

7 Divide the fillets between four plates. Spoon over the onion compote. Serve with broccoli and lemon wedges, if you like.

Per portion Energy 672kcal/2805kJ; Protein 35.9g; Carbohydrate 43.5g, of which sugars 23.7g; Fat 34.1g, of which saturates 12.3g; Cholesterol 114mg; Calcium 186mg; Fibre 2.8g; Sodium 460mg.

FRIED MUSTARD HERRINGS WITH MANGETOUTS

THE SWEDISH MUSTARD AND DILL THAT ARE USED IN THE SAUCE GIVE THIS DISH A CLASSIC SCANDINAVIAN CHARACTER. THE HERRINGS HAVE TO BE FRESH AS THEY LOSE THEIR DELICIOUS FLAVOUR IF THEY ARE KEPT FOR TOO LONG. THE MANGETOUTS CAN BE REPLACED WITH SUGAR SNAP PEAS.

SERVES SIX

INGREDIENTS
    6 fresh herrings, filleted
    50g/2oz/1 cup fresh breadcrumbs
    150g/5oz/1¼ cups plain
      (all-purpose) flour
    50g/2oz/¼ cup butter
    15ml/1 tbsp vegetable oil
    450g/1lb mangetouts
      (snow peas)
    salt and ground black pepper
    mashed potatoes, to serve
For the mustard and dill sauce
    100g/4oz Swedish mustard
    100g/4oz/½ cup sugar
    15ml/1 tbsp cider vinegar
    5ml/1 tsp salt
    ground black pepper
    300ml/½ pint/1¼ cups
      vegetable oil
    100g/4oz chopped fresh
      dill fronds

1 To make the mustard and dill sauce, put the Swedish mustard, sugar and cider vinegar, with salt and pepper to season, into a bowl.

2 Mix the ingredients together, then very slowly drizzle the vegetable oil into the mixture, whisking it all the time until you have achieved a thick, shiny sauce. Add the chopped fresh dill and stir well.

3 If necessary, remove any fins or scales from the herring fillets, then rinse under cold running water and dry on kitchen paper.

4 Cut the fillets in half lengthways, then add to the bowl of sauce. Place in the refrigerator overnight to marinate.

5 Put the breadcrumbs and flour on to a large plate and season with salt and pepper. Coat the fish fillets, on both sides, in the mixture.

6 Heat the butter and oil in a large frying pan, add the herring fillets and fry on both sides until golden brown and cooked through.

7 Meanwhile, put the mangetouts in a steamer and cook for 5 minutes. Serve the herrings with the mangetouts and mashed potatoes.

Per portion Energy 730kcal/3032kJ; Protein 25.1g; Carbohydrate 30.7g, of which sugars 4.5g; Fat 57.2g, of which saturates 11.9g; Cholesterol 68mg; Calcium 152mg; Fibre 2.7g; Sodium 728mg.

FRIED EEL <u>WITH</u> POTATOES <u>IN</u> CREAM SAUCE

A LEGACY OF DENMARK'S RURAL PAST, FRIED EEL IS NOW A CHOICE DELICACY. SERVED WITH BOILED OR CREAMED POTATOES AND ACCOMPANIED BY REFRESHING ICY AQUAVIT AND BEER, THIS SEASONAL DISH, CALLED STEGT ÅL MED FLØDESTUVEDE KARTOFLER, IS A MUCH-LOVED SUMMER SPECIALITY.

SERVES FOUR

INGREDIENTS
 1kg/2¼lb eel, skinned and cleaned
 1 egg
 5ml/1 tsp water
 25g/1oz/½ cup fine
  breadcrumbs, toasted
 10ml/2 tsp salt
 2.5ml/½ tsp ground white pepper
 40g/1½oz/3 tbsp butter
 2 lemons, sliced into wedges,
  to garnish
For the potatoes
 800g/1¾lb potatoes, peeled
 5ml/1 tsp salt
 40g/1½oz/3 tbsp butter
 20g/¾oz/3 tbsp plain
  (all-purpose) flour
 475ml/16fl oz/2 cups single
  (light) cream
 salt and ground white pepper, to taste
 45ml/3 tbsp chopped fresh parsley,
  to garnish

1 Cut the eel into 10cm/4in lengths. Whisk together the egg and water in a shallow dish. Place the breadcrumbs in a second shallow dish. Dip the eel first into the egg mixture, then into the breadcrumbs to coat both sides evenly. Sprinkle with salt and pepper. Leave the fish to rest for at least 10 minutes.

2 Melt the butter in a large pan over a medium-high heat. Add the eel and cook for about 10 minutes on each side, until golden brown and tender.

3 Remove from the pan and drain on kitchen paper. Keep warm.

4 Meanwhile, boil the potatoes in salted water for about 20 minutes, until tender. Drain, slice and keep warm.

5 Melt the butter in a pan and stir in the flour. Cook, stirring, for 5 minutes until the roux is pale beige. Slowly stir in the cream and cook for about 5 minutes, stirring constantly, until the sauce has thickened. Season to taste with salt and pepper.

6 Stir the potato slices into the cream sauce. Serve with the fried eel, sprinkled with parsley and garnished with lemon wedges. Serve with broccoli, if you like.

COOK'S TIPS
• A balloon whisk will help keep the roux smooth and free of lumps.
• Look for fresh eel in Asian markets.

Per portion Energy 978kcal/4074kJ; Protein 50.2g; Carbohydrate 43.7g, of which sugars 5.6g; Fat 68.2g, of which saturates 32.3g; Cholesterol 483mg; Calcium 184mg; Fibre 2.3g; Sodium 448mg.

FRIED MACKEREL WITH RHUBARB CHUTNEY

MACKEREL HAS A WONDERFUL FLAVOUR AND, AS AN OILY FISH, IS VERY GOOD FOR YOU. BECAUSE OF ITS OILINESS AND DISTINCTIVE FLAVOUR IT IS BEST SERVED WITH SOMETHING TART SUCH AS A SQUEEZE OF LEMON OR, AS IN THIS SWEDISH RECIPE, RHUBARB.

SERVES SIX

INGREDIENTS
   60ml/4 tbsp plain
     (all-purpose) flour
   6 mackerel fillets
   30ml/2 tbsp vegetable oil
   25g/1oz/2 tbsp butter
   salt and ground black pepper
   boiled new potatoes, to serve
For the rhubarb chutney
   150g/5oz fresh rhubarb
   50g/2oz/¼ cup caster
     (superfine) sugar
   5ml/1 tsp cider vinegar
   a knob (pat) of butter

1 To make the rhubarb chutney, cut the rhubarb into small pieces, then put it in a pan with the caster sugar and cider vinegar.

2 Simmer for 6 minutes until the rhubarb is soft but not mushy. Stir in the butter.

3 Put the flour in a bowl and dust the mackerel fillets with it on both sides. Season them with salt and ground black pepper.

4 Heat the oil and butter in a frying pan, add the mackerel and fry them for 2–3 minutes on each side until golden. Serve with the chutney and new potatoes.

Per portion Energy 353kcal/1470kJ; Protein 19.9g; Carbohydrate 16.7g, of which sugars 9.1g; Fat 23.4g, of which saturates 5.9g; Cholesterol 63mg; Calcium 54mg; Fibre 0.7g; Sodium 90mg.

JANSSON'S TEMPTATION

THIS SWEDISH ANCHOVY PIE IS ANOTHER WARMING DISH FOR THE WINTER MONTHS. THE DISH IS NAMED AFTER A WELL-KNOWN SWEDISH OPERA SINGER, WHO SERVED IT TO HIS GUESTS AFTER A PERFORMANCE AT THE OPERA HOUSE IN STOCKHOLM.

3 Drain well and put in a bowl. Add the sliced onion and mix together, then put in a shallow, ovenproof dish.

4 Mix together the milk and cream. Put both the liquid and the fish from the can of anchovies into the milk mixture and stir together. Pour the mixture over the potatoes and season with salt and pepper.

5 Bake in the oven for 50 minutes until golden brown and bubbling.

COOK'S TIPS
• This dish is delicious served on its own or with a salad and is also perfect when eaten with cold sliced ham.
• If you cannot get Swedish anchovies, use ordinary salted anchovies and soak them in milk for a couple of hours to remove the saltiness.

SERVES SIX

INGREDIENTS
  6 large potatoes
  1 Spanish (Bermuda) onion,
   thinly sliced
  120ml/4fl oz/½ cup milk
  250ml/8fl oz/1 cup double
   (heavy) cream
  100g/3½oz can Swedish anchovies
  salt and ground black pepper

1 Preheat the oven to 180°C/350°F/Gas 4. Peel and grate the potatoes.

2 Put the grated potatoes in a colander and wash under cold running water to remove any excess starch.

Per portion Energy 400kcal/1669kJ; Protein 9.4g; Carbohydrate 36.5g, of which sugars 6.1g; Fat 25.1g, of which saturates 14.6g; Cholesterol 69mg; Calcium 115mg; Fibre 2.5g; Sodium 696mg.

WHOLE GLAZED TROUT <u>WITH</u> CUCUMBER SALAD

THE PRESENTATION OF THE TROUT IN THIS RECIPE LOOKS SPLENDID, AND THE SWEET-SOUR CUCUMBER SALAD IS NOT ONLY A GREAT ACCOMPANIMENT BUT ALSO AN ESSENTIAL DISH FOR THE NORWEGIAN COLD TABLE. A WHOLE SALMON CAN BE PREPARED IN THE SAME WAY AND LOOKS EQUALLY GOOD.

SERVES FOUR

INGREDIENTS
1 whole trout, total weight
    about 1.5kg/3¼lb
1 packet powdered aspic
500ml/17fl oz/2¼ cups clear
    fish stock or water
salt and ground white pepper
For every 1 litre/1¾ pints/4 cups water
1 bay leaf
1 bunch fresh parsley
30ml/2 tbsp salt
10 black peppercorns
1 lemon, sliced
fresh dill or parsley sprigs, to garnish
For the cucumber salad
1 cucumber
105ml/7 tbsp fresh lemon juice
    or white wine vinegar
105ml/7 tbsp water
30–45ml/2–3 tbsp sugar
30ml/2 tbsp chopped fresh parsley
salt and ground black pepper

1 Put the fish in a fish kettle or, if possible, bend the fish into a semi-circle to fit a suitably sized pan, with the backbone uppermost. Add enough water to just cover the fish.

2 Tie the bay leaf and parsley together with string. Add to the pan with the salt, peppercorns and half the lemon slices.

3 Bring slowly to the boil and then simmer for 1 minute. Remove the pan from the heat but leave the fish in the cooking liquid. Set the pan aside, in a cool place, until the fish is cold.

4 Meanwhile, prepare the cucumber for the salad. Peel the skin off the cucumber if it is tough or if you prefer. Otherwise the skin can be left on or scored down its length with a fork or cannelle knife. Slice it finely.

5 Put the sliced cucumber in a colander, sprinkling each layer generously with salt. Put a saucer then a weight on top and leave to drain for 1–2 hours.

6 To make the dressing, mix together the lemon juice or vinegar, water, sugar to taste, pepper and a pinch of salt if necessary. Stir well to dissolve the sugar.

7 Dissolve the aspic powder in the stock or water, according to packet instructions. Check the seasoning and add salt and pepper to taste only if necessary.

8 Carefully remove the fish from the stock and place on a serving dish.

9 Gently ease the skin off the fish; leave the head and tail intact. Remove the fat from along the backbone. Allow to drain completely, then dry with kitchen paper.

10 As the aspic begins to thicken, brush it over the whole trout. Leave to set. Garnish with dill or parsley sprigs and the remaining lemon slices. Rinse the cucumber under cold running water then squeeze dry. Put in a serving dish and pour over the dressing. Sprinkle over the parsley and serve with the fish.

Per portion Energy 375kcal/1580kJ; Protein 59.1g; Carbohydrate 9.3g, of which sugars 9.2g; Fat 11.5g, of which saturates 2.6g; Cholesterol 240mg; Calcium 133mg; Fibre 1.1g; Sodium 224mg.

SALMON STEAKS WITH WARM POTATO SALAD

SALMON IS A POPULAR FISH IN DENMARK FOR SPECIAL OCCASIONS, FESTIVALS AND SIGNIFICANT ANNIVERSARIES. IT WAS ONCE PLENTIFUL IN THE WILD, BUT MOST OF THE SALMON EATEN IN SCANDINAVIA TODAY IS FARMED. SIMPLY POACHED, SALMON'S SAVOURY TASTE SHINES THROUGH, ENRICHED BY THE WINE AND LEMON JUICE FLAVOURS IN THE POACHING LIQUID. WARM POTATO SALAD IS ANOTHER DANISH FAVOURITE, AND ITS BUTTERY, TANGY DRESSING COMPLEMENTS THE SALMON. SERVE WITH ASPARAGUS.

SERVES SIX

INGREDIENTS
    3 bunches fresh dill
    6 salmon steaks, each about
        2.5cm/1in thick (1.3kg/3lb
        total weight)
    475ml/16fl oz/2 cups water
    250ml/8fl oz/1 cup dry white wine
    15ml/1 tbsp white vinegar or
        lemon juice
    5ml/1 tsp salt
    5 allspice berries
    2 bay leaves
    6 small dill sprigs, to garnish
    6 lemon slices, to garnish
For the warm potato salad
    1.2kg/2½lb potatoes
    175g/6oz chopped onion
    175ml/6fl oz/¾ cup water
    45ml/3 tbsp cider vinegar
    10ml/2 tsp caster (superfine) sugar
    5ml/1 tsp mustard powder
    salt and ground white pepper
    25g/1oz/2 tbsp butter
    45ml/3 tbsp chopped parsley

2 Peel the potatoes and boil them whole in lightly salted water for 20–25 minutes, until tender.

3 To make the dressing, place the onion in a pan with the water. Bring to the boil over a medium-high heat, and cook for about 5 minutes, until the onion is transparent.

4 Stir in the vinegar, sugar and mustard and season to taste with salt and pepper, adding a little more water if necessary. Stir in the butter until melted and keep warm.

5 Drain the cooked potatoes and allow them to cool slightly. While they are still quite warm, cut them into 1cm/½in slices and layer them in a large bowl.

6 Pour the dressing over the sliced potatoes, add the chopped parsley, then gently toss everything together to coat the potatoes evenly in the dressing without breaking them up.

7 When the fish is opaque and flakes easily with a fork, skim off any scum and lift out the fish, drain and allow to cool slightly.

8 Remove the skin from the salmon, then place it on a serving platter or on individual serving plates. Garnish the salmon steaks with dill sprigs and lemon slice twists, and serve with the warm potato salad.

COOK'S TIPS
• It is best, if possible, to buy wild salmon rather than farmed. These fish are more expensive, but have firmer skin with a deep pink flesh. Ethical fishmongers will advise you which are wild salmon and which are farmed. Wild salmon is available from late spring to late summer.
• The quality of farmed salmon can be variable. Look out for firm, dark pink flesh with creamy marbling.
• Salmon steaks can also be poached in the oven. Preheat the oven to 200°C/400°F/Gas 6. Place the fish and poaching liquid in the kettle and cook for 20–25 minutes.

1 Place the dill sprigs in the bottom of a 23 x 33cm/9 x 13in rectangular baking dish or small fish kettle. Arrange the salmon steaks over the dill sprigs or on the tray of a fish kettle. Combine the water with the wine, vinegar or lemon juice and salt and add the allspice berries and bay leaves. Pour over the salmon, then bring to a simmer, lower the heat, cover and cook for 10–15 minutes, until tender.

Per portion Energy 578kcal/2420kJ; Protein 47.6g; Carbohydrate 36.3g, of which sugars 6g; Fat 27.9g, of which saturates 6.5g; Cholesterol 117mg; Calcium 67mg; Fibre 2.4g; Sodium 146mg.

POACHED SALMON STEAKS WITH SANDEFJORD BUTTER

FOR SHEER SIMPLICITY RAISED TO A HIGH STANDARD, THIS DISH, KOKT LAKS MED SANDEFJORDSMØR, TAKES A LOT OF BEATING. SANDEFJORD BUTTER IS NAMED AFTER A TOWN NEAR THE MOUTH OF THE OSLOFJORD. A SHIPPING CENTRE SINCE THE 14TH CENTURY, IT IS NOW A SEASIDE RESORT. THIS CLASSIC BUTTER SAUCE IS THE TRADITIONAL NORWEGIAN ACCOMPANIMENT TO MANY FISH DISHES.

SERVES FOUR

INGREDIENTS

    4 salmon steaks, each about 175g/6oz
    45ml/3 tbsp salt
    5ml/1 tsp whole black peppercorns
    1 lemon slice
    1 onion slice, rings separated
    about 1 litre/1¾ pints/4 cups water
For the Sandefjord butter
    100ml/3½fl oz/scant ½ cup double
      (heavy) cream
    225g/8oz/1 cup chilled unsalted
      butter, cut into small cubes
    30–45ml/2–3 tbsp chopped fresh
      parsley or chives
To serve
    boiled potatoes
    cucumber salad

1 Put the fish steaks, in a single layer, in a pan. Add the salt, peppercorns, lemon and onion slice. Add the water to cover the steaks. If there is not enough water, add a little more. Bring to the boil, then lower the heat to below simmering point. (The water should just throw up the occasional bubble.)

2 Poach the fish for 6–8 minutes, until the flesh easily loosens from the backbone.

3 To make the Sandefjord butter, pour the cream into a pan and slowly bring to the boil. Lower the heat and add the butter, in small pieces, whisking all the time until well incorporated before adding another piece. Do not allow the sauce to boil or it will separate. If you wish, the sauce can be kept warm by putting it in a bowl standing over a pan of gently simmering water.

4 Just before serving, add the parsley or chives to the sauce. Serve the fish with boiled potatoes and a cucumber salad, accompanied with the Sandefjord butter.

Per portion Energy 771kcal/3184kJ; Protein 26.3g; Carbohydrate 1.1g, of which sugars 1g; Fat 73.6g, of which saturates 40g; Cholesterol 217mg; Calcium 71mg; Fibre 0.6g; Sodium 406mg.

SALMON ROLLS WITH ASPARAGUS AND BUTTER SAUCE

ASPARAGUS HAS BEEN A POPULAR INGREDIENT IN NORWAY FOR MANY YEARS AND ITS GREEN SPEARS APPEAR EACH YEAR AS A WELCOME SIGN OF SPRING. THE GREEN CONTRASTS BEAUTIFULLY WITH THE PINK FLESH OF THE SALMON IN THIS RECIPE, LAKSERULADER MED ASPARGES, MAKING IT A DELIGHTFULLY PRETTY DISH. BOTH THE ASPARAGUS AND SALMON HAVE A SWEETNESS OF FLAVOUR THAT MARRY PERFECTLY.

SERVES FOUR

INGREDIENTS

4 thick or 8 thin asparagus spears
4 very thin slices salmon fillet,
  each weighing about 115g/4oz
juice of 1 lemon
salt and ground black pepper
1 bunch fresh parsley, chopped,
  to serve

For the butter sauce
1 shallot, finely chopped
6 black peppercorns
120ml/4fl oz/½ cup dry white wine
60ml/4 tbsp double (heavy) cream
200g/7oz/scant 1 cup butter,
  cut into small cubes
salt and ground black pepper

1 Steam the asparagus spears for 6–8 minutes, according to their size, until tender. Refresh under cold running water, drain and set aside.

2 The slices of salmon should be wide enough to roll around the asparagus. Don't worry if they have to be patched together. Place the salmon slices on a clean work surface, season with salt and pepper, lay one or two asparagus spears across each slice and then roll the salmon around them.

3 Place the rolls on a rack over a pan of boiling water, sprinkle with lemon juice, and cover and steam for 3–4 minutes until tender.

4 To make the butter sauce, put the shallot, peppercorns and wine in a small pan and heat gently until the wine has reduced to a tablespoonful. Strain and return the liquid to the pan. Add the cream, bring to the boil, and then lower the heat.

5 Add the butter to the sauce in small pieces, whisking all the time until well incorporated before adding another piece. Do not allow the sauce to boil or it will separate. Season the sauce with salt and pepper to taste, if necessary. If you wish, the sauce can be kept warm by putting it in a bowl, standing over a pan of gently simmering water. Add the chopped parsley to the sauce and serve with the salmon rolls.

COOK'S TIP

If you can't get the salmon sliced, buy a 600g/1¼lb piece cut from the thick end of the fillet. Use a knife to cut across the salmon, slanting slightly down, as though slicing smoked salmon but more thickly.

Per portion Energy 694kcal/2867kJ; Protein 25.7g; Carbohydrate 2.4g, of which sugars 2.1g; Fat 62.5g, of which saturates 33.4g; Cholesterol 187mg; Calcium 55mg; Fibre 0.6g; Sodium 362mg.

SALTED SALMON WITH POTATOES IN DILL SAUCE

RIMMAD LAX OR SALTED SALMON IS A REFRESHING ALTERNATIVE TO THE MORE COMMONLY KNOWN GRAVLAX RECIPE. THIS TYPE OF CURED SALMON IS PLUMPER, SMOOTHER AND FRESHER, MAKING IT A LOVELY LIGHT SUPPER. THIS DISH IS FROM SWEDEN AND IS DELICIOUS WITH CREAMY POTATOES AND DILL, WHICH COUNTERACTS THE SALTINESS OF THE FISH.

3 The next day, make a brine by mixing the remaining salt and the water in a bowl. Place the salmon in the brine and leave in the refrigerator for another night.

4 Remove the salmon from the brine and cut into 5mm/¼in slices. If large, cut the potatoes in half, then cook in boiling water for about 20 minutes until tender.

SERVES SIX TO EIGHT

INGREDIENTS
    200g/7oz/2 cups sea salt
    50g/2oz/¼ cup caster (superfine) sugar
    1kg/2¼lb salmon, scaled, filleted
      and boned
    1 litre/1¾ pints/4 cups water
    675–900g/1½–2lb new potatoes
For the béchamel and dill sauce
    25g/1oz/2 tbsp butter
    45ml/3 tbsp plain (all-purpose) flour
    750ml/1¼ pints/3 cups milk
    120ml/4fl oz/½ cup double
      (heavy) cream
    a little freshly grated nutmeg (optional)
    25g/1oz/¼ cup chopped fresh dill
    salt and ground black pepper

1 Mix together 100g/4oz/1 cup of the salt and the sugar.

2 Cover the salmon fillets with the mixture and put in a plastic bag. Seal the bag and put the fish on a plate in the refrigerator overnight.

5 Meanwhile, make the béchamel sauce. Melt the butter in a pan, add the flour and cook over a low heat for 1 minute, stirring to make a roux. Remove from the heat and slowly add the milk, stirring all the time, to form a smooth sauce. Return to the heat and cook, stirring, for 2–3 minutes until the sauce boils and thickens. Stir in the cream, nutmeg if using, salt and pepper to taste and heat gently.

6 Drain the cooked potatoes and add to the sauce with the chopped dill. Serve the salted salmon with the potatoes in béchamel and dill.

Per portion Energy 407kcal/1699kJ; Protein 26.4g; Carbohydrate 22.6g, of which sugars 5.9g; Fat 24g, of which saturates 9.7g; Cholesterol 85mg; Calcium 155mg; Fibre 1g; Sodium 118mg.

LAX PUDDING

THIS MOUTHWATERING WINTER WARMER — A CLASSIC DISH FROM THE SWEDISH HUSMANSKOST, OR HOME COOKING — IS AN EXCELLENT WAY TO USE UP ANY REMAINING SMOKED SALMON OR GRAVLAX. THIS IS A GOOD ALTERNATIVE TO FISH PIE, WITH SIMILAR INGREDIENTS, BUT A QUITE DIFFERENT PREPARATION METHOD. THE DILL IS WHAT MAKES LAX PUDDING SO ESSENTIALLY SWEDISH.

SERVES EIGHT

INGREDIENTS
    250g/9oz new potatoes
    25g/1oz/2 tbsp butter
    1 leek, sliced
    200g/7oz gravlax, about 8 slices
    a little chopped fresh dill
    2 eggs
    250ml/8fl oz/1 cup milk
    30ml/2 tbsp double (heavy) cream
    salt and ground black pepper

1 Cook the new potatoes in boiling salted water for 15–20 minutes until tender. Drain the potatoes and set them aside to cool.

2 Meanwhile, melt the butter in a pan. Add the sliced leek and sauté gently until softened.

3 Preheat the oven to 180°C/350°F/Gas 4. Thinly slice the cooled potatoes. Sprinkle a little dill in the bottom of an ovenproof terrine. Top with a layer of potatoes.

COOK'S TIP
The terrine can be finished with a garnish of 25g/1oz melted butter to which 30ml/2 tbsp chopped fresh parsley has been added.

4 Add 1–3 slices of gravlax and then add a layer of leeks. Repeat these layers, using all the ingredients, finishing with a neat layer of potatoes. Sprinkle over the chopped dill.

5 Beat the eggs in a jug (pitcher) or bowl. Add the milk and cream and beat together. Season with salt and pepper. Pour the egg mixture into the terrine. Bake for 30 minutes until golden brown.

Per portion Energy 137kcal/573kJ; Protein 9.9g; Carbohydrate 7.2g, of which sugars 2.4g; Fat 7.8g, of which saturates 3.9g; Cholesterol 70mg; Calcium 59mg; Fibre 0.8g; Sodium 525mg.

CREAMED SHELLFISH <u>IN A</u> SPINACH RING

SHELLFISH FROM THE NORTH SEA ARE GREATLY LOVED IN NORWAY. LOBSTER, PRAWNS AND CRABS ALL FORM PART OF A COLD TABLE OR ARE USED IN A VARIETY OF SOUPS AND SAUCES. THE MIXTURE THAT FOLLOWS CAN BE SERVED WITH RICE, USED AS A FILLING FOR PASTRY OR AN OMELETTE OR, AS IN THIS RECIPE, SKALLDYRSTUING MED SPINATRAND, AS THE FILLING FOR A SPINACH RING.

SERVES FOUR

INGREDIENTS

  1–2 cooked lobsters, 300g/11oz
    cooked prawns (shrimp) in their
    shell, or white and brown meat of
    1–2 cooked crabs
  25g/1oz/2 tbsp shellfish butter
    (see below)
  30ml/2 tbsp plain (all-purpose) flour
  300ml/½ pint/1¼ cups fish stock
  150ml/¼ pint/⅔ cup double
    (heavy) cream
  30ml/2 tbsp brandy
  30ml/2 tbsp chopped fresh dill
  salt and ground black pepper
For the shellfish butter
  shells from 1 of the above shellfish
  40g/1½oz/3 tbsp butter
For the spinach ring
  butter, for greasing
  500g/1¼lb fresh spinach leaves,
    washed, or 225g/8oz frozen
    chopped spinach, thawed
  4 large (US extra large) eggs
  200ml/7fl oz/scant 1 cup milk
  200ml/7fl oz/scant 1 cup single
    (light) cream
  pinch of freshly grated nutmeg
  pinch of ground allspice
  salt and ground black pepper

1 Remove the flesh from the shellfish and cut, if necessary, into bitesize pieces. Keep the flesh in the refrigerator for use later and reserve the shells for the shellfish butter.

2 To make the shellfish butter, using a mortar and pestle, pound the reserved shells thoroughly. Add the butter and work into the shell fragments.

3 Put the shell and butter mixture in a pan and cook over a low heat for 15 minutes, without browning.

4 Add water to just cover the shells, bring to the boil, then reduce the heat and simmer for 1 minute.

5 Strain the liquid through a fine sieve (strainer) and leave to cool.

6 When cold, put the liquid in the refrigerator and leave to chill until the butter has set on the surface, about 2–3 hours.

7 Preheat the oven to 180°C/350°F/ Gas 4. Lift the butter off the surface of the liquid.

8 Generously butter a 1 litre/1¾ pint ring mould. If using fresh spinach, plunge it into a pan of boiling water, then drain immediately.

9 Refresh under cold running water, drain and squeeze until the spinach is dry. Chop it finely either by hand or in a blender.

10 Lightly beat the eggs, then add the milk and cream and stir well.

11 Add the chopped spinach and season with the nutmeg, allspice, salt and a little pepper.

12 Pour the mixture into the prepared mould and place it in a roasting pan. Fill with hot water to reach three-quarters of the way up the sides of the mould. Bake for 35 minutes or until a knife, inserted in the ring, comes out clean.

13 To make the creamed shellfish, melt the shellfish butter in a pan, stir in the flour and cook over a low heat for 1–2 minutes. Remove from the heat and gradually stir in the fish stock to form a smooth sauce. Stir in the cream. Return to the heat and, stirring, cook until it boils and thickens. Simmer over a low heat for 2–3 minutes.

14 Add the brandy. Season with salt and pepper. Add the reserved shellfish and heat gently, without boiling, until heated through. Stir in the chopped dill.

15 When the spinach ring is cooked, leave to stand for 2–3 minutes, then run a knife around the edge of the mould and invert the ring on to a serving plate. Fill the centre with the creamed shellfish and serve hot.

Per portion Energy 620kcal/2573kJ; Protein 34.5g; Carbohydrate 12g, of which sugars 6.1g; Fat 46.9g, of which saturates 26.3g; Cholesterol 393mg; Calcium 431mg; Fibre 2.9g; Sodium 650mg.

SHELLFISH SALAD

THIS SALAD WAS CREATED TO TAKE FULL ADVANTAGE OF THE MANY TYPES OF DELICIOUS SHELLFISH THAT CAN BE CAUGHT OFF THE WEST COAST OF NORWAY. IT APPEARS ON ALL NORWEGIAN COLD TABLES FOR SPECIAL OCCASIONS, WITH THE SHELLFISH CHOSEN ACCORDING TO ITS AVAILABILITY AND TASTE. WHEN FRESH SHELLFISH IS SCARCE OR EXPENSIVE, FROZEN OR CANNED IS AN ALTERNATIVE.

SERVES FOUR

INGREDIENTS
   115g/4oz/1¾ cups mushrooms
   juice of ½ lemon
   1 lobster, about 450g/1lb, cooked
     and with meat extracted
   115g/4oz/1 cup cooked fresh
     or canned asparagus
   1 crisp lettuce, shredded
   16 cooked mussels
   115g/4oz/½ cup cooked peeled
     prawns (shrimp)
   2 tomatoes, skinned and quartered
   dill fronds, to garnish
For the dressing
   30ml/2 tbsp white wine vinegar
   90–120ml/6–8 tbsp olive oil
   pinch of sugar
   1 garlic clove, crushed (optional)
   salt and ground black pepper

1 Chill all the salad ingredients in the refrigerator before use.

2 To make the dressing, put the white wine vinegar, olive oil, sugar and crushed garlic, if using, in a bowl and mix well together.

3 Season the dressing with salt and pepper to taste and mix again.

4 Slice the mushrooms, then place them in a serving bowl and sprinkle over the lemon juice. Cut the lobster meat into bitesize pieces and add to the bowl.

5 Cut the cooked or canned asparagus into 5cm/2in pieces. Add to the bowl with the mushrooms. Add the shredded lettuce, then the mussels, prawns and quartered tomatoes.

6 Pour the dressing over the salad ingredients and toss everything together. Garnish with dill fronds and serve immediately.

Per portion Energy 280kcal/1166kJ; Protein 23.2g; Carbohydrate 4.4g, of which sugars 3g; Fat 19g, of which saturates 2.9g; Cholesterol 127mg; Calcium 96mg; Fibre 1.8g; Sodium 357mg.

DILLFLOWER CRAYFISH

EATING CRAYFISH IN AUGUST AND SEPTEMBER IS ALMOST A SACRED RITUAL IN SWEDEN. FOR YEARS IT WAS POSSIBLE TO EAT LOCAL CRAYFISH BUT THEY ARE NOW ALMOST EXTINCT AND HAVE BEEN REPLACED BY A HARDY AMERICAN TYPE CALLED THE SIGNAL CRAYFISH. THIS DISH, KRÄFTOR MED KRONDILL, IS EATEN AS A CELEBRATION, AT WHICH SNAPS AND BEER ARE SERVED AND AMUSING SONGS ARE SUNG.

SERVES SIX TO EIGHT

INGREDIENTS
  2kg/4½lb live freshwater crayfish
  3 litres/5 pints/12 cups water
  100g/4oz/1 cup coarse sea salt
  2 sugar lumps
  1 onion, chopped
  350ml/12fl oz bottle stout
  1 large bunch dill or dill flowers
    (dill flowers are available from
    florists in the summer season
    or use dill seeds to infuse the
    crayfish with a similar flavour)
  Västerbotten or mature (sharp)
    Cheddar cheese and toasted
    bread, to serve

1 Put the live crayfish into strong plastic bags, about 10–15 per bag, seal the bags and place them in the freezer for 2 hours to put the crayfish to sleep. (This is the most humane and least traumatic way of killing live crayfish. Many people, however, are convinced that crayfish taste far superior when they are cooked fresh, in which case this step should be missed out and they should be added live at step 4.)

2 Put the water, salt and sugar in a large pan and bring to the boil over a high heat.

3 Meanwhile, put the dill or dill flowers in a large bowl, reserving some for the garnish, and add the chopped onion and stout.

4 Remove a bag of crayfish from the freezer, unseal the bag and immediately drop the unconscious crayfish into the boiling water.

5 Cover the pan, return to the boil and cook for about 8 minutes, until the crayfish turn a bright orange colour.

6 Using a slotted spoon, remove the crayfish from the water and place on top of the dill. Repeat with the remaining crayfish until they are all cooked.

COOK'S TIP
The best way to eat crayfish is with a crayfish knife, a sharp pointed knife that always has a red handle. However, many people simply break the shell with their teeth and then suck out the juice.

7 Pour the hot cooking liquid over the crayfish and allow to cool in the liquid, then leave to marinate in the refrigerator overnight. The strong flavour of the dill will infuse the crayfish.

8 Drain the crayfish and serve, garnished with the reserved fresh dill and accompanied with cheese and toast. Serve with snaps and beer!

Per portion Energy 115kcal/481kJ; Protein 21.7g; Carbohydrate 1.1g, of which sugars 0.9g; Fat 1.8g, of which saturates 0.5g; Cholesterol 78mg; Calcium 141mg; Fibre 0.1g; Sodium 1527mg.

CRAB GRATIN

THIS DISH, GRATINERAD KRABBA, IS A FILLING MAIN COURSE AND A REMNANT OF AN OLDER ERA, BUT SUCH TRADITIONAL COMFORT FOOD STILL HOLDS PRIDE OF PLACE IN MANY KITCHENS. THIS RECIPE IS DEFINITELY ONE TO IMPRESS YOUR FRIENDS. CRAB IS PROLIFIC ON THE WEST COAST OF SWEDEN, BUT THE DISH CAN ALSO BE MADE USING AROUND 18 LANGOUSTINES INSTEAD OF THE CRAB. IN THIS CASE, COOK THEM FOR ABOUT 10 MINUTES, UNTIL THEY TURN A BRIGHT ORANGE.

SERVES SIX

INGREDIENTS

6 large live crabs
3 litres/2½ pints/6¼ cups water
350ml/12fl oz beer
100g/4oz/1 cup coarse sea salt
2 sugar lumps
40g/1½oz Cheddar cheese, grated
boiled basmati rice and salad, to serve
For the sauce
25g/1oz/2 tbsp butter
15ml/1 tbsp plain (all-purpose) flour
475ml/16fl oz/2 cups double
(heavy) cream
2 egg yolks
30ml/2 tbsp brandy
10ml/2 tsp liquid from a can of
Swedish anchovies, or other
fish stock
salt and ground black pepper

1 Put the crabs in individual, strong plastic bags, seal and place in the freezer for 2 hours to put them to sleep (this is the most humane and least traumatizing way of killing them).

2 Put the water, beer, sea salt and sugar in a very large pan and bring to the boil.

COOK'S TIPS
• Instead of boiling the live crabs yourself, you could use 500g/1¼lb fresh crab meat, thawed if frozen. You will then also need 300ml/½ pint/1¼ cups fish stock to make the sauce.
• The dish can also be made using three lobsters or 18 langoustines as an alternative to the crab. Prepare them in the same way but when you remove a lobster from the freezer, weigh it quickly and calculate the cooking time by allowing 18 minutes for the first 500g/1¼lb and an extra 11 minutes for every additional 500g/1¼lb. Cook the langoustine for about 10 minutes, until they turn a bright orange colour.

3 Remove 1–2 crabs, depending upon the size of your pan, from the freezer, unseal the bag and immediately drop the unconscious crabs into the boiling water. Cover the pan, return to the boil and cook for 15 minutes, allowing an extra 10 minutes for each additional crab.

4 Remove the cooked crab from the water and transfer to a large bowl. Repeat with the remaining crabs until they are all cooked.

5 Pour the hot cooking liquid over the crabs, allow to cool in the liquid and then leave in the refrigerator overnight.

6 Remove the crabs from the liquid and reserve 300ml/½ pint/1¼ cups. Put the crab on a chopping board on its back to extract the meat. Hold a claw firmly in one hand and twist to remove it. Remove the remaining claw and legs in the same way.

7 Break the claws in half by bending them backwards, then crack the shells with a nutcracker or rolling pin and hook out the meat with a skewer.

8 Remove the stomach sac and mouth and discard. Hold the shell firmly and press the body section upwards and gently pull them apart. Remove the grey gills and discard, then cut the body into small pieces and hook out the meat. Finally, scoop the brown meat out of the shell.

9 Preheat the oven to 200°C/400°F/ Gas 6. To make the sauce, melt the butter in a pan, add the flour and cook over a low heat for 1 minute, stirring to make a roux.

10 Remove from the heat and slowly add the reserved liquid, stirring all the time, to form a smooth sauce. Return to the heat and cook, stirring, for 2–3 minutes until the sauce boils and thickens.

11 Remove from the heat, stir in the cream, then add the egg yolks, brandy and anchovy liquid or stock and season to taste with salt and pepper.

12 Add the extracted crab meat to the sauce and then put the mixture into the empty crab shells.

13 Sprinkle the grated Cheddar cheese on top and bake in the oven for 10–15 minutes until the crab meat mixture is golden brown. Serve hot, with boiled rice and salad.

Per portion Energy 544kcal/2244kJ; Protein 10.9g; Carbohydrate 6.1g, of which sugars 4.2g; Fat 51.7g, of which saturates 30.8g; Cholesterol 209mg; Calcium 112mg; Fibre 0.1g; Sodium 216mg.

DOMESTIC MEATS

Throughout Scandinavia, there is little pollution, imports are strictly controlled and pesticides and antibiotics are rarely used. This ensures that Norway, Sweden and Denmark produce domestic meat with a wonderful flavour. Gotland, a small Swedish island, produces famously delicious lamb, while Denmark's favourite meat is succulent, satisfying pork. In Norway beef is used to make the Scandinavian classic meatball and gravy dish, which is found in many forms.

BRAISED CHICKEN

Braising is a favourite method of cooking chicken in Denmark. Once the chicken is browned, the dish can be cooked on top of the stove or in the oven. Serve gammeldags kylling with boiled new potatoes to create a classic Danish meal.

SERVES FOUR TO SIX

INGREDIENTS
    1 roasting chicken, about 1.6–2kg/
      3½–4½lb, jointed
    juice of ½ lemon
    25g/1oz/2 tbsp butter
    475ml/16fl oz/2 cups chicken stock
    250g/9oz sliced leeks
    6 small carrots, sliced
    175ml/6fl oz/¾ cup double
      (heavy) cream
    salt and ground black pepper

1 Rinse the chicken and pat dry, inside and out, with kitchen paper. Rub the skin with lemon juice, salt and pepper.

2 Melt the butter in a heavy pan, which has a tight-fitting lid, over a medium heat.

3 Add the chicken pieces and cook for about 15 minutes, turning, until they are browned all over.

4 Pour half the stock over the chicken, add the squeezed lemon half, and cover. Simmer, basting with the remaining stock, for 30 minutes.

5 Add the leeks and carrots and cook for a further 30 minutes, or until the juices run clear when the chicken is pierced. Lift out the chicken and vegetables and keep warm. Discard the lemon half.

6 Raise the heat, bring the stock to the boil, and reduce the liquid to a slightly thickened gravy. Add the cream and heat through until thick and smooth. Season to taste. Return the chicken and vegetables to the pan to warm through.

7 Serve the chicken with the vegetables and gravy together with some boiled new potatoes, if you like.

COOK'S TIP
To prepare this dish in the oven, brown the chicken on the stove, then cover and place the pan in a preheated oven at 180°C/350°F/Gas 4. Cook for 45 minutes, until the juices run clear. Half-way through the cooking time, add the vegetables.

Per portion Energy 853kcal/3585kJ; Protein 34.7g; Carbohydrate 87.7g, of which sugars 62.1g; Fat 43.3g, of which saturates 17.8g; Cholesterol 211mg; Calcium 65mg; Fibre 1.6g; Sodium 764mg.

BRAISED CHICKEN WITH MASHED SWEDE

THIS TRADITIONAL NORWEGIAN WAY OF COOKING CHICKEN CREATES FABULOUS FLAVOUR AND PRODUCES DELICIOUS JUICES IN THE DISH. IT IS SERVED WITH A MIXTURE OF MASHED SWEDE AND POTATO, BOTH ABSORBING THE BUTTER TO GIVE A CREAMY PURÉE.

SERVES FOUR

INGREDIENTS
 75g/3oz/6 tbsp butter
 1 small bunch fresh parsley
 1.6kg/3½lb chicken
 salt and ground black pepper
For the mashed swede (rutabaga)
 450g/1lb swede (rutabaga),
  cut into cubes
 675g/1½lb potatoes, cut into cubes
 115g/4oz/½ cup butter
 pinch of ground allspice
 salt and ground black pepper

1 Put 50g/2oz/4 tbsp of the butter, the parsley, and some salt and pepper inside the chicken. Heat the remaining butter in a pan. Add the chicken and brown on all sides. Season.

2 Lower the heat, cover the pan and simmer gently for 1 hour. Test by inserting the point of a sharp knife into the thigh near the body until the juices are clear.

3 To prepare the mashed swede, put the swede in a large pan, cover with water and season with salt. Bring to the boil, lower the heat and simmer for 15 minutes.

4 Add the potatoes to the pan of swede and simmer for 15 minutes. Drain, reserving a little water and return the vegetables to the pan. Mash well, then add the butter and allspice. Season the mashed vegetables with salt and pepper.

5 When cooked, transfer the chicken to a warmed serving dish. Add a little water to the pan to make a simple gravy, stirring to deglaze the pan and to scrape up any sediment from the bottom. Serve the chicken with the gravy and mashed swede.

Per portion Energy 821kcal/3410kJ; Protein 43.5g; Carbohydrate 33g, of which sugars 7.9g; Fat 58g, of which saturates 24.9g; Cholesterol 269mg; Calcium 91mg; Fibre 3.8g; Sodium 372mg.

ROAST CHICKEN WITH LINGONBERRIES

TRADITIONAL SUNDAY DINNER IN DENMARK OFTEN FEATURES SLICED, ROAST CHICKEN SERVED COLD WITH POTATO SALAD, AND A SAUCE OF TART-SWEET LINGONBERRIES; A MEAL THAT'S EASY ON THE COOK. THE BERRIES, SMALL CRANBERRY-LIKE FRUIT, GROW WILD THROUGHOUT SCANDINAVIA'S MOUNTAINOUS NORTHERN CLIMES. LOOK FOR FROZEN, UNSWEETENED LINGONBERRIES, WHICH CAN BE SWEETENED TO TASTE WITH THE ADDITION OF SOME SUGAR.

4 Lower the oven temperature to 180°C/350°F/Gas 4. Pour the remaining stock or water into the pan. Baste the chicken with the remaining melted butter and the pan juices and continue to cook for a further 30–40 minutes, until the juices run clear when the thickest part of the thigh is pierced. Remove from the oven, cover and leave to cool. Refrigerate the cooled chicken until ready to slice for serving.

SERVES SIX TO EIGHT

INGREDIENTS
    1 roasting chicken, about
       1.6–2kg/3½–4½lb
    ½ lemon
    60ml/4 tbsp chopped fresh parsley
    65g/2½oz/5 tbsp butter, softened
    250ml/8fl oz/1 cup chicken stock
       or water
    350g/12oz/1½ cups unsweetened
       lingonberries
    100–150g/3¾–5oz/½–¾ cup caster
       (superfine) sugar, to taste
    salt and ground black pepper
    potato salad, to serve

1 Preheat the oven to 220°C/425°F/Gas 7. Rinse the chicken and pat dry inside and out with kitchen paper. Rub with lemon. Season with salt and pepper.

2 Mix together the parsley and 40g/1½oz/3 tbsp of the butter and spread this inside the chicken. Close the opening with a skewer or fine string.

3 Pour half the chicken stock or water into a roasting pan and place the chicken, breast side up, on a rack in the pan. Melt the remaining butter and brush half of it over the chicken. Roast for 30 minutes.

5 Place the lingonberries in a bowl. Add the sugar a little at a time, stirring until the sugar thoroughly dissolves and the fruit is mashed. Add more sugar to taste and chill the lingonberries until ready to serve.

6 Remove the chicken from the refrigerator half an hour before serving so that the meat is not too chilled. Just before you are ready to eat, carve the chicken and arrange the slices, together with the whole legs and wings, on a serving platter. Serve with potato salad and the lingonberry sauce.

Per portion Energy 405kcal/1682kJ; Protein 24.9g; Carbohydrate 15.3g, of which sugars 15.3g; Fat 27.4g, of which saturates 10.2g; Cholesterol 145mg; Calcium 36mg; Fibre 1.4g; Sodium 151mg.

ROAST DUCK WITH PRUNES AND APPLES

CHRISTMAS EVE DINNER IN DENMARK TRADITIONALLY FEATURED A PLUMP ROAST GOOSE STUFFED WITH SLICED APPLES AND PRUNES — A BIRD THAT SIGNALLED A FAMILY'S PROSPERITY AND WELLBEING. TODAY, DUCK HAS REPLACED ITS LARGER COUSIN AS THE HOLIDAY BIRD AND THE SAME CLASSIC APPLE AND PRUNE STUFFING WORKS EQUALLY WELL. AT CHRISTMAS, SERVE WITH ROAST POTATOES, LINGONBERRY SAUCE, AND BRAISED RED CABBAGE; AT OTHER TIMES SERVE MORE SIMPLY WITH STEAMED CABBAGE.

SERVES FOUR

INGREDIENTS
1 duck, about 1.8–2.5kg/4–5½ lb, with giblets
150g/5oz stoned (pitted) prunes, sliced
2 medium eating apples, peeled and chopped
20g/¾oz fine breadcrumbs
475ml/16fl oz/2 cups chicken stock
small bay leaf
30ml/2 tbsp plain (all-purpose) flour
15ml/1 tbsp single (light) cream
salt and ground black pepper

1 Preheat the oven to 240°C/475°F/Gas 9. Rinse the duck and pat dry with kitchen paper. Score the breast with a crosshatch pattern. Season well.

2 Toss the prunes and apples with the breadcrumbs in a bowl and spoon this mixture into the duck cavity, packing it firmly. Close the opening with skewers or sew up with fine string.

3 Pour 250ml/8fl oz/1 cup of the chicken stock into a roasting pan. Place the duck on a rack in the roasting pan, breast side down, and cook for 20 minutes.

4 Put the giblets in a pan with 475ml/16fl oz/2 cups water and the bay leaf. Bring to a rolling boil for 20–30 minutes until reduced. Strain and set aside.

5 Lower the oven heat to 180°C/350°F/Gas 4. Remove the roasting pan from the oven and turn the duck breast side up. Pour the remaining stock into the pan. Continue to cook for 40 minutes per kg/20 minutes per lb, until the juices run clear when the thickest part of the leg is pierced. Transfer the duck to a serving dish and leave in a warm place to rest for 10 minutes before carving.

6 To make the gravy, pour off the fat from the roasting pan and whisk the flour into the remaining meat juices. Cook the mixture over a medium heat for 2–3 minutes until light brown. Gradually whisk in the giblet stock and stir in the cream. Cook the gravy, stirring, for a further 3 minutes, then pour into a sauceboat and serve with the duck.

Per portion Energy 663kcal/2757kJ; Protein 31.6g; Carbohydrate 24g, of which sugars 14.6g; Fat 49.6g, of which saturates 14g; Cholesterol 100mg; Calcium 55mg; Fibre 2.8g; Sodium 222mg.

ROAST PORK, CRACKLING AND GLAZED POTATOES

PORK IS THE FAVOURITE MEAT IN DENMARK, AND ROAST PORK WITH GOLDEN CRACKLING IS A MUCH-LOVED DISH, ESPECIALLY DURING WINTER. FOR THIS DANISH RECIPE, SELECT A BONE-IN PORK LOIN WITH THE SKIN LEFT ON FOR THE CRACKLING.

SERVES EIGHT TO TEN

INGREDIENTS

  1 bone-in pork loin, weighing
    about 2.25kg/5lb
  10ml/2 tsp mustard powder
  15 whole cloves
  2 bay leaves
  900ml/1½ pints/3¾ cups water
  175ml/6fl oz/¾ cup single (light)
    cream (optional)
  salt and ground white pepper
  braised red cabbage, to serve
For the glazed potatoes
  900g/2lb small potatoes
  50g/2oz/¼ cup caster
    (superfine) sugar
  65g/2½oz/5 tbsp butter
For the apples with redcurrant jelly
  750ml/1¼ pints/3 cups water
  115g/4oz/generous ½ cup soft
    light brown sugar
  5ml/1 tsp lemon juice
  4–5 tart eating apples, peeled,
    cored and halved
  60–75ml/4–5 tbsp redcurrant jelly

1 Preheat the oven to 200°C/400°F/ Gas 6. Use a sharp knife to score the pork skin in a diamond pattern.

2 Rub the pork rind with the salt, pepper and mustard powder, then push the cloves and bay leaves into the skin.

3 Place the pork loin, skin side up, on a rack in a roasting pan and cook for about 1 hour, until the skin is crisp and golden.

4 Pour the water into the bottom of the roasting pan, then return the pork to the oven and cook for a further 30 minutes, until cooked through.

5 Boil the potatoes in salted water for 15–20 minutes, or until they are soft. Drain the potatoes, peel them and keep them warm.

6 Melt the caster sugar in a large frying pan over a low heat until it turns light brown in colour. Add the cooked potatoes and the butter, stirring to coat the potatoes, and cook for about 6–8 minutes, until the potatoes are rich golden brown in colour. Set the glazed potatoes aside and keep them warm while you prepare the apples with redcurrant jelly.

7 To cook the apples, bring the water to the boil in a large pan and stir in the brown sugar. Add the lemon juice and the apple halves, lower the heat and poach gently until the apples are just tender.

8 Remove the apples from the pan. Carefully spoon 7.5ml/1½ tsp redcurrant jelly into the hollow of each apple half and set them aside, keeping them warm.

9 When the pork loin is cooked through, transfer it to a serving dish and set it aside in a warm place to rest for about 15 minutes before carving it.

10 Meanwhile, to make the gravy, transfer the meat juices from the roasting pan into a pan and cook over a medium heat until reduced. Whisk in a little single cream if you wish, and season with salt and pepper to taste.

11 Serve the pork with the gravy, caramelized potatoes and poached apple halves. You can remove the crackling from the pork, and serve it separately, while still warm. Alternatively, impress your guests by leaving the crackling on the pork, then remove it at the table.

Per portion Energy 654kcal/2735kJ; Protein 36.9g; Carbohydrate 39.5g, of which sugars 26.2g; Fat 39.9g, of which saturates 16.1g; Cholesterol 124mg; Calcium 36mg; Fibre 1.5g; Sodium 152mg.

STUFFED LOIN OF PORK WITH PRUNES AND HASSELBACK POTATOES

THE SWEDES LOVE THE TASTE OF PORK AND THIS RECIPE IS A REAL CLASSIC. HERE, THE ROAST PORK IS SERVED WITH HASSELBACK POTATOES, WHICH ARE THE SWEDISH VERSION OF ROAST POTATOES. THEY HAVE A WONDERFUL CRISPY CRUST AND A SOFT, BUTTERY INSIDE.

SERVES SIX TO EIGHT

INGREDIENTS
   200g/7oz/scant 1 cup Agen prunes
   15g/½oz/1 tbsp butter
   1 Spanish (Bermuda) onion, chopped
   15ml/1 tbsp chopped fresh parsley
   500g/1¼lb boned loin of pork,
      with rind on
   salt and ground black pepper
For the hasselback potatoes
   1.3–1.8kg/3–4lb small
      roasting potatoes
   100g/4oz/½ cup butter, melted
   30ml/2 tbsp fresh breadcrumbs

1 Soak the prunes in cold water overnight. The next day, chop the prunes into small pieces.

2 Melt the butter in a frying pan, add the onion and fry for about 5 minutes until beginning to soften.

3 Add the chopped prunes and chopped fresh parsley to the frying pan and fry, stirring occasionally, until the onions are very soft and the mixture is slightly sticky.

4 Season the mixture with salt and pepper to taste, then set aside and allow to cool while you prepare the hasselback potatoes.

5 Preheat the oven to 220°C/425°F/ Gas 7. Peel the potatoes so that they are all evenly sized and oval in shape.

6 Put the potatoes, one at a time, in the bowl of a wooden spoon and slice across their width at 3mm/⅛in intervals, through the potato until you hit the wooden spoon. This stops you slicing all the way through.

7 Then put the potatoes in a roasting pan and pour over the melted butter. Roast in the top of the oven for 10 minutes.

8 Meanwhile, open out the pork and place it, skin side down, on a chopping board. Spread the prune stuffing over the pork.

9 Roll it up and tie at regular intervals with string. Using a sharp knife score the skin, then sprinkle with salt.

10 When the potatoes have roasted for 10 minutes, baste with the butter. Reduce the oven temperature to 180°C/350°F/Gas 4 and roast the pork in the oven, below the potatoes, for 40 minutes.

11 Remove the potatoes from the oven, baste them and sprinkle over the breadcrumbs. Return them to the oven and roast the potatoes and pork for a further 20 minutes, until the meat is cooked through.

12 Remove the cooked pork from the oven and leave it to rest for 15 minutes.

13 Meanwhile, increase the oven temperature to 220°C/425°F/Gas 7 and roast the potatoes for a further 15 minutes until golden brown and opened up like a fan.

14 To serve, remove the crackling from the pork and carve the meat. Serve with the hasselback potatoes.

COOK'S TIP
Hasselback potatoes, with their delicious crispy shells, are named after the 'Hasselbacken' restaurant of Stockholm where they were first served. The cooking times are adapted here to fit with the recipe, but if you are cooking them on their own, just put them in an oven preheated at 220°C/425°F/Gas 7 for 35–40 minutes.

Per portion Energy 538kcal/2247kJ; Protein 16.7g; Carbohydrate 42.8g, of which sugars 15.1g; Fat 34.6g, of which saturates 18.5g; Cholesterol 95mg; Calcium 46mg; Fibre 4g; Sodium 248mg.

FRIED PORK AND APPLES

EPLEFLESK IS A SIMPLE DISH THAT TURNS AN INEXPENSIVE CUT OF MEAT INTO A MOST ENJOYABLE MEAL.
IT IS IDEAL FOR A QUICK SUPPER. NORWEGIAN APPLES ARE CRISP WITH A BEAUTIFUL FLAVOUR; THE
SUMMER IS NOT VERY WARM BUT THE FRUIT RIPENS NICELY WITH ALMOST 24 HOURS OF SUNSHINE A DAY.

SERVES FOUR

INGREDIENTS
  600g/1lb 6oz lightly salted or fresh
    belly of pork, cut into thin slices
  500g/1¼lb crisp eating apples
  30ml/2 tbsp soft light brown sugar
  salt and ground black pepper
  chopped fresh parsley or chives,
    to garnish (optional)
To serve
  boiled potatoes
  a green vegetable

COOK'S TIP
Cut the apple rings to a depth of 5mm/
¼in across the apple. Most apples will
make four rings.

1 Heat a large frying pan, without any
oil or fat, until hot. Add the pork slices
and fry over a low heat for 3–4 minutes
on each side, until golden brown.
Season the pork slices with salt and
pepper. Transfer to a warmed serving
dish and keep warm.

2 Core the apples but do not peel, then
cut the apples into rings.

3 Add the apple rings to the frying
pan and fry gently in the pork fat for
3–4 minutes on each side until they
are just beginning to turn golden
and translucent.

4 Sprinkle the slices with the sugar
and turn once more for a couple of
minutes until the sugar side starts
to caramelize.

5 Serve the pork slices with the apple
rings. Accompany with a green
vegetable, garnished with chopped
fresh parsley or chives, if you like.

Per portion Energy 645kcal/2676kJ; Protein 23.4g; Carbohydrate 19g, of which sugars 19g; Fat 53.4g, of which saturates 19.7g; Cholesterol 108mg; Calcium 21mg; Fibre 2g; Sodium 113mg.

BRAISED PIG'S CHEEKS WITH MASHED SWEDES

*THIS CLASSIC SWEDISH DISH, BRÄSERAD GRISKIND MED KÅLROTSMOS, IS TRADITIONALLY MADE WITH
HAM HOCK BUT THIS METHOD INSTEAD USES PIG'S CHEEKS AS THE MAIN INGREDIENT. PIG'S CHEEK IS
DELICIOUSLY TENDER AND IS TODAY BECOMING A REGULAR SIGHT IN FASHIONABLE RESTAURANTS.*

SERVES EIGHT

INGREDIENTS
8 salted pig's cheek oysters
1 leek, halved widthways
1 carrot, halved widthways
1 bay leaf
bouquet garni (see Cook's Tip)
2 large swedes (rutabagas)
250ml/8fl oz/1 cup crème fraîche
25g/1oz/2 tbsp butter
salt and ground black pepper

1 Put the salted pig's cheeks into a
large pan and add enough cold water
to cover.

2 Add the leek, carrot, bay leaf and
bouquet garni, bring to the boil, then
lower the heat and simmer for 2 hours
until tender.

3 Meanwhile, chop the swedes into
large chunks.

4 Half an hour before the pig's cheeks
are cooked, cook the prepared swedes
in boiling salted water for 30 minutes
until soft.

5 Drain, transfer to a bowl and mash well.
Beat in the crème fraîche, butter, and
plenty of black pepper with a spoon.

6 Finally, beat the mashed swedes
gently with a wooden spoon to make
the mixture as light, smooth and fluffy
as possible.

7 When the pig's cheeks are cooked
through, drain them, slice and serve
immediately, accompanied by the
mashed swedes.

COOK'S TIP
Make a bouquet garni by tying together a
sprig of thyme, some parsley stalks and
a sprig of marjoram.

Per portion Energy 272kcal/1131kJ; Protein 18.1g; Carbohydrate 8.6g, of which sugars 8.2g; Fat 18.6g, of which saturates 11.2g; Cholesterol 89mg; Calcium 99mg; Fibre 3.2g; Sodium 101mg.

CHRISTMAS HAM WITH SWEDISH MUSTARD

AT CHRISTMAS TIME IN SWEDEN EVERY POSSIBLE USE IS MADE OF ALMOST ALL PARTS OF THE PIG. THIS DISH IS ALWAYS MADE WITH 'GREEN', OR SALTED GAMMON, RATHER THAN THE SMOKED VARIETY. ON CHRISTMAS EVE IT IS TRADITIONAL TO EAT HAM SUCH AS THIS FOR SUPPER AFTER HAVING EATEN A CHRISTMAS PORRIDGE, WHICH IS SIMILAR TO RICE PUDDING.

2 Bring to the boil, then reduce the heat and simmer gently for 1 hour. Remove from the heat and leave to cool overnight in the pan.

3 Preheat the oven to 220°C/425°F/ Gas 7. Remove the ham from the pan (don't discard the stock but see Cook's Tip) and remove the rind from the ham, leaving the fat.

4 Spread the mustard over the fat and sprinkle the breadcrumbs on top so that they stick to the mustard.

5 Put the ham in a roasting pan and bake in the oven for about 20 minutes until golden brown and crisp on the outside. Serve the ham either hot or cold, accompanied by boiled peas and Cumberland sauce.

COOK'S TIP
Make good use of the stock from this recipe in a soup, known as Dopp i grytan. Bring the stock to the boil for about a minute and serve with a Swedish sweet bread, such as vörtbröd.

SERVES SIX TO EIGHT

INGREDIENTS
  1kg/2¼lb unsmoked gammon
    (ham) joint
  1 onion, halved
  2 apples, quartered
  2 bay leaves
  5ml/1 tsp whole white peppercorns
  2 sprigs fresh thyme
  2–3 sprigs fresh parsley
  5ml/1 tsp cumin seeds
  30ml/2 tbsp Swedish mustard
  30ml/2 tbsp fresh breadcrumbs
  boiled peas and Cumberland sauce,
    or other fruit sauce, to serve

1 Put the gammon joint in a large pan. Add the onion, apples, bay leaves, peppercorns, fresh thyme, fresh parsley and cumin seeds and add enough water to cover.

Per portion Energy 214kcal/893kJ; Protein 23.9g; Carbohydrate 4.9g, of which sugars 1g; Fat 11.7g, of which saturates 3.2g; Cholesterol 29mg; Calcium 32mg; Fibre 0.2g; Sodium 1313mg.

BAKED SAUSAGE TERRINE

THIS DISH, KORVTERRIN, CAN BE MADE WITH READY-MADE SAUSAGE MEAT, OR IF YOU PREFER YOU CAN MAKE YOUR OWN, AS SHOWN HERE, USING A MIXTURE OF OATMEAL, PIG'S LIVER, PORK AND RAISINS. THE OATMEAL CREATES A TEXTURE JUST LIKE THE SAUSAGE MEAT. SWEET LINGONBERRY CONSERVE IS A PERFECT SCANDINAVIAN ACCOMPANIMENT.

SERVES SIX TO EIGHT

INGREDIENTS
115g/4oz/1 cup oatmeal
750ml/1¼ pints/3 cups water
750ml/1¼ pints/3 cups milk
15g/½oz/1 tbsp butter
1 red onion, finely chopped
200g/7oz pig's liver, minced (ground)
200g/7oz minced (ground) pork
150g/5oz/1 cup raisins
5ml/1 tsp chopped fresh marjoram
5ml/1 tsp ground allspice
salt and ground black pepper
lingonberry conserve and toast,
  to serve

1 Preheat the oven to 180°C/350°F/ Gas 4, then line the base and sides of a 20cm/8in loaf tin (pan) with baking parchment.

2 Put the oatmeal, water and milk in a large pan, bring to the boil, then reduce the heat and cook for 3–4 minutes until soft. Leave to cool.

3 Melt the butter in a pan, add the finely chopped onion and fry for 5–10 minutes until the onion is softened and translucent.

4 Transfer the onion to a large bowl, add the cooled oatmeal, pig's liver, minced pork, raisins, marjoram, allspice, salt and pepper and mix well together.

5 Pour the mixture into the prepared tin, level the top and bake in the oven for 40 minutes–1 hour until lightly browned. Serve hot or cold, with lingonberry conserve and toast.

Per portion Energy 238kcal/1003kJ; Protein 15.6g; Carbohydrate 28.5g, of which sugars 17.8g; Fat 7.7g, of which saturates 3.1g; Cholesterol 91mg; Calcium 134mg; Fibre 1.5g; Sodium 105mg.

MOCK HARE, REDCURRANT JELLY SAUCE AND HASSELBACK POTATOES

THIS HEARTY DANISH MEATLOAF IS INTENDED TO IMITATE HARE OR RABBIT. SERVED WITH GRAVY SUBTLY SWEETENED WITH REDCURRANT JELLY, ALONG WITH BUTTERY FANS OF HASSELBACK POTATOES, THE MEATLOAF MAKES A RICH MEAL WITH LUXURIOUS FLAVOURS.

SERVES SIX

INGREDIENTS
   450g/1lb lean minced (ground) beef
   450g/1lb minced (ground) pork
   75g/3oz/1½ cups fine breadcrumbs
   25g/1oz/2 tbsp finely chopped onion
   2 eggs
   75ml/5 tbsp double (heavy) cream
   3–4 streaky (fatty) bacon
     rashers (strips)
   salt and ground black pepper
For the hasselback potatoes
   12 medium-sized oval or round
     potatoes (about 1.8kg/4lb
     total weight)
   50g/2oz/¼ cup butter
   25g/1oz/½ cup fine breadcrumbs
   25g/1oz/⅓ cup freshly grated
     Parmesan cheese
   salt and ground white pepper
For the sauce
   15g/½oz/1 tbsp butter
   25g/1oz/¼ cup plain
     (all-purpose) flour
   120ml/4fl oz/½ cup single
     (light) cream
   60ml/4 tbsp redcurrant jelly
   salt and ground white pepper

1 Preheat the oven to 190°C/375°F/ Gas 5. Put the minced beef and minced pork in a large bowl and mix together thoroughly.

2 Stir in the breadcrumbs, chopped onion, eggs, double cream, salt and pepper.

3 Turn the mixture into a 12.5 x 23cm/ 5 x 9in loaf tin (pan), pressing it in firmly with your hands. Arrange the bacon rashers over the top and bake the terrine for 1 hour.

4 Meanwhile, lightly grease a baking dish. Peel the potatoes and rinse them under cold water.

5 Cut each potato crossways into 8–10 thin, even slices, taking care not to cut all the way through to the bottom, so the slices hold together. This can be done by placing the potato against the edge of a chopping board so that the knife hits the chopping board before cutting all the way through the potato. Alternatively, place the potato on a wooden spoon and slice across its width until you hit the wooden spoon. This way, the knife will not cut all the way through the potato.

6 Place the hasselback potatoes, sliced side up, in the prepared baking dish.

7 Dot evenly with butter and sprinkle with salt and pepper. Roast for about 1–1½ hours, or until tender and light brown, basting with butter during cooking. Sprinkle with breadcrumbs and grated cheese 20 minutes before the end of the cooking time.

8 When the meat loaf is cooked through, pour off the fat and reserve. Leave the loaf to cool for 15 minutes while you make the sauce.

9 Pour 75ml/2½fl oz/⅓ cup of reserved fat into a pan, add the butter and heat until it melts. Whisk in the flour, and cook, stirring, for 2–4 minutes until well blended.

10 Stir in the cream, redcurrant jelly, salt and pepper. Cook until smooth and heated through.

11 Slice the meat loaf and serve it drizzled with the redcurrant sauce and accompanied by the crispy hasselback potatoes.

Per portion Energy 935kcal/3903kJ; Protein 41.2g; Carbohydrate 69.2g, of which sugars 12.1g; Fat 56.7g, of which saturates 28.6g; Cholesterol 199mg; Calcium 136mg; Fibre 3.5g; Sodium 478mg.

Norwegian Beef Stew

Lapskaus is a traditional Norwegian casserole of beef cooked with root vegetables, which makes it a complete meal in a pot. Cooking the vegetables separately from the meat for part of the time is an unusual technique, which allows them to keep more of their own flavour than would be possible if added to the meat at the beginning.

SERVES FOUR TO SIX

INGREDIENTS

- 1.2kg/2½lb stewing beef, cut into large cubes
- 1.2 litres/2 pints/5 cups beef stock
- 450g/1lb carrots, cut into bitesize pieces
- 1 small swede (rutabaga) or turnip, cut into bitesize pieces
- 675g/1½lb potatoes, cut into bitesize pieces
- 1 onion, finely chopped
- salt and ground black pepper

1 Put the beef in a large pan, add enough water to cover, season with salt and pepper and bring slowly to the boil.

2 Lower the heat, cover and simmer for 1 hour.

3 When the beef has been cooking for 30 minutes, bring the beef stock to the boil in a separate pan. Add the carrots and swede or turnip and simmer for 15 minutes.

4 Add the potatoes to the stock and simmer for a further 15 minutes.

5 When the beef has been cooking for 1 hour, strain the cubes, reserving the stock for a soup or another dish.

6 Add the beef to the vegetables with the onion. Check the seasoning, adding salt and pepper only if necessary.

7 Simmer the casserole for a further 15–30 minutes, depending on the quality of the meat, until the meat and vegetables are tender. Serve hot.

Per portion Energy 475kcal/1987kJ; Protein 48.4g; Carbohydrate 28.2g, of which sugars 10.8g; Fat 19.4g, of which saturates 7.8g; Cholesterol 116mg; Calcium 73mg; Fibre 4.3g; Sodium 170mg.

SAILOR'S STEAK

ALSO KNOWN AS SEAMAN'S BEEF, THIS DISH, CALLED SJÖMANSBIFF, IS FROM SWEDEN. IT USED TO BE ASSOCIATED WITH SAILORS BECAUSE IT REQUIRES VERY FEW KITCHEN UTENSILS AND JUST ONE POT TO MAKE IT. COOKING THE MEAT AND VEGETABLES TOGETHER, IN CONTRAST TO NORWEGIAN BEEF STEW, GIVES THE DISH A DELICIOUS AND HEARTY STEW-LIKE COMBINATION OF TEXTURES AND FLAVOURS.

SERVES EIGHT

INGREDIENTS

8 thin slices entrecôte (sirloin) steak, about 600g/1lb 6oz
8 medium potatoes
15g/½oz/1 tbsp butter
4 onions, chopped
15ml/1 tbsp chopped fresh parsley, plus extra to garnish
1 sprig fresh thyme
3 bay leaves
500ml/17fl oz bottle ale
salt and ground black pepper
pickled beetroot (beet) or pickled gherkins, to serve

1 Preheat the oven to 180°C/350°F/Gas 4. Using a rolling pin or heavy wooden mallet, beat the steaks until they are flattened.

2 Peel the potatoes, cut in half and then into 1cm/½in slices.

3 Melt the butter in a large frying pan. Add the onions and fry for about 10 minutes until golden brown.

4 Push the onions to one side of the pan, add the steaks and fry until sealed on both sides.

5 Transfer to a casserole and add the sliced potatoes, parsley, thyme, bay leaves, salt and pepper. Pour over the ale, cover and bake in the oven for about 1 hour until the potatoes are tender. Garnish with chopped parsley and serve with pickled beetroot or pickled gherkins.

Per portion Energy 279kcal/1170kJ; Protein 19.4g; Carbohydrate 29.9g, of which sugars 9.7g; Fat 6.6g, of which saturates 3.2g; Cholesterol 50mg; Calcium 38mg; Fibre 2.3g; Sodium 70mg.

BEEF PATTIES <u>WITH</u> ONIONS <u>AND</u> FRIED EGG

FRIED BEEF PATTIES ARE A VERY OLD, TRADITIONAL DANISH DISH, A WORKERS' MEAL STILL ENJOYED TODAY ALL AROUND THE COUNTRY. MOST OFTEN SERVED FOR LUNCH, THE PATTIES ARE ACCOMPANIED BY BUTTERED FLAT BREAD AND PICKLED RED CABBAGE OR GHERKINS.

2 Gradually stir in the milk until thoroughly blended to make a soft, moist mixture. Season with salt and pepper. Refrigerate for 15–30 minutes.

3 Melt 40g/1½oz/3 tbsp of the butter in a pan over a medium heat. Divide the meat mixture into four and form rounded patties.

4 Place the patties in the pan and cook for 8–10 minutes, turning once, until browned. Remove from the pan and keep warm.

5 Melt the remaining butter in the pan, add the sliced onions and cook, stirring often, for 6–8 minutes, until soft and golden.

6 When the onions are ready, fry the remaining eggs in a little hot oil in a separate frying pan.

7 To serve, place the patties on four serving plates and top each with a spoonful of cooked onions. Place a fried egg on top of the onions and serve immediately.

SERVES FOUR

INGREDIENTS
  450g/1lb lean minced (ground) beef
  45ml/3 tbsp breadcrumbs
  20g/¾oz/¼ cup finely
    chopped onions
  5 eggs
  15g/½oz/¼ cup chopped fresh parsley
  120ml/4fl oz/½ cup milk
  65g/2½oz/5 tbsp butter
  3 medium onions, sliced
  vegetable oil, for frying
  salt and ground black pepper

1 Put the beef in a mixing bowl, add the breadcrumbs, chopped onions, one of the eggs and the parsley and mix well.

Per portion Energy 527kcal/2189kJ; Protein 32.7g; Carbohydrate 11.8g, of which sugars 2.9g; Fat 39.3g, of which saturates 18.5g; Cholesterol 342mg; Calcium 104mg; Fibre 0.5g; Sodium 375mg.

BEEF MEATBALLS IN GRAVY

THIS IS THE NORWEGIAN VERSION OF MEATBALLS, ALTHOUGH EVERYONE HAS THEIR OWN RECIPE. IT IS CALLED KJØTTKAKER MED KÅLSTUING. TRADITIONALLY MADE WITH BEEF, SOME COOKS WILL USE A MIXTURE OF BEEF AND PORK, WHILE OTHERS WILL ADD CHOPPED ONIONS OR VARY THE SEASONINGS.

SERVES FOUR

INGREDIENTS

500g/1¼ lb finely minced
(ground) beef
large pinch of freshly grated nutmeg
large pinch of ground allspice
large pinch of ground ginger
15ml/1 tbsp potato flour
200ml/7fl oz/scant 1 cup milk
or water
1 egg, lightly beaten
30ml/2 tbsp vegetable oil
25g/1oz/2 tbsp butter
25g/1oz/¼ cup plain
(all-purpose) flour
600ml/1 pint/2½ cups beef stock
30ml/2 tbsp double (heavy) cream
salt and ground black pepper

1 Put the minced beef in a bowl and add the grated nutmeg, ground allspice, ground ginger, potato flour, 5ml/1 tsp salt and pepper and beat well.

2 Add the milk or water, little by little, beating after each addition. Add the beaten egg and beat well again until thoroughly combined.

3 With wet hands, shape the mixture into balls. (The balls can be any size you like but the larger the balls, the longer it will take to cook them.)

4 Heat the oil in a large frying pan, add the meatballs, in batches if necessary, and fry over a medium heat until cooked. Remove them and transfer to a plate.

5 When the meatballs are cooked, add the butter to the pan and heat until melted. Add the flour, stirring with a wooden spoon to deglaze the pan, scraping up any sediment.

6 Gradually add the stock, stirring all the time to form a smooth sauce. When all the stock has been added, bring slowly to the boil, stirring, until the sauce thickens.

7 Check the seasonings, adding salt and pepper only if necessary, then simmer for 10 minutes.

8 Add the double cream to the sauce, then add the cooked meatballs and simmer for a further 10 minutes. Serve hot.

Per portion Energy 454kcal/1882kJ; Protein 26.9g; Carbohydrate 5g, of which sugars 0.3g; Fat 36.4g, of which saturates 15.5g; Cholesterol 146mg; Calcium 32mg; Fibre 0.2g; Sodium 157mg.

SWEDISH HASH

THIS CLASSIC DISH IS KNOWN IN SWEDEN AS PYTT I PANNA, LITERALLY MEANING 'PUT IN THE PAN'. ORIGINALLY INTRODUCED AS AN ECONOMY DISH MADE WITH LEFTOVERS, ITS POPULARITY HAS MEANT THAT IT IS NOW INVARIABLY MADE FROM FRESH INGREDIENTS.

SERVES THREE TO FOUR

INGREDIENTS

    4 large potatoes
    about 25g/1oz/2 tbsp butter
    15ml/1 tbsp vegetable oil
    1 large onion, finely chopped
    150g/5oz gammon (smoked or cured
      ham) or bacon, finely chopped
    100g/4oz smoked frankfurters,
      finely chopped
    500g/1¼lb cold cooked lamb or
      beef, cubed
    3–4 very fresh eggs
    salt and ground black pepper
    chopped fresh parsley, to garnish
    Worcestershire sauce, to serve

1 Peel the potatoes, then cut them into small cubes measuring about 3mm/⅛in.

2 Heat the butter and oil in a large frying pan, add the potato cubes and fry for about 20 minutes, stirring frequently, until golden brown.

3 Remove the potatoes from the pan with a slotted spoon, put in a bowl and keep warm.

4 Put the onion in the pan, adding more butter if necessary, and fry until golden brown. Remove from the pan and add to the potatoes.

5 Add the gammon or bacon and the frankfurter sausages, fry until cooked and put them in the bowl.

6 Fry the beef or lamb until heated through and add to the other fried ingredients. Season the mixture with salt and pepper to taste and mix well.

7 Divide the mixture among warmed, individual serving plates. Break the eggs, one at a time, separating the yolks from the whites, and putting an egg yolk in half its shell in the centre of each plate. Garnish with chopped parsley and serve with Worcestershire sauce.

COOK'S TIPS
• 1–2 tbsp capers can be included in the mixture. Add them to the pan with the meat.
• Make sure that the eggs are very fresh and, because the recipe contains raw egg yolks, do not serve the dish to infants, the elderly, pregnant women, and convalescents.
• The dish can also be served with fried eggs and beetroot (beets) or sour pickled gherkins.

Per portion Energy 930kcal/3866kJ; Protein 55.9g; Carbohydrate 18.7g, of which sugars 3.6g; Fat 70.9g, of which saturates 28.8g; Cholesterol 427mg; Calcium 68mg; Fibre 1.3g; Sodium 1992mg.

LAMB STEW IN A CREAMY DILL SAUCE

The Baltic island of Gotland, off the south-east coast of Sweden, is famous for the herds of sheep that roam across its rugged landscape and, consequently, its lamb production. This delectable dish, known as dillkött, is strongly associated with the region.

SERVES SIX TO EIGHT

INGREDIENTS
  1kg/2¼lb lamb neck fillet or
    boned leg, cubed
  1 Spanish (Bermuda) onion,
    roughly chopped
  1 carrot, chopped
  1 celery stick, chopped
  1 bay leaf
  2 sprigs fresh thyme
For the sauce
  1 bunch fresh dill
  250ml/8fl oz/1 cup water
  90g/3½oz/½ cup sugar
  120ml/4fl oz/½ cup white vinegar
  10g/¼oz/½ tbsp butter, softened
  10g/¼oz/½ tbsp plain
    (all-purpose) flour
  1 egg yolk
  120ml/4fl oz/½ cup double
    (heavy) cream
  salt and ground black pepper

1 Put the cubed lamb in a large pan and then add the onion, carrot, celery, bay leaf and thyme. Pour in enough cold water to cover the ingredients fully, bring to simmering point and then simmer for about 40 minutes to 1 hour until the meat is tender.

2 To make the sauce, remove the dill fronds from the main stalks, reserving the stalks, chop finely and set aside.

3 Put the reserved stalks in a pan and add the water, sugar and vinegar. Bring to the boil, then boil over a high heat for 5 minutes.

4 Put the butter in a bowl and work in the flour with a fork until smooth to make a beurre manié. In a separate bowl, mix the egg yolk and cream.

5 When the lamb is cooked, put 1 litre/1¾ pints/4 cups of the stock from the lamb in a pan. Strain in the sugar and vinegar liquid, then bring the mixture to simmering point.

6 Add small knobs (pats) of the beurre manié, whisking vigorously, and allow each knob to melt before adding another, to thicken the sauce. Bring to the boil, then simmer for about 10 minutes.

7 Stir the egg and cream mixture and the chopped dill fronds into the sauce. Do not allow the mixture to boil or the sauce will curdle. Pour over the lamb and serve with potatoes, if you like.

Per portion Energy 509kcal/2125kJ; Protein 34.4g; Carbohydrate 22.6g, of which sugars 20.1g; Fat 31.8g, of which saturates 16g; Cholesterol 191mg; Calcium 56mg; Fibre 1.2g; Sodium 169mg.

EASTER RACK OF LAMB

GATHERING WITH FAMILY MEMBERS AND SHARING AN EASTER FEAST FEATURING A MAGNIFICENT RACK OF LAMB, SIMPLY COOKED, MARKS THE HOLIDAY FOR MANY DANES. ACCOMPANY THIS DISH, PÅSKE LAM, WITH STEAMED ASPARAGUS AND LINGONBERRY SAUCE.

3 Place the lamb in the preheated oven and immediately lower the temperature to 180°C/350°F/Gas 4. Roast for 1½ hours. Do not cover or baste during the cooking time.

4 Remove the pan from the oven and arrange the potatoes, onions and carrots under the rack. Cook for about 30 minutes more, or until the meat is done to your liking and the vegetables are tender.

5 Transfer the lamb and vegetables to a serving dish and keep warm. Skim the fat from the pan juices. To make the gravy, pour 45ml/3 tbsp pan juices into a pan over a medium heat.

6 Whisk the flour into the pan juices and cook for 3–4 minutes until well blended and smooth.

7 Slowly stir in the remaining pan juices and the stock; cook until thickened. Season to taste with salt and pepper.

8 Serve the lamb and vegetables hot with the gravy.

SERVES EIGHT TO TEN

INGREDIENTS

   1.8–2kg/4–4½lb racks of lamb,
     fat trimmed from bones
   900g/2lb red potatoes, peeled
     and halved
   3 medium onions, quartered
   900g/2lb carrots, halved lengthways
   40g/1½oz/⅓ cup plain
     (all-purpose) flour
   250ml/8fl oz/1 cup good lamb stock
   salt and ground black pepper
   chopped parsley, to garnish

COOK'S TIPS
• When purchasing a rack of lamb, calculate four to five ribs per person, depending on the size of the lamb.
• For medium-rare lamb, allow 60 minutes per kilogram/30 minutes per pound cooking time; for medium lamb, allow 70 minutes per kilogram/35 minutes per pound.

1 Preheat the oven to 220°C/425°F/Gas 7. To prepare the meat, make a slit in the membrane on each rib and arrange the racks in a circle with the bone ends curving outward.

2 Tie the ribs with fine string to secure them in the crown position. (You can ask your butcher to prepare the crown roast for you.) Wrap the bone ends with foil to prevent them from burning. Rub the meat with salt and pepper, and place on a rack in a roasting pan.

Per portion Energy 493kcal/2050kJ; Protein 25.6g; Carbohydrate 28.7g, of which sugars 10.7g; Fat 31.5g, of which saturates 15.1g; Cholesterol 97mg; Calcium 62mg; Fibre 3.9g; Sodium 113mg.

STUFFED ROAST SHOULDER ᴼᶠ LAMB

BONING AND STUFFING A JOINT OF LAMB NOT ONLY ADDS EXTRA FLAVOUR BUT MAKES IT MUCH EASIER TO CARVE. THE STUFFING IN THIS NORWEGIAN RECIPE IS SIMPLE BUT TASTY. GLAZED ONIONS ARE AN EXCELLENT ACCOMPANIMENT AND ARE POPULAR WITH ROASTED MEAT DISHES.

SERVES SIX TO EIGHT

INGREDIENTS
   2.25kg/5lb shoulder of lamb, boned,
      with bones reserved
   1 bunch fresh parsley, chopped
   2 garlic cloves, finely chopped
   2–3 fresh rosemary sprigs,
      finely chopped
   salt and ground black pepper
For the stock
   1 celery stick
   1 bunch fresh parsley
   1 carrot
   1 leek
   1 small onion
   1 fresh thyme sprig
   1 bay leaf
   6 black peppercorns
   5ml/½ tsp salt
For the sauce
   60ml/4 tbsp potato flour
   200ml/7fl oz/scant 1 cup
      whipping cream
   100ml/3½fl oz/scant ½ cup
      medium sherry
For the glazed onions
   675g/1½lb small onions or shallots,
      in their skins
   25g/1oz/2 tbsp butter
   30ml/2 tbsp sugar
   salt and ground black pepper

1 To make the stock, tie the celery and the bunch of parsley together with string. Put in a large pan with the lamb bones, carrot, leek, onion, thyme, bay leaf, peppercorns and salt. Add water to cover, bring to the boil, then reduce the heat and simmer for 1½–2 hours.

2 Strain and remove the fat from the top. Measure 800ml/1 pint 7fl oz/ 3¼ cups of the stock and reserve.

3 Preheat the oven to 180°C/350°F/Gas 4. Open out the lamb and spread the parsley, garlic and rosemary over the surface. Season with salt and pepper. Roll up and secure with string. Roast for 1–1½ hours, basting often with the cooking juices, until tender.

4 To prepare the glazed onions, put the onions or shallots in a pan and cover with water. Bring to the boil, then reduce the heat and simmer for 5 minutes. Drain. Refresh under cold running water, then drain again. Remove the skins.

5 Melt the butter in a large pan. Add the onions and shake the pan to cover them in the butter. Cook over a low heat for 15–20 minutes until tender. Add the sugar, shaking the pan, and cook until the onions have caramelized slightly. Do not overcook the onions or they will not hold their shape.

6 When the meat is cooked, remove it from the pan, transfer to a warmed serving dish, cover with foil and leave in a warm place to rest.

7 Meanwhile, add a little of the reserved stock to the roasting pan, stirring to deglaze the pan and scraping up any sediment from the base. Add the rest of the stock, then strain the juices through a sieve (strainer) into a large pan.

8 In a small bowl, blend the potato flour with a little cold water to form a smooth paste, then add a little of the hot stock. Stir into the pan and bring to the boil, stirring all the time until thickened. Add the cream and sherry and season to taste with salt and pepper. Serve the lamb with the sauce and glazed onions.

Per portion Energy 731kcal/3033kJ; Protein 41.9g; Carbohydrate 17.6g, of which sugars 10g; Fat 53.7g, of which saturates 27g; Cholesterol 205mg; Calcium 65mg; Fibre 1.4g; Sodium 178mg.

LAMB <u>IN</u> BUTTERMILK <u>WITH</u> ROASTED SHELL POTATOES

THIS NORWEGIAN RECIPE SHOWS HOW MARINATING MEAT WAS A GOOD WAY OF KEEPING IT FRESH, ALTHOUGH ONLY IF THE INTENTION WASN'T TO KEEP THE MEAT FOR TOO LONG. TODAY, LAMB IS STILL MARINATED IN BUTTERMILK, NATURAL YOGURT OR SOUR MILK. IT MAKES THE MEAT VERY MOIST AND TENDER AND GIVES IT A SWEET FLAVOUR. THE POTATOES ARE A SIMPLE BUT DELICIOUS VARIATION ON BAKED POTATOES. THE PREPARATION CAN BE DONE BEFOREHAND AND THE FILLED POTATOES REHEATED IN THE OVEN WITH THE LAMB.

SERVES FOUR TO SIX

INGREDIENTS
   1 leg of lamb, knuckle end trimmed,
      total weight about 2kg/4½lb
   3.5–4.8 litres/6–8 pints/15–20 cups
      buttermilk or natural (plain) yogurt
   15ml/1 tbsp salt
   250ml/8fl oz/1 cup water
For the sauce
   600ml/1 pint/2½ cups chicken
      or vegetable stock
   5ml/1 tsp potato flour
   150ml/¼ pint/⅔ cup sour cream
   salt and ground black pepper
To serve
   a green vegetable, such as
      green beans
   rowan jelly or cranberry sauce
For the potatoes
   4–6 baking potatoes
   50–75g/2–3oz/4–6 tbsp butter
   45–60ml/3–4 tbsp double
      (heavy) cream
   1 bunch spring onions (scallions),
      white and pale green parts
      only, chopped
   45ml/3 tbsp grated Jarlsberg cheese
   salt and ground black pepper

1 Put the leg of lamb in a large bowl and add enough buttermilk or natural yogurt to cover the meat. Keep in the refrigerator for 4–6 days, turning the meat three or four times a day.

2 To prepare the potatoes, preheat the oven to 200°C/400°F/Gas 6. Prick the potatoes all over with a fork and bake in the oven for 1 hour until tender.

3 Cut a slice off the top of each potato and scoop out the insides into a bowl, leaving a sturdy shell. Add the butter to the cooked potato and mash well together. Add the cream and spring onions, and season to taste with salt and pepper. Replace the cooked potato inside the potato shells and top with the grated cheese.

4 When ready to cook the lamb, preheat the oven to 160°C/325°F/Gas 3. Remove the meat from the buttermilk or yogurt, dry on kitchen paper and rub with salt.

5 Place in a roasting pan, standing on a rack, and pour the water into the roasting pan.

6 Roast in the oven for about 1½ hours until tender. A meat thermometer should read 76°C/169°F and the meat should only just be cooked. During cooking, keep the water in the roasting pan topped up.

7 About 20 minutes before the lamb is cooked, arrange the potato shells on a baking tray and reheat in the oven.

8 When the lamb is cooked, remove the meat from the pan, transfer to a warmed serving dish, cover with foil and leave in a warm place while preparing the sauce.

9 Add a little of the stock to the roasting pan, stirring to deglaze the pan and scraping up any sediment from the bottom of the pan. Add enough of the remaining stock to make up to about 1.2 litres/2 pints/5 cups in total. Pour the juices through a sieve (strainer) into a large pan.

10 In a small bowl, blend the potato flour with a little cold water to form a smooth paste and add a little of the hot liquid. Stir into the pan and heat, stirring until thickened. Remove from the heat before it boils and stir in the sour cream. Season with salt and pepper to taste. Serve the lamb with the sauce, the potatoes, a green vegetable and rowan jelly or cranberry sauce.

Per portion Energy 634kcal/2637kJ; Protein 41.8g; Carbohydrate 12.8g, of which sugars 2.5g; Fat 46.3g, of which saturates 20.9g; Cholesterol 195mg; Calcium 102mg; Fibre 1g; Sodium 235mg.

GOTLAND LAMB BURGERS STUFFED WITH BLUE CHEESE

LAMB BURGERS ARE HEALTHIER THAN BEEF BURGERS BECAUSE THEY CONTAIN LESS SATURATED FAT. THE LAMB ADDS A GAMEY, RICH QUALITY TO THESE SWEDISH BURGERS, A DISH ORIGINATING FROM THE ISLAND OF GOTLAND, AND THE BLUE CHEESE AND CRÈME FRAÎCHE GIVE THEM A CREAMY CONSISTENCY.

SERVES EIGHT

INGREDIENTS
  2 potatoes
  60ml/4fl oz/½ cup milk
  50g/2oz/¼ cup butter
  1 egg, beaten
  1 red onion, chopped
  100ml/4floz/½ cup crème fraîche
  15ml/1 tbsp mustard seeds
  400g/14oz minced (ground) lamb
  225g/8oz/1 cup blue cheese
    such as Gorgonzola or Stilton
  salt and ground black pepper

1 Peel the potatoes, cut into quarters and cook in boiling water for about 20 minutes until tender.

2 Drain the potatoes, return to the pan and mash well. Heat the milk with 25g/1oz/2 tbsp of the butter and beat them well into the potato mash.

VARIATION
The burgers can be made with minced (ground) venison. They are also good served with mashed potatoes and leeks sliced and lightly fried in butter.

3 Put the mashed potatoes in a large bowl. Add the egg, chopped onion, crème fraîche, mustard seeds, salt and pepper and mix well together. Add the minced lamb and mix again.

4 Form the mixture into 16 round, flat burgers. Spoon a little blue cheese on the centre of eight of the burgers and then place the remaining burgers on top to make eight larger burgers.

5 Melt the remaining butter in a large frying pan. Add the burgers and fry for 3 minutes on each side, until golden and the cheese has melted. Serve hot.

Per portion Energy 345kcal/1433kJ; Protein 18g; Carbohydrate 7g, of which sugars 1.2g; Fat 27.2g, of which saturates 16.5g; Cholesterol 116mg; Calcium 116mg; Fibre 0.5g; Sodium 310mg.

STUFFED FOIE GRAS WITH APPLE AND LINGONBERRY CHUTNEY

THIS DISH IS A GREAT SWEDISH FAVOURITE. IT IS EXPENSIVE, BUT CERTAINLY WORTH IT ONCE YOU HAVE TASTED IT, AND IT IS SPECIAL BECAUSE IT USES PIG'S CHEEK, WHICH IS AN UNDERUSED CUT OF MEAT. THE RECIPE IS QUITE COMPLICATED, BUT THE REWARD IS DELICIOUS!

SERVES EIGHT

INGREDIENTS
    4 salted pig's cheek oysters
    1 small onion
    1 bay leaf
    1 large fresh foie gras,
        about 250g/9oz
    sprigs of fresh thyme
    105ml/7 tbsp Sauternes or other
        sweet wine
    salt and ground black pepper
    sliced brioche, toasted, to serve
For the apple and lingonberry chutney
    4 crisp eating apples,
        such as Braeburn
    50g/2oz lingonberry conserve
    50g/2oz mango chutney

1 Preheat the oven to 140°C/275°F/ Gas 1. Thoroughly wash and rinse two jam jars and dry in the oven whilst preparing the chutney.

2 To prepare the chutney, peel, core and chop the apples into small cubes. Put in a bowl and add the lingonberry conserve and the mango chutney. Put in the hot jars and cover immediately with airtight tops. Leave to cool, then keep in the refrigerator for 2–3 days before using.

COOK'S TIP
You can buy whole foie gras at some food markets, or you can order them over the internet. If you can't find pig's cheeks, ask your butcher for pig's jowls.

3 Meanwhile, sprinkle salt and pepper on the foie gras and place in a polythene bag with the thyme and wine. Seal the bag and leave it in the refrigerator overnight.

4 Put the pig's cheek oysters in a pan of water with the onion and bay leaf and poach for 1–2 hours until tender. Drain and leave to cool.

5 Preheat the oven to 110°C/225°F/ Gas ¼. Open the polythene bag, drain off the wine and cut the foie gras in half lengthways. Put the foie gras in an ovenproof dish and roast in the oven for about 30 minutes, until the liver is very soft and starts to melt.

6 Put half of the foie gras in the bottom of a terrine. Arrange the pig's cheeks down the centre, then place the rest of the foie gras on top. Cover with baking parchment and put a heavy weight on top to press it down. Leave in the refrigerator overnight to chill and set.

7 To serve the foie gras, turn it out on to a board and, using a warm knife, carefully cut into 1cm/½in thick slices. Serve with the apple and lingonberry chutney and toasted brioche.

Per portion Energy 185kcal/774kJ; Protein 9.7g; Carbohydrate 12.3g, of which sugars 12g; Fat 10.1g, of which saturates 3g; Cholesterol 69mg; Calcium 13mg; Fibre 0.9g; Sodium 279mg.

SWEETBREADS WITH PANCETTA

LAMB'S SWEETBREADS TEND TO BE MORE FREQUENTLY USED THAN OTHER TYPES OF PANCREAS, BUT THIS RECIPE USES CALF'S SWEETBREADS. THESE HAVE A MILD TASTE BUT THE ADDITION OF PANCETTA, SALTED BELLY OF PORK FROM ITALY, ADDS A DELICIOUS CONTRASTING FLAVOUR TO THE DISH.

4 Cut the sweetbreads into small pieces.

5 Melt the butter in a frying pan. Add the sweetbreads and fry for 2–3 minutes. Remove from the pan and set aside.

SERVES SIX TO EIGHT

INGREDIENTS
500g/1¼lb fresh or frozen
 calf's sweetbreads
25g/1oz/2 tbsp butter
15ml/1 tbsp plain (all-purpose) flour
200ml/7fl oz/scant 1 cup double
 (heavy) cream
30ml/2 tbsp dry Amontillado sherry
200g/7oz thinly sliced pancetta
salt and cayenne pepper
toast, to serve
chopped fresh parsley, to garnish

1 Put the calf's sweetbreads in a large bowl, cover with cold water, and leave to soak overnight.

2 The next day, drain and put the sweetbreads in a pan. Cover with cold water, add 5ml/1 tsp salt and bring to the boil. Lower the heat and simmer for 5 minutes.

3 Drain the sweetbreads and leave them to cool. When cool enough to handle, peel off any outer membrane and remove any veins.

6 Stir the flour into the pan, then slowly add the cream, stirring to form a smooth sauce. Add the sherry and bring to the boil, stirring until the sauce thickens. Reduce the heat. Simmer for 5 minutes.

7 Meanwhile, cut the pancetta into strips. Put in a frying pan and fry in its own fat until crisp. Add the sweetbreads to the sauce and season with salt and cayenne pepper. Serve the sweetbreads on toast with the pancetta and parsley on top.

Per portion Energy 309kcal/1280kJ; Protein 14.1g; Carbohydrate 2g, of which sugars 0.5g; Fat 26.8g, of which saturates 13.9g; Cholesterol 220mg; Calcium 22mg; Fibre 0.1g; Sodium 387mg.

BURNING LOVE

No one seems to know how this dish, brændende kærlighed, got its name, but it's solid evidence of the Danish passion for bacon. Easy to prepare, the hearty combination was popular as a family meal in rural Denmark. Use thick-sliced bacon for the best flavour.

SERVES FOUR TO SIX

INGREDIENTS

1.2kg/2½lb potatoes, peeled
  and cut into chunks
40g/1½oz/3 tbsp butter
300ml/½ pint/1¼ cups single
  (light) cream or milk
pinch of freshly grated nutmeg
450g/1lb streaky (fatty) bacon, diced
3 medium onions, diced
salt and ground black pepper
parsley sprigs, to garnish

1 Boil the potatoes in salted water for 15–20 minutes, until soft when pierced with a fork. Drain and mash.

2 Heat the butter and cream or milk in a pan, whisking them together. When they come to the boil immediately remove from the heat and stir the mixture gradually into the mashed potatoes, beating vigorously after each addition. Season with nutmeg, salt and pepper. Cover and keep warm.

3 Place the bacon in a large frying pan and cook over medium-low heat until crisp. Drain on paper towels, leaving the bacon fat in the pan.

4 Add the onions to the pan and cook for about 10 minutes, until soft and transparent. Remove with a slotted spoon, reserving the fat.

5 To serve, mound the mashed potatoes on to a serving platter and make a hollow in the middle. Pour the remaining bacon fat from the frying pan into the hollow.

6 Surround the potato mound with the bacon and onions. Garnish with parsley sprigs. Serve with pickled beetroot, if you like.

Per portion Energy 531kcal/2213kJ; Protein 17.8g; Carbohydrate 42.2g, of which sugars 10.3g; Fat 33.5g, of which saturates 15.9g; Cholesterol 92mg; Calcium 88mg; Fibre 3.4g; Sodium 1045mg.

WILD MEATS

Norway and Sweden are noted for the quality of their wild meat. Hunting remains a popular activity in the late autumn months, with the main animals being elk, reindeer, roe deer, red deer and fallow deer. There is less wild game available in Denmark, although venison is still very much enjoyed as part of the national culinary repertoire. Wild hare is also a favourite in Scandinavia, as well as guinea fowl, pheasant and quail.

PHEASANT STUFFED <u>WITH</u> MOUNTAIN FRUITS

THE LEAN, TENDER MEAT OF THE PHEASANT HAS ALWAYS BEEN A GREAT EUROPEAN DELICACY. THE SWEETNESS OF THE FRUIT STUFFING IN THIS RECIPE, FARSERT ORRFUGLSTEK I GRYTE, BASED ON AN IDEA BY THE NORWEGIAN CHEF, ARNE BRIMI, BALANCES THE BIRD'S GAMEY FLAVOUR.

SERVES SIX TO EIGHT

INGREDIENTS
- 1.8–2.25kg/4–5lb pheasant or black grouse, plucked and drawn
- 15ml/1 tbsp unsalted butter
- 75ml/2½fl oz/⅓ cup medium white wine
- 1 rosemary sprig
- 100ml/3½fl oz/scant ½ cup sour cream or crème fraîche
- salt and ground black pepper

For the stuffing
- 115g/4oz/½ cup pitted prunes
- 2 apples
- juice of 1 lemon
- 115g/4oz/1 cup fresh blueberries or dried cranberries
- 5ml/1 tsp chopped fresh rosemary
- salt and ground black pepper

To serve
- boiled new potatoes
- a green vegetable or salad

1 Cut the prunes into small pieces and put in a bowl. Peel, core and finely dice the apples and add to the prunes. Pour over the lemon juice. Add the berries and rosemary, season and mix together.

2 Fill the bird with the stuffing and truss with string.

3 Melt the butter in a flameproof casserole and fry the bird until browned all over.

4 Stand the bird on a small rack in the casserole. Add the wine to cover the rack, and add the rosemary.

5 Cover the casserole and simmer gently for about 1 hour. Insert the point of a sharp knife into the thigh near the body – if the juices are clear, the bird is cooked. Remove the bird and rack from the casserole, put on a warmed serving dish and keep warm.

6 Discard the rosemary sprig and add the sour cream or crème fraîche to the pan juices. Heat the juices, stirring well, until the sauce has reduced to a good pouring consistency.

7 Carve the bird, arrange on a dish and garnish with the stuffing and a little sauce. Accompany with the remaining sauce, boiled potatoes and a green vegetable or salad.

Per portion Energy 213kcal/893kJ; Protein 21.3g; Carbohydrate 8.6g, of which sugars 8.6g; Fat 10g, of which saturates 4.5g; Cholesterol 12mg; Calcium 58mg; Fibre 1.7g; Sodium 85mg.

QUAIL <u>IN</u> CREAM SAUCE

THIS IS A GOOD WAY OF COOKING SMALL BIRDS, SUCH AS QUAIL, PTARMIGAN, PIGEON AND POUSSIN. THE SLOW COOKING IN CREAM, BUTTER AND THE JUICES FROM THE BIRDS GIVES THEM A WONDERFUL FLAVOUR, MAKES THE FLESH TENDER AND PRODUCES A VELVETY SAUCE. THIS DISH IS FROM NORWAY.

SERVES FOUR

INGREDIENTS
    about 225g/8oz/1 cup butter
    1 large bunch fresh parsley
    6–8 quail, 2 ptarmigan, 4 pigeons
      or 2–4 poussins, depending on size
    2–8 sugar lumps
    300ml/½ pint/1¼ cups double
      (heavy) cream
    salt and ground black pepper
To serve
    boiled new potatoes
    green beans

1 Melt about 50g/2oz/4 tbsp of the butter in a flameproof casserole dish. When the butter stops frothing, add the parsley and cook until soft. Remove from the heat.

2 Season the inside of each bird, then stuff each one using the parsley, 15g/ ½oz/1 tbsp butter and a lump of sugar.

3 Return the casserole dish to the heat, add the remaining butter and heat until melted. Add the birds and fry until browned on all sides. Season the birds.

4 Add a little cream to the casserole dish, then cover, leaving a small gap for steam to escape, and simmer very gently, adding a little more cream from time to time, until the flesh almost falls off the bone. The cooking time will depend on the birds' size. The quail will take 30–40 minutes, the ptarmigan or pigeons will take about 1½ hours and the poussins will take about 1 hour 15 minutes.

5 Remove the cooked birds from the casserole dish and transfer to a warmed serving dish.

6 Lightly whip the remaining cream and add to the cooking juices. Heat gently and serve with the birds. Accompany with boiled new potatoes and green beans.

Per portion Energy 1033kcal/4264kJ; Protein 30.8g; Carbohydrate 1.6g, of which sugars 1.6g; Fat 100.4g, of which saturates 54.4g; Cholesterol 223mg; Calcium 64mg; Fibre 0g; Sodium 468mg.

STUFFED GUINEA FOWL <u>WITH</u> WILD MUSHROOMS

Guinea fowl meat is white like chicken but tastes more like pheasant, although with a less gamey flavour. In this Swedish dish, pärlhöna med blandad svamp, the meat is combined with the earthy taste of wild mushrooms and served with pearl barley risotto.

SERVES EIGHT

INGREDIENTS
   40g/1½oz/3 tbsp butter
   250g/9oz mixed wild
    mushrooms, chopped
   30ml/2 tbsp chopped fresh parsley
   5ml/1 tsp soy sauce
   8 guinea fowl breast portions, skinned
   about 750ml/1¼ pints/3 cups
    chicken stock for poaching
   15ml/1 tbsp plain (all-purpose) flour
   salt and ground black pepper
For the pearl barley risotto
   200g/7oz pearl barley (see Cook's Tips)
   15ml/1 tbsp olive oil
   100g/4oz mixed wild mushrooms
   2 garlic cloves, crushed
   100g/4oz fresh parsley, chopped
For the roasted vegetables
   200g/7oz parsnips and carrots,
    or seasonal vegetables
   120ml/4fl oz/½ cup olive oil

1 Cook the pearl barley in a pan of lightly salted water for 1–2 hours until tender.

2 Melt 25g/1oz/2 tbsp of the butter in a pan, add the 250g/9oz mushrooms and sauté until the juices have evaporated. Add the parsley and soy sauce and leave to cool.

3 Put the guinea fowl portions between two sheets of clear film (plastic wrap) and bash until flattened with a wooden rolling pin.

4 Spread the cold mushroom stuffing on to the guinea fowl portions, then roll them up carefully. Wrap each portion individually in clear film.

5 Preheat the oven to 180°C/350°F/ Gas 4. Cut the vegetables into strips or cubes and put in an oiled roasting pan. Drizzle with the olive oil, sprinkle with salt and roast in the oven for approximately 20 minutes until tender.

6 Thirty minutes before the barley is cooked, put the wrapped breasts in a pan in a single layer and pour over the stock. Bring to the boil and simmer gently for 30 minutes.

7 Ten minutes before the barley is cooked, prepare the pearl barley risotto. Heat the oil in a pan, add the mushrooms and sauté gently.

8 Remove the cooked breasts from the stock and keep warm. Pour the stock into a jug (pitcher) and make up to 600ml/1 pint/2½ cups if required.

COOK'S TIPS
• There are two ways to prepare pearl barley: either soak it in cold water for at least 4 hours before cooking for an hour; or cook it straight from the packet for approximately 2 hours.
• Pearl barley risotto can also be eaten as a dish on its own, sprinkled with grated Parmesan cheese and drizzled with truffle oil.

9 Melt the remaining butter, add the flour, and cook, stirring over a low heat for 1 minute to make a roux. Remove from the heat and add the reserved stock to form a gravy. Return to the heat and stir for 2–3 minutes until the gravy thickens. Season to taste.

10 Drain the pearl barley and add to the mushrooms with the garlic and parsley. Stir together.

11 Unwrap the breasts, slice carefully and place on warmed serving plates. Serve with the gravy, roasted vegetables and pearl barley risotto.

Per portion Energy 348kcal/1462kJ; Protein 27.7g; Carbohydrate 26g, of which sugars 2.4g; Fat 15.6g, of which saturates 3.6g; Cholesterol 77mg; Calcium 49mg; Fibre 1.8g; Sodium 226mg.

ROAST HARE WITH LINGONBERRIES

FRESH HARE IS AVAILABLE IN NORWAY THROUGHOUT THE SHOOTING SEASON, WHICH RUNS FROM AUGUST UNTIL THE END OF FEBRUARY. A YOUNG HARE IS THE BEST CHOICE AS IT IS THE MOST TENDER. ALL HARES HAVE A DELICIOUS GAMEY TASTE BUT AS THEY GET OLDER, THE FLESH BECOMES TOUGHER. ALTHOUGH A YOUNG HARE DOES NOT NEED TO BE MARINATED, DOING THIS DOES ADD MORE FLAVOUR.

SERVES FOUR TO SIX

INGREDIENTS

   1 hare (jack rabbit), skinned and
     jointed into serving pieces
   40g/1½oz/3 tbsp butter
   45–60ml/3–4 tbsp Dijon mustard
   30–45ml/2–3 tbsp lingonberries
     or crushed cranberries
   475ml/16fl oz/2 cups chicken stock
   salt and ground black pepper
For the marinade
   750ml/1¼ pints/3 cups red wine
     or 350ml/12fl oz/1½ cups red
     wine vinegar
   90ml/6 tbsp olive oil
   1 small onion, sliced
   15ml/1 tbsp black peppercorns
   1 bay leaf
   1 thyme sprig
For the sauce
   5ml/1 tsp potato flour
   15ml/1 tbsp water
   45ml/3 tbsp double (heavy) cream
   30ml/2 tbsp port (optional)
   15ml/1 tbsp lingonberries or
     crushed cranberries
   salt and ground black pepper

1 To make the marinade, put the red wine or vinegar, olive oil, onion, peppercorns, bay leaf and thyme in a large bowl.

2 Remove the whitish-blue membrane and any fine skin on the hare.

3 Add the joints to the marinade and leave to marinate at room temperature for 2–3 hours.

4 Remove the joints from the marinade and drain on kitchen paper.

5 Preheat the oven to 180°C/350°F/Gas 4. Melt the butter. Season the joints with salt and pepper and brush with the mustard.

6 Put only the leg joints of the marinated hare into a roasting pan and baste them with a little of the melted butter. Add the lingonberries or crushed cranberries to the roasting pan.

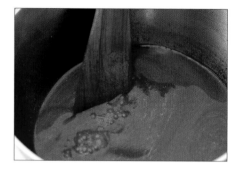

7 Roast the joints in the oven for 10 minutes, then add the back pieces to the pan, baste with more melted butter and continue roasting for about 1 hour until the meat is tender. Continue basting with the melted butter every 10 minutes throughout the cooking time and when all the butter has been used, baste the hare with the chicken stock instead.

8 When the hare is cooked, transfer the pieces to a warmed serving dish and keep warm.

9 Strain the juices from the roasting pan into a pan and bring to the boil.

10 In a small bowl, blend the potato flour with the water to form a smooth paste then add a little of the hot meat juices.

11 Stir into the pan with the rest of the meat juices and heat over a medium heat (do not boil), stirring all the time until thickened.

12 Taste the sauce to check the seasoning, adding salt and pepper only if necessary. Add the double cream, port (if using) and the lingonberries or crushed cranberries, and serve the sauce with the hare.

Per portion Energy 274kcal/1140kJ; Protein 22.6g; Carbohydrate 2g, of which sugars 1.1g; Fat 19.6g, of which saturates 6.5g; Cholesterol 25mg; Calcium 28mg; Fibre 0.2g; Sodium 293mg.

CARPACCIO <u>OF</u> CURED VENISON

TUNT SKIVAD GRAVAD HJORT IS A MODERN SWEDISH CURED-MEAT DISH. IT IS A GOOD ALTERNATIVE TO GRAVLAX AND IS PREPARED IN A SIMILAR WAY, THE ONLY DIFFERENCE BEING THAT FRESH THYME FLAVOURS THE MEAT INSTEAD OF DILL. YOU CAN USE ELK, REINDEER OR ANY OTHER VENISON INSTEAD.

3 Wrap the fillet in the foil and leave in the refrigerator to cure for 48 hours, turning every 12 hours.

4 Transfer the fillet to the freezer and store it in the freezer for up to 1 week before serving.

5 Thinly slice the meat while it is still frozen, when it is much easier to slice.

6 Thaw the fillet for a minimum of 10 hours in the refrigerator.

7 Just before serving, place the sliced meat on individual serving plates and drizzle with a little olive oil and lemon juice.

8 Serve with a crisp green salad and Melba toast.

SERVES SIX TO EIGHT

INGREDIENTS
   1kg/2¼lb venison fillet
   50g/2oz/½ cup coarse salt
   50g/2oz/¼ cup caster
     (superfine) sugar
   1 bunch fresh thyme, leaves stripped
   5ml/1 tsp ground black pepper
   olive oil and lemon juice, for drizzling
   crisp green salad and Melba toast,
     to serve

1 Remove all stringy parts from the venison then place on a sheet of foil.

2 Mix the salt and sugar together and sprinkle the mixture over the fillet. Add the thyme leaves and season with pepper.

Per portion Energy 153kcal/651kJ; Protein 27.8g; Carbohydrate 6.5g, of which sugars 6.5g; Fat 2.8g, of which saturates 1g; Cholesterol 63mg; Calcium 10mg; Fibre 0g; Sodium 69mg.

REINDEER TERRINE <u>WITH</u> JUNIPER BERRIES

This simple stewing venison recipe from Norway makes a hearty terrine. It is rich and tasty, and is ideal for a picnic or a cold table. Preparation starts a day before cooking and it is best eaten two to three days after making it to allow the flavours to mature.

SERVES SIX TO EIGHT

INGREDIENTS

500g/1¼lb reindeer or stewing venison, finely chopped
500g/1¼lb fat belly of pork, minced (ground)
10ml/2 tsp chopped fresh thyme
10ml/2 tsp chopped fresh rosemary
6 juniper berries, well crushed
a little freshly grated nutmeg
50ml/2fl oz/¼ cup aquavit or brandy
1 garlic clove
10ml/2 tsp coarse salt
1 bay leaf
6–8 rashers (slices) unsmoked streaky (fatty) bacon, rind removed
200ml/7fl oz/scant 1 cup double (heavy) cream
ground black pepper

1 Put the meat, herbs, juniper berries, nutmeg, pepper and aquavit or brandy in a bowl. Mix together well.

2 Crush the garlic with the salt and add to the mixture. Cover and leave to chill in the refrigerator.

3 The next day, preheat the oven to 150°C/300°F/Gas 2. Put the bay leaf in the bottom of a 1kg/2¼lb loaf tin (pan).

4 With a knife back, stretch the streaky bacon and line the tin.

5 Add the cream to the meat mixture and mix in well. Turn the mixture into the tin and flip the ends of the bacon over the mixture.

6 Place the tin in a roasting pan and fill with hot water to come halfway up the sides of the tin.

7 Bake the terrine in the preheated oven for about 1½ hours or until the terrine starts to come away from the sides of the tin.

8 Remove the tin from the oven and put on a heatproof tray, dish or pan with sides. Place a board on top and weight it down so the juices overflow. Leave the terrine to cool.

9 Remove the cooled terrine from the tin, wrap in foil and chill in the refrigerator before serving.

Per portion Energy 492kcal/2039kJ; Protein 26.8g; Carbohydrate 0.4g, of which sugars 0.4g; Fat 41.4g, of which saturates 18.6g; Cholesterol 123mg; Calcium 22mg; Fibre 0g; Sodium 322mg.

BRAISED VENISON WITH ROASTED ROOT VEGETABLES

Braising is a slightly gentler way of cooking compared to roasting and is ideal if you are unsure of the age of your game. Boning the leg makes it easier for carving and the meat will serve more people than if left on the bone. This recipe is from Norway.

SERVES SIX TO EIGHT

INGREDIENTS
  2.5–3kg/5½–6½lb leg of
    venison, boned
  7.5ml/1½ tsp unsalted butter
  15ml/1 tbsp vegetable oil
  1 carrot, halved lengthways
  1 onion, halved
  120ml/4fl oz/½ cup beef or
    venison stock
  4–5 black peppercorns
  salt
For the stuffing
  10g/¼oz dried wild mushrooms
  40g/1½oz/3 tbsp unsalted butter
  5 shallots, chopped
  150g/5oz/2 cups mushrooms, sliced
  10ml/2 tsp juniper berries, crushed
  5ml/1 tsp chopped fresh marjoram
  salt and ground black pepper
For the sauce
  475ml/16fl oz/2 cups beef or
    venison stock
  90ml/3½fl oz/scant ½ cup
    medium white wine
  300ml/½ pint/1¼ cups
    whipping cream
  10ml/2 tsp arrowroot (optional)
For the roasted root vegetables
  5 onions, quartered
  5 carrots, cut into 5cm/2in pieces
  3 parsnips, cut into 5cm/2in pieces
  1 medium-sized celeriac, cut into
    5cm/2in pieces
  1 turnip or small swede (rutabaga),
    cut into 5cm/2in pieces
  45ml/3 tbsp olive oil
  salt and ground black pepper

1 To make the stuffing, put the dried mushrooms in a bowl and pour over boiling water to cover. Leave to soak for about 15–20 minutes, then drain and chop finely.

2 Preheat the oven to 180°C/350°F/Gas 4. Melt the butter for the stuffing in a pan, add the shallots and sauté for 3 minutes.

3 Add the fresh mushrooms and the soaked and chopped mushrooms to the pan and stir over a high heat for 5–7 minutes until browned.

4 Add the juniper berries and chopped marjoram. Season generously with salt and pepper.

5 Put the stuffing inside the leg of venison and either sew or tie with string into a neat parcel.

6 Heat the butter and the oil in a flameproof casserole, add the meat and fry until browned on all sides.

7 Add the halved carrot and onion, the beef or venison stock, peppercorns and salt to season.

8 Cover the casserole with a lid and cook in the oven for about 1½ hours until the meat is tender. If you are using a meat thermometer, the internal temperature of the meat should read 65°C/150°F.

9 For the roasted root vegetables, put the prepared vegetables in a shallow ovenproof dish, drizzle over the olive oil, season with salt and pepper and toss together to coat evenly in the oil. Roast in the oven, tossing occasionally, for about 1 hour until all the vegetables are tender.

10 When tender, remove the venison from the casserole and put on a warmed serving dish. Skim off any fat from the cooking juices, then strain the juices into a pan to make the sauce.

11 Add the stock and wine, bring to the boil and cook until reduced slightly. Add the cream and reduce further until the sauce is a good pouring consistency.

12 If you like, to thicken the sauce, blend the arrowroot with a little cold water to form a smooth paste then add a little of the hot sauce. Stir into the pan and bring to the boil until thickened. Serve the venison with the sauce and root vegetables.

Per portion Energy 459kcal/1919kJ; Protein 44.8g; Carbohydrate 15.2g, of which sugars 10.7g; Fat 25.1g, of which saturates 14.2g; Cholesterol 146mg; Calcium 98mg; Fibre 4.4g; Sodium 195mg.

VENISON TENDERLOINS WITH CHERRY SAUCE

SERVED MAINLY IN AUTUMN OR WINTER DURING THE HUNTING SEASON, VENISON'S RICH, EARTHY FLAVOUR HAS LED TO A REVIVAL IN ITS POPULARITY. CREAMED PARSNIPS GO WELL WITH THIS DANISH DISH TOGETHER WITH BRAISED LEEKS AND ROAST POTATOES.

SERVES FOUR TO SIX

INGREDIENTS
  2–2.5kg/4½–5½lb venison tenderloin
  25g/1oz/2 tbsp butter, softened
  250ml/8fl oz/1 cup water
  salt and ground black pepper
For the cherry sauce
  250ml/8fl oz/1 cup cherry juice
  120ml/4fl oz/½ cup water
  25ml/1½ tbsp cornflour (cornstarch)
  425g/15oz canned or frozen
    unsweetened stoned (pitted) cherries
  90g/3½oz/½ cup sugar, or to taste
  salt

1 Preheat the oven to 230°C/450°F/ Gas 8. Tie the venison at 2.5cm/1in intervals with fine string to hold its shape while roasting.

2 Sprinkle with salt and pepper, and spread with butter. Place on a rack in a shallow roasting pan, and pour in the water. Cook in the hot oven for 20 minutes to brown the surface.

3 Lower the heat to 180°C/350°F/Gas 4. Continue to cook the tenderloin, basting at intervals with the pan juices, for a further 1¼ hours, until barely pink in the centre (65°C/150°F on a meat thermometer).

4 Leave the meat in a warm place to rest for 10 minutes before slicing.

5 Meanwhile, to make the sauce, bring the cherry juice to the boil in a pan over a medium-high heat.

6 Whisk together the water and cornflour in a small bowl, and stir into the cherry juice.

7 Cook, stirring constantly, until the mixture thickens. Stir in the sugar.

8 Stir in the cherries and bring the sauce back to the boil. Serve with the venison.

Per portion Energy 518kcal/2197kJ; Protein 74.6g; Carbohydrate 37.5g, of which sugars 33.7g; Fat 10.8g, of which saturates 4.8g; Cholesterol 176mg; Calcium 45mg; Fibre 0.4g; Sodium 220mg.

VENISON CHOPS WITH ALMOND POTATOES

ALMOND POTATOES ARE YELLOW, WAXY POTATOES, WHICH ARE AVAILABLE IN SWEDEN IN THE AUTUMN, WHICH MEANS THEY COINCIDE WITH THE SHOOTING SEASON. THEY ARE DELICIOUS WITH WILD MUSHROOMS, GATHERED AT THE SAME TIME OF YEAR.

SERVES EIGHT

INGREDIENTS
  1.6kg/3½lb almond or pink fir apple
    new potatoes, unpeeled
  75g/3oz/6 tbsp butter
  8 venison chops
  250g/9oz chanterelle mushrooms,
    roughly chopped
  salt and ground black pepper

1 Boil the potatoes in salted water for about 20 minutes until tender.

2 Meanwhile, melt 25g/1oz/2 tbsp of the butter in a large frying pan. Add the chops and fry over a low heat for about 8 minutes on each side. Do not overcook the chops as they should still be slightly pink in the middle.

3 Season the chops well, then transfer them to a warmed serving dish. Cover with foil and keep warm.

COOK'S TIP
This dish is also delicious served with lingonberries or lingonberry conserve, which is available from Swedish food shops.

4 In a separate large frying pan, melt 25g/1oz/2 tbsp of the butter, add the mushrooms and fry for about 5 minutes until golden.

5 Season the mushrooms well with salt and pepper to taste.

6 When the potatoes are cooked, drain them, then mash them well with their skins on. Add the remaining 25g/1oz/ 2 tbsp butter and season the potatoes with salt and pepper to taste. Serve the chops with the mashed potatoes and mushrooms.

Per portion Energy 368kcal/1553kJ; Protein 37.3g; Carbohydrate 32.3g, of which sugars 2.7g; Fat 11.7g, of which saturates 6.5g; Cholesterol 97mg; Calcium 23mg; Fibre 2.4g; Sodium 176mg.

REINDEER STROGANOFF

The fillet used in this Swedish dish is the best cut of reindeer. The bitter gin flavour of the juniper berries is a strong complement to the wild meat. Beef is an excellent substitute meat or, for a more authentic taste, you could use roe deer which is similar to reindeer in both texture and taste. The dish is called red stroganoff in Swedish.

2 Add the chopped onions and crushed juniper berries to the pan.

3 Stir the flour into the pan then, over a low heat, add the tomato purée, mustard and finally the cream and stir together. Simmer for about half an hour until the meat is tender.

4 Garnish the dish with chopped parsley and serve with boiled rice or pearl barley.

COOK'S TIP
Garnishing the reindeer stroganoff with chopped parsley gives the dish more colour and freshness.

SERVES SIX TO EIGHT

INGREDIENTS
  1kg/2¼lb reindeer, roe deer
    or beef fillet
  15g/½oz/1 tbsp butter
  15ml/1 tbsp vegetable oil
  2 Spanish (Bermuda) onions,
    chopped
  8 juniper berries, crushed
  15ml/1 tbsp plain (all-purpose) flour
  45ml/3 tbsp tomato purée (paste)
  45ml/3 tbsp Dijon mustard
  475ml/16fl oz/2 cups double
    (heavy) cream
  chopped fresh parsley, to garnish
  boiled rice or pearl barley, to serve

1 Cut the meat into 5mm/¼in x 5cm/2in strips. Heat the butter and oil in a large frying pan, add the strips of meat and fry them for about 5 minutes until golden brown on all sides.

Per portion Energy 486kcal/2019kJ; Protein 30.2g; Carbohydrate 7.8g, of which sugars 5.1g; Fat 38.2g, of which saturates 22g; Cholesterol 148mg; Calcium 57mg; Fibre 0.9g; Sodium 274mg.

ROE DEER CUTLETS WITH MUSHROOMS

WILD ROE DEER, A SPECIES OF EUROPE AND ASIA MINOR, IS VERY POPULAR IN SWEDEN AND ITS FLESH HAS THE LOWEST FAT CONTENT OF ANY RED MEAT. ROE DEER IS A GOOD SUBSTITUTE FOR REINDEER AND IS VERY TENDER. BLACKBERRIES, REDCURRANTS AND JUNIPER BERRIES ARE ALL CLASSIC FLAVOURS TO ADD TO ROE DEER OR OTHER VENISON DISHES — THIS RECIPE USES JUNIPER BERRIES.

SERVES SIX

INGREDIENTS
    75g/3oz/6 tbsp butter
    200g/7oz chanterelle mushrooms,
      halved if large
    200g/7oz trumpet mushrooms
      (trompette des morts)
    2kg/4½lb saddle of roe deer
      (12 cutlets), trimmed by
      the butcher
    1 litre/1¾ pints/4 cups water
    3 shallots, chopped
    5 juniper berries, crushed
    1 fresh thyme sprig, chopped
    1 bay leaf
    225g/8oz potatoes, cut into
      5mm/¼in cubes
    6 small carrots, cut into
      5mm/¼in cubes
    120ml/4fl oz/½ cup double
      (heavy) cream
    salt and ground black pepper

1 In a large frying pan, melt 25g/1oz/
2 tbsp of the butter, add all the
mushrooms and sauté until browned.

2 Meanwhile, season the roe deer
cutlets with salt and pepper. Melt 25g/
1oz/2 tbsp of the butter in a separate
large frying pan, then add the cutlets
and fry for 2–3 minutes until browned
on both sides.

3 Add the water, shallots, juniper
berries, thyme and bay leaf to the
cutlets. Bring to the boil, then simmer
for 10 minutes to reduce the liquid.

4 Meanwhile, melt half the remaining
butter in a frying pan. Add the potatoes
and fry for 20 minutes, stirring often,
until golden. Transfer to a serving dish
and keep warm. Fry the carrots in the
remaining butter until golden.

5 Add the cream to the casserole and
continue to cook for 20 minutes.

6 Finally, add the sautéed mushrooms.
Cook until heated through, then serve
hot, with the fried potatoes and carrots.

Per portion Energy 455kcal/1903kJ; Protein 40.7g; Carbohydrate 19.3g, of which sugars 6.8g; Fat 25.4g, of which saturates 14.7g; Cholesterol 137mg; Calcium 50mg; Fibre 3g; Sodium 193mg.

SADDLE OF ROE DEER WITH GLAZED CARROTS

THE SADDLE OF ROE DEER IS THE CHOICEST CUT, YIELDING TWO LENGTHS OF TENDERLOIN. THERE IS NO WASTE AND THE MEAT IS TENDER AND MELTS IN THE MOUTH. THE SADDLE OF LARGER DEER CAN BE COOKED IN THE SAME WAY BUT ALLOW LONGER FOR THE ROASTING. THIS IS A NORWEGIAN RECIPE.

SERVES SIX

INGREDIENTS

2kg/4½lb saddle of venison,
  preferably roe deer, boned,
  with bones reserved
1 carrot, roughly chopped
1 small leek, roughly chopped
1 celery stick, roughly chopped
½ onion
1 bunch fresh parsley
75–100g/3–4oz/6–8 tbsp unsalted
  butter, softened
120ml/4fl oz/½ cup red wine
5ml/1 tsp potato flour or arrowroot
15ml/1 tbsp water
300ml/½ pint/1¼ cups whipping
  cream or sour cream
salt and ground black pepper
For the glazed carrots
  475ml/16fl oz/2 cups water
  9 carrots, each cut into 4 pieces
  75g/3oz/6 tbsp butter
  25ml/1½ tbsp sugar
  7.5ml/1½ tsp salt
  chopped fresh parsley, to garnish
To serve
  boiled potatoes
  baked onions
  a green vegetable
  rowan or redcurrant jelly

1 Put the reserved meat bones in a large pan with the carrot, leek, celery, onion and parsley, salt and pepper.

2 Add water to cover, bring to the boil, simmer for 1½–2 hours, then strain and skim off any fat. Reserve 600ml/1 pint/2½ cups of the strained stock.

3 To prepare the carrots, boil the water in a pan. Add the carrots, butter, sugar and salt, return to the boil and cook, uncovered, for 40 minutes until the water has almost evaporated. Shake the pan occasionally to coat the carrots in the glaze.

4 Preheat the oven to 200°C/400°F/Gas 6. Slip a small, sharp knife underneath the membrane on the saddle and remove it. Trim the meat of all sinews and gristle.

5 Heat 25g/1oz/2 tbsp of the butter in a frying pan, add the meat and fry until brown. Season and spread the remaining 50g/2oz/4 tbsp of butter over the meat.

6 Place the meat on a rack in a roasting pan and roast for 10–15 minutes. Press the meat to test how well cooked it is – it should be slightly underdone and should give slightly when pressed, as it will continue to cook after being removed from the oven. Transfer to a warmed serving dish, cover with foil and leave to rest for 15–20 minutes.

7 Pour the wine into a pan, bring to the boil and boil until reduced by half.

8 In a small bowl, blend the potato flour or arrowroot with the water to form a smooth paste.

9 Add the reserved stock to the roasting pan, stirring to deglaze the pan and scraping up any sediment. Strain the juices into a pan and add the reduced wine. Add a little hot liquid to the flour paste and stir into the pan. Bring to just below the boil, stirring until thickened.

10 Add the cream and reheat gently, not allowing the mixture to boil. Season if necessary.

11 Serve the meat cut into thick slices with the sauce, the carrots garnished with chopped parsley, boiled potatoes, baked onions, a green vegetable and rowan jelly.

COOK'S TIPS

• Underneath the saddle are slim little fillets. Reserve these for another occasion.
• If using potato flour, do not allow the sauce to re-boil or it may go stringy.

Per portion Energy 576kcal/2390kJ; Protein 31.4g; Carbohydrate 12.9g, of which sugars 12.4g; Fat 43.9g, of which saturates 26.8g; Cholesterol 172mg; Calcium 68mg; Fibre 2.4g; Sodium 264mg.

ROE DEER MEDALLIONS WITH REDCURRANTS

THIS NORWEGIAN DISH IS SERVED ON SPECIAL OCCASIONS. THE EQUIVALENT CUT OF BEEF WOULD BE TOURNEDOS FROM THE FILLET. WITH VENISON OR ROE DEER THE FILLET IS MUCH SMALLER, SO ASK FOR THE MEDALLIONS TO BE CUT FROM THE THICK END OF THE FILLET AND ALLOW TWO PER PERSON.

SERVES SIX

INGREDIENTS
    about 800g/1¾lb venison fillet,
      preferably roe deer, cut into
      8 medallions
    15g/½oz/1 tbsp butter
    15ml/1 tbsp vegetable oil
    salt and ground black pepper
For the sauce
    200ml/7fl oz/scant 1 cup venison
      or beef stock
    150ml/¼ pint/⅔ cup port
    100ml/3½fl oz/scant ½ cup double
      (heavy) cream
    30ml/2 tbsp redcurrants
    a knob (pat) of butter
To serve
    baked onions
    a green salad
    boiled potatoes (optional)

1 Preheat the oven to 200°C/400°F/ Gas 6. Season the venison medallions with salt and pepper.

2 Heat the butter and vegetable oil in a large frying pan, then add the medallions of venison fillet. Quickly sear them on both sides, then transfer them to a baking tray and set aside while you make the sauce.

3 Add the stock to the pan, stirring to deglaze and scraping up any sediment from the bottom of the pan. Add the port and cream, stir well together, then cook until reduced by half.

4 Season the sauce with salt and pepper to taste. Add the redcurrants and a knob of butter.

5 Roast the medallions in the oven for 4–5 minutes, according to size, until slightly underdone (see Cook's Tip).

6 Place the medallions on individual warmed serving plates or a serving dish, pour a little sauce over each and serve the remaining sauce separately. Accompany with baked onions and a green salad, and potatoes, if you like.

COOK'S TIP
The meat should be served slightly underdone, which means the medallions should give slightly when pressed.

Per portion Energy 337kcal/1407kJ; Protein 30.1g; Carbohydrate 3.8g, of which sugars 3.8g; Fat 20.3g, of which saturates 10.9g; Cholesterol 106mg; Calcium 23mg; Fibre 0.2g; Sodium 95mg.

ELK KALOPS

KALOPS IS THE SWEDISH WORD FOR MEAT PIECES OR STEW, AND THIS RECIPE USES ELK, WHICH GIVES THIS DISH ITS NAME ÄLGKALOPS. IT IS NOT NECESSARY TO USE THE THIGH CUT, BUT IT DOES REDUCE THE COOKING TIME. YOU MAY NEED TO COOK IT FOR LONGER IF USING A DIFFERENT CUT OF MEAT.

SERVES SIX TO EIGHT

INGREDIENTS

1kg/2¼lb elk (moose) thigh
15g/½oz/1 tbsp butter
15ml/1 tbsp vegetable oil
2 Spanish (Bermuda) onions,
 roughly chopped
2 carrots, roughly chopped
3 bay leaves
5ml/1 tsp ground allspice
5ml/1 tsp ground white pepper
15ml/1 tbsp plain (all-purpose) flour
250ml/8fl oz/1 cup red wine
500ml/17fl oz/2¼ cups beef stock
salt
pickled beetroot (beet), to serve

1 Cut the meat into 1cm/½in cubes. Heat the butter and oil in a large frying pan. Add the meat and fry for about 5 minutes until browned on all sides.

2 Using a slotted spoon, remove from the pan and set aside.

3 Add the onions to the pan and fry for 10 minutes, stirring often, until softened.

4 Add the carrots and fry for a further 2–3 minutes, then add the bay leaves, allspice, pepper and salt.

5 Stir in the flour, then return the meat to the pan.

6 Slowly stir in the red wine and beef stock, bring to the boil, then cover and simmer for about 2 hours until very tender.

7 Serve the elk kalops with pickled beetroot, if you like.

COOK'S TIP
Pickled beetroot (beet) is a classic Swedish accompaniment to meat. It can be bought ready prepared or made fresh, and can be stored in the refrigerator for up to three weeks.

Per portion Energy 136kcal/571kJ; Protein 14.6g; Carbohydrate 5.5g, of which sugars 3.1g; Fat 4.4g, of which saturates 1.7g; Cholesterol 35mg; Calcium 21mg; Fibre 0.9g; Sodium 52mg.

ELK MEATBALLS WITH LINGONBERRY CONSERVE

MEATBALLS ARE PROBABLY THE BEST-KNOWN SWEDISH DISH AND ARE ESPECIALLY DELICIOUS WHEN HOME-MADE. WHEN COOKING THEM YOURSELF, IT IS A GOOD IDEA TO MAKE A LARGE QUANTITY BECAUSE THEY TAKE QUITE A WHILE TO PREPARE. THIS METHOD SUGGESTS USING HALF THE MEATBALLS AND FREEZING THE REST. THIS DISH IS KNOWN AS ÄLGKÖTTBULLAR MED LINGON IN SWEDEN.

THE MEATBALLS SERVE 12 TO 14;
THE SAUCE SERVES SIX

INGREDIENTS

1 large potato, peeled
100g/4oz/½ cup butter
1kg/2¼ lb red onions, finely chopped
150g/5oz/2½ cups fresh breadcrumbs
300ml/½ pint/1¼ cups double
  (heavy) cream
105ml/7 tbsp full-fat (whole) milk
5ml/1 tsp sugar
ground white pepper
10ml/2 tsp salt
3kg/6¾ lb minced (ground) elk
  (moose) or 1kg/2¼ lb best quality
  minced (ground) pork and
  2kg/4½ lb best quality minced
  (ground) steak
6 eggs, beaten
handful of finely chopped
  fresh parsley
about 45ml/3 tbsp vegetable oil
mashed potatoes and lingonberry
  conserve, to serve
For the cream sauce
  120ml/4fl oz/½ cup
    Amontillado sherry
  250ml/8fl oz/1 cup double
    (heavy) cream
  30ml/2 tbsp soy sauce (optional)

1 Cut the potato into quarters and cook in boiling water for 15–20 minutes until tender, then drain and mash.

2 Melt 75g/3oz/6 tbsp of the butter in a frying pan, add the onions and fry until softened.

3 Put the mashed potato, onions, breadcrumbs, cream and milk in a large bowl and mix together. Leave to swell for a few minutes.

4 Add the sugar, season generously with pepper and add the salt. Add the elk or pork and steak mince, the eggs and parsley and mix thoroughly together.

5 Leave to stand for 1 hour to allow the flavours to infuse.

6 Using your hands, roll the mixture into meatballs that are about the size of a small apricot. (At this stage, if it is more convenient you can freeze half the quantity of meatballs to use on another occasion.)

7 Heat the remaining butter and the oil in a large frying pan, add the meatballs and fry in batches to avoid over-crowding the pan, for about 10 minutes until browned. (You may need to add a little more oil to the pan but this will depend on how much fat there is in the meat.)

8 Using a slotted spoon, remove the meatballs from the pan, transfer to a warmed serving dish and keep warm.

COOK'S TIP
To make good quality minced (ground) pork, buy a boneless leg of pork and for minced steak, buy topside or braising steak. Trim off the fat, then mince (grind) the meat in a food processor or mincer.

9 To make the cream sauce, add the sherry and stir to deglaze the pan.

10 Stir in the cream, add the soy sauce if using, and heat gently.

11 Pour the sauce over the meatballs and serve hot, with mashed potatoes and lingonberry conserve.

Per portion Energy 828kcal/3430kJ; Protein 39.8g; Carbohydrate 20.4g, of which sugars 6.6g; Fat 64.6g, of which saturates 32.4g; Cholesterol 276mg; Calcium 103mg; Fibre 1.6g; Sodium 333mg.

DESSERTS

Scandinavians of all ages love their desserts, and the sweet treats of Norway, Denmark and Sweden share many similarities. Fruits, particularly summer berries, are a key ingredient in many cakes, tarts, puddings and sweet soups. Almonds are a Scandinavian favourite, featuring in many recipes and starring in the ubiquitous marzipan or almond paste. The dessert menu would not be complete without waffles, pancakes and creamy rice pudding.

COLD BUTTERMILK SOUP

LIGHT AND FROTHY, WITH SUBTLE SWEETNESS AND LEMONY NOTES, THIS REFRESHING COLD SOUP IS DELIGHTFULLY SIMPLE TO PREPARE. DON'T BE PUT OFF BY THE BUTTERMILK BASE: IT GIVES NO SOUR TASTE, ONLY A CREAMY RICHNESS. KÆRNEMÆLKS KOLDSKÅL IS A SUMMER FAVOURITE FOR MANY DANES.

SERVES SIX

INGREDIENTS
  2 large (US extra large) eggs, separated
  1.5ml/¼ tsp cream of tartar
  130g/4½oz/⅔ cup caster
    (superfine) sugar
  5ml/1 tsp vanilla extract
  2.5ml/½ tsp grated lemon rind,
    plus extra to decorate
  1.5 litres/2½ pints/6¼ cups
    buttermilk
  50g/2oz/¼ cup flaked (sliced)
    almonds, toasted, to decorate

1 Beat the egg whites until frothy in a medium bowl. Add the cream of tartar. Beat until stiff peaks form. Set aside.

2 In a second bowl, beat the egg yolks with the sugar. Add the vanilla extract and lemon rind. Stir in the buttermilk and blend the mixture thoroughly.

3 Gently fold the egg whites into the buttermilk mixture, stirring to blend.

4 Serve immediately, decorated with toasted almonds and grated lemon rind.

COOK'S TIP
Toast the almonds in a dry frying pan over a low heat. Be careful not to burn them.

NOTE
Raw eggs are not recommended for very young children, pregnant women, convalescents or anyone suffering from an illness. Make sure the eggs are very fresh.

Per portion Energy 241kcal/1017kJ; Protein 12.5g; Carbohydrate 34.2g, of which sugars 34g; Fat 7.3g, of which saturates 1.2g; Cholesterol 73mg; Calcium 346mg; Fibre 0.6g; Sodium 136mg.

ROSEHIP SOUP

IN SCANDINAVIA FRUIT SOUPS ARE OFTEN EATEN AS A DESSERT — ROSEHIP SOUP, OR NYPONSOPPA, IS THE MOST POPULAR IN SWEDEN. THOSE WHO LIKE THIS SOUP CAN PICK WILD ROSEHIPS EVERY AUTUMN — IT IS HIGHLY NUTRITIOUS AND A WELCOME SWEET TREAT IN THE WINTER MONTHS.

SERVES FOUR TO SIX

INGREDIENTS
600–700g/1lb 6oz–1lb 9oz
    fresh or 400–500g/14oz–1¼lb
    dried rosehips
2 litres/3½ pints/8 cups water
15ml/1 tbsp cornflour (cornstarch)
100g/4oz/½ cup sugar
whipped double (heavy) cream
    or vanilla ice cream, to serve

1 If using fresh rosehips, cut in half then scoop out every trace of the seeds and prickly hairs. If using dried rosehips, put in a mortar and grind with a pestle.

2 Put the rosehips in a small pan, add the water, bring to the boil and simmer for about 30 minutes until they are soft.

3 Bring to the boil and boil for 15 minutes to reduce the liquid.

4 Strain the cooked rosehips through muslin (cheesecloth) and reserve the cooking liquid.

5 In a small bowl, blend the cornflour with a little of the rosehip liquid to form a smooth paste.

VARIATION
The soup is also good served with a spoonful of freshly ground blanched almonds instead of the whipped cream or ice cream.

6 Pour the reserved liquid into a pan and add the sugar. Slowly stir in the cornflour mixture and bring to the boil, stirring. Simmer for 10–15 minutes. Serve warm or cold topped with cream or ice cream.

Per portion Energy 92kcal/391kJ; Protein 0.8g; Carbohydrate 22.8g, of which sugars 20.5g; Fat 0.3g, of which saturates 0.1g; Cholesterol 0mg; Calcium 16mg; Fibre 1g; Sodium 11mg.

RED BERRY SOUP <u>WITH</u> CREAM

SOME CALL THIS RUBY-RED BERRY SOUP, RØDGRØD MED FLØDE, DENMARK'S NATIONAL DESSERT. SIMPLE TO PREPARE, IT CAN BE MADE USING A BLEND OF RED BERRIES, BUT CURRANTS AND RASPBERRIES ARE THE TRADITIONAL COMBINATION. SERVE COLD WITH A SWIRL OF CREAM IN EACH BOWL.

2 Bring the mixture to the boil and cook over a medium-high heat for 3 minutes.

3 Pour the fruit and juice through a sieve (strainer) set over a pan. Use a wooden spoon to press through as much berry juice as possible.

4 In a small bowl, mix the cornflour with the remaining blackcurrant juice. Stir the cornflour mixture into the berry juice. Place the pan over a medium heat and bring the juice to the boil, stirring, until it thickens slightly.

5 Pour the cream into a bowl and stir in the vanilla sugar. Pour the soup into individual bowls and spoon 30ml/2 tbsp cream into each bowl, swirling it slightly. Sprinkle each bowl with a few raspberries and serve.

VARIATION
Chopped, fresh rhubarb blended with berries can also be used to make this dessert. Potato flour can be substituted for cornflour, but do not boil the soup after adding it or it will become rubbery.

SERVES SIX

INGREDIENTS
  400g/14oz/3½ cups redcurrants
  450g/1lb/2⅔ cups raspberries
  100–150g/3¾–5oz/½–¾ cup
    sugar (depending on the sweetness
    of the fruit)
  550ml/18fl oz/2½ cups
    blackcurrant juice
  45ml/3 tbsp cornflour (cornstarch)
  250ml/8fl oz/1 cup double
    (heavy) cream
  10ml/2 tsp vanilla sugar
  raspberries, to decorate

1 Put the berries, sugar and 500ml/ 17fl oz/generous 2 cups of the blackcurrant juice into a pan and add 750ml/1¼ pints/3 cups water.

Per portion Energy 383kcal/1606kJ; Protein 3.1g; Carbohydrate 44g, of which sugars 37.1g; Fat 23g, of which saturates 14.1g; Cholesterol 57mg; Calcium 84mg; Fibre 3.6g; Sodium 25mg.

DANISH DRIED FRUIT SOUP

THROUGHOUT SCANDINAVIA, SOUPS MADE WITH DRIED FRUIT USED TO BE ESPECIALLY WELCOME DURING THE LONG, DARK WINTER MONTHS. ANY COMBINATION OF DRIED FRUIT CAN BE USED IN VARM FRUGTSUPPE; PEARS AND PEACHES ARE A MODERN ADDITION, BUT FAITHFUL TO THE SOUP'S HERITAGE.

SERVES SIX TO EIGHT

INGREDIENTS
- 50g/2oz/¼ cup currants
- 50g/2oz/¼ cup sultanas (golden raisins)
- 115g/4oz/½ cup dried apricots
- 115g/4oz/½ cup prunes
- 115g/4oz/½ cup dried apples
- 115g/4oz/½ cup dried peaches
- 115g/4oz/½ cup dried pears
- 15ml/1 tbsp grated lemon rind
- 7.5cm/3in cinnamon stick
- 5 whole cloves
- 40g/1½oz/¼ cup quick-cook tapioca
- 250ml/8fl oz/1 cup double (heavy) cream

3 Remove the pan from the heat. Remove the cinnamon stick and discard. Let the fruit mixture cool slightly.

4 Beat the double cream until soft peaks form. Serve the warm fruit soup with a dollop of cream in each bowl.

1 Chop all the dried fruit and place in a large pan together with 1 litre/ 1¾ pints/4 cups water. Cover with a lid, and leave to stand for at least 2 hours or overnight.

2 Stir the lemon rind, cinnamon stick, cloves and tapioca into the dried fruit mixture. Bring to the boil, cover and simmer gently for about 1 hour, stirring occasionally.

Per portion Energy 305kcal/1277kJ; Protein 2.7g; Carbohydrate 37.4g, of which sugars 31.5g; Fat 17.1g, of which saturates 10.4g; Cholesterol 43mg; Calcium 51mg; Fibre 4g; Sodium 17mg.

GLÖGG JELLY WITH CLOVE CREAM

As the story goes, this delicious sweet was the result of a happy accident — some Glögg wine left over after a party and the inspired idea to make jelly with it. It is a classic Swedish dish, which is simple to make and perfect as a Christmassy dessert.

SERVES SIX TO EIGHT

INGREDIENTS
   5 gelatine leaves
   750ml/1¼ pints/3 cups Swedish
      Glögg or mulled wine
   15ml/1 tbsp sugar
For the spiced cream
   200ml/7fl oz/scant 1 cup double
      (heavy) cream
   5ml/1 tsp icing
      (confectioners') sugar
   pinch of ground cloves

1 Soak the gelatine leaves in cold water until soft.

2 Pour the Glögg wine into a pan and heat gently.

3 Stir the sugar into the wine until dissolved, then add the softened gelatine leaves, which should melt.

4 Pour the mixture into individual heatproof serving glasses, leave to cool, then place in the refrigerator for about an hour to set.

5 Whisk the cream until stiff, then add the icing sugar. Just before serving, add a spoonful of the cream, topped with ground cloves, to each glass of jelly.

COOK'S TIP
Swedish Glögg is a mulled wine that is usually enjoyed at Christmas. It is served hot and has a robust alcohol content.

Per portion Energy 197kcal/815kJ; Protein 0.5g; Carbohydrate 3.1g, of which sugars 3.1g; Fat 13.5g, of which saturates 8.4g; Cholesterol 34.3mg; Calcium 20mg; Fibre 0g; Sodium 12.3mg.

LEMON MOUSSE

LIGHT AND AIRY, THIS HEAVENLY DESSERT IS EASY TO MAKE AS WELL AS BEING REFRESHING.
ITS DANISH NAME, CITRONFROMAGE, ALLUDES TO THE INFLUENCE OF FRENCH CULINARY TRADITIONS
IN DENMARK IN THE 1800S. IT LOOKS ATTRACTIVE WITH GRATED LEMON RIND SCATTERED ON TOP.

SERVES SIX TO EIGHT

INGREDIENTS
50ml/2fl oz/¼ cup apple juice
  or water
30ml/2 tbsp powdered gelatine
30ml/2 tbsp grated lemon rind
90ml/6 tbsp fresh lemon juice
4 eggs, separated
175g/6oz/1½ cup icing
  (confectioners') sugar
250ml/8fl oz/1 cup double
  (heavy) cream

1 Pour the apple juice or water into a bowl, then add the gelatine until softened.

2 Add 120ml/4fl oz/½ cup boiling water to the bowl and stir to dissolve the gelatine, then stir in half the lemon rind and all the juice.

3 Combine the egg yolks with 150g/5oz/1¼ cups of the icing sugar in a bowl, and beat until frothy.

4 Fold the gelatine mixture into the egg yolks. Refrigerate for at least 1 hour.

5 Beat the egg whites until stiff and fold them into the egg yolk mixture.

6 Beat the cream until stiff peaks form, and stir in the remaining icing sugar. Fold half the cream into the egg and lemon mixture.

7 Spoon the mousse into a deep, 2-litre/3½-pint/8¾-cup glass bowl or 6 individual bowls. Chill until set. Serve decorated with the remaining whipped cream and lemon rind.

VARIATION
Crumble macaroons into the bottom of dessert glasses and spoon over the mousse.

NOTE
Raw eggs are not recommended for very young children, pregnant women, convalescents or anyone with an illness.

Per portion Energy 278kcal/1159kJ; Protein 3.7g; Carbohydrate 23.4g, of which sugars 23.4g; Fat 19.6g, of which saturates 11.2g; Cholesterol 138mg; Calcium 41mg; Fibre 0g; Sodium 43mg.

OLD-FASHIONED APPLE CAKE

IN DANISH THIS CAKE IS SOMETIMES CALLED BONDEPIGE MED SLØR, MEANING 'PEASANT GIRL IN A VEIL'. IT IS SERVED ON ST MARTIN'S DAY, 11 NOVEMBER. USE A GLASS BOWL TO SHOW THE DIFFERENT LAYERS, AND ASSEMBLE ABOUT AN HOUR BEFORE SERVING SO THE BREADCRUMBS STAY CRISP.

2 Melt the butter in a frying pan. Stir in the breadcrumbs and brown sugar, tossing to coat the crumbs evenly with the butter. Cook, stirring, for about 4 minutes until the crumbs are lightly browned and toasted. Remove from the heat and set aside.

3 Beat the double cream until soft peaks form and stir in the icing and vanilla sugars.

4 Place a thin layer of breadcrumbs in the bottom of six serving glasses or bowls, cover the breadcrumbs with a layer of apple, then a layer of cream. Repeat the layers, ending with cream.

5 Chill, then decorate with the chopped nuts or grated chocolate before serving.

SERVES SIX

INGREDIENTS

   1kg/2¼lb tart eating apples,
      peeled and cored
   90g/3½oz/½ cup sugar, or to taste
   5ml/1 tsp cinnamon
   1.5ml/¼ tsp freshly grated nutmeg
   1.5ml/¼ tsp ground cloves (optional)
   25g/1oz/2 tbsp butter
   175g/6oz/3 cups fresh breadcrumbs
   25g/1oz/2 tbsp soft light brown sugar
   250ml/8fl oz/1 cup double
      (heavy) cream
   10ml/2 tsp icing (confectioners') sugar
   5ml/1 tsp vanilla sugar
   chopped nuts or grated chocolate,
      to decorate

1 Cut the apples into chunks. Place in a heavy pan with 250ml/8fl oz/1 cup water, the sugar, cinnamon, nutmeg and cloves (if using). Cover and cook over a low heat, stirring occasionally, for 25 minutes, until soft but still chunky. Remove from the heat and leave to cool.

Per portion Energy 498kcal/2090kJ; Protein 4.7g; Carbohydrate 64.3g, of which sugars 42.5g; Fat 26.5g, of which saturates 16.1g; Cholesterol 66mg; Calcium 79mg; Fibre 3.3g; Sodium 261mg.

NATIONAL DAY DESSERT

THIS FROTHY PINK PUDDING, GRUNDLOVSDESSERT, CELEBRATES DENMARK'S NATIONAL DAY, COMMEMORATING THE CHANGE FROM A CONSTITUTIONAL MONARCHY TO A PARLIAMENTARY DEMOCRACY WHEN FREDERICK IX SIGNED THE NEW CONSTITUTION ON 5 JUNE 1953.

SERVES SIX

INGREDIENTS

    675g/1½lb rhubarb
    115g/4oz/½ cup caster
     (superfine) sugar
    30ml/2 tbsp lemon juice
    250ml/8fl oz/1 cup milk
    1 vanilla pod (bean)
    30ml/2 tbsp powdered gelatine
    4 eggs, separated
    1 drop red food colouring
    250ml/8fl oz/1 cup double
     (heavy) cream
    flaked (sliced) almonds, to decorate

1 Cut the rhubarb into 2.5cm/1in pieces and place in a pan. Add half the sugar, the lemon juice and 250ml/8fl oz/1 cup water. Bring to the boil, then reduce the heat and simmer gently for 15 minutes until the rhubarb is soft.

2 Pour the milk into a pan. Slit open the vanilla pod and scrape the seeds into the milk; add the vanilla pod. Bring the milk to the boil, reduce the heat and simmer for 2 minutes.

3 Remove from the heat to cool and discard the vanilla pod.

4 First soften the gelatine in 30ml/ 2 tbsp cold water, then pour on 120ml/4fl oz/½ cup boiling water and stir until the gelatine has dissolved.

VARIATION
Crumble almond macaroons in the bottom of the bowls before adding the rhubarb.

5 Combine the egg yolks with the remaining sugar in a mixing bowl and beat until light and thick.

6 Stir the gelatine mixture into the egg yolks with the vanilla-flavoured milk and leave to thicken.

7 Beat the egg whites into stiff peaks and fold gently into the thickened egg yolk and milk mixture.

8 Add a drop of red food colouring and blend until the pudding is coloured pale pink.

9 Beat the double cream until stiff.

10 Fold half the cream into the egg mixture. Divide the rhubarb among six bowls and spoon over the pudding. Top with a spoonful of the remaining whipped cream and sprinkle with almonds. Chill until ready to serve.

Per portion Energy 375kcal/1566kJ; Protein 11.6g; Carbohydrate 23.6g, of which sugars 23.6g; Fat 26.9g, of which saturates 15.4g; Cholesterol 186mg; Calcium 204mg; Fibre 1.6g; Sodium 78mg.

CARAMEL PUDDING

EVERY COUNTRYSIDE HOME IN NORWAY USED TO HAVE AT LEAST ONE COW IN THE GROUNDS AND MILK REMAINS A STAPLE OF THE COUNTRY'S DIET. THIS SIMPLE BUT DELICIOUS PUDDING IS A GREAT NORWEGIAN FAVOURITE. IT'S A WARM, STICKY, COMFORTING PUDDING FOR COLD WINTER EVENINGS.

SERVES FOUR

INGREDIENTS

115g/4oz/½ cup plus
  30ml/2 tbsp sugar
30ml/2 tbsp hot water
3 large (US extra large) eggs
3 large (US extra large) egg yolks
600ml/1 pint/2½ cups full-fat
  (whole) milk, or a mixture of milk
  and single (light) cream
1 vanilla pod (bean), split lengthways
chopped blanched almonds,
  to decorate

COOK'S TIP

The creamy texture of the custard depends on slow cooking. Filling the roasting pan with cold water coming three-quarters of the way up the sides of the caramel dish helps to filter the heat.

1 Preheat the oven to 160°C/325°F/ Gas 3. For the caramel, put the 115g/4oz/½ cup sugar in a pan over a medium heat until golden. Add the hot water carefully. Stir together.

2 Pour the caramel into a round, ovenproof dish and swirl the caramel around to coat the bottom and a little way up the sides. It will set instantly.

3 Mix the eggs and egg yolks and the remaining sugar in a bowl (don't whisk).

4 Using the caramel pan, heat the milk with the split vanilla pod to just below boiling.

5 Remove the vanilla pod from the milk and whisk the milk into the egg and sugar.

6 Strain through a sieve (strainer), then pour into the caramel dish.

7 Place in a roasting pan and fill with cold water to come about three-quarters of the way up the sides.

8 Bake the custard for 45 minutes to 1 hour, until set. Leave until cool, then chill for 2–3 hours.

9 Having run a knife around the edge, place a serving dish over the top of the custard and invert the caramel on to the dish.

10 Decorate the top of the pudding with chopped almonds.

Per portion Energy 296kcal/1248kJ; Protein 13.1g; Carbohydrate 37.1g, of which sugars 37.1g; Fat 11.8g, of which saturates 4.2g; Cholesterol 337mg; Calcium 239mg; Fibre 0g; Sodium 136mg.

BLUEBERRY ICE CREAM PARFAIT

AUTUMN IN NORWAY IS THE SEASON FOR HUNTING WILD BERRIES. WILD BILBERRIES ARE RELATED TO THE LARGER, CULTIVATED BLUEBERRY, AND YOU CAN USE THEM IN THIS RECIPE, KNOWN AS BLÅBÆRIS, FOR EXTRA FLAVOUR. YOU COULD USE ALMOST ANY SOFT BERRY, SUCH AS RASPBERRIES OR BLACKBERRIES.

SERVES FOUR

INGREDIENTS

   2 large (US extra large) eggs, separated
   115g/4oz/1 cup icing
    (confectioners') sugar
   200g/7oz/1¾ cup blueberries
   300ml/½ pint/1¼ cups double
    (heavy) cream
   30ml/2 tbsp aquavit (optional)

1 Put the egg yolks and half the sugar in a bowl and whisk together until pale and thick.

2 Beat in about three-quarters of the blueberries and reserve the remainder for decorating. Blend in the berries so that they burst and spread their colour.

3 Whisk the egg whites until they form soft peaks. Whisk in the remaining sugar.

VARIATION
This basic recipe can be used with any number of different flavourings, such as the grated rind of 1 orange, 30ml/2 tbsp chopped stem ginger or 30ml/2 tbsp raisins and 30ml/2 tbsp rum.

4 Fold the egg whites and sugar mixture into the blueberry mixture.

5 Whisk the cream with the aquavit, if using, until it just holds its shape, and fold into the blueberry mixture.

6 Transfer to a mould or freezer container and freeze for 6–8 hours until firm.

7 Unless the berries were very juicy, it should be possible to serve the ice cream parfait straight from the freezer. However, if the berries produced a lot of juice, it is better to put the parfait in the refrigerator for about 20 minutes to allow it to soften slightly before being served.

8 To serve, dip the mould briefly in hot water before turning out on to a serving platter. Decorate with the reserved blueberries.

Per portion Energy 536kcal/2228kJ; Protein 4.9g; Carbohydrate 34.6g, of which sugars 34.6g; Fat 43.1g, of which saturates 25.8g; Cholesterol 198mg; Calcium 96mg; Fibre 1.8g; Sodium 55mg.

WILD BERRY TART

THE SWEDISH FORESTS ABOUND IN WILD BERRIES, SUCH AS LINGONBERRIES, CLOUDBERRIES, BILBERRIES AND STRAWBERRIES. THE COOL CLIMATE AND EVENING SUNSHINE CREATE THEIR MAGICAL TASTE, WHICH IMPROVES THE FURTHER NORTH YOU GO. WHEN COOKING, SWEDES FAVOUR SMALL, IRREGULAR BERRIES WHOSE FLAVOUR THEY REGARD AS SUPERIOR TO THOSE WITH PERFECT, UNIFORM SHAPES.

2 Stir in the sugar, add the egg to the mixture and combine to form a dough. Wrap the dough in baking parchment and place in the refrigerator to chill for 1 hour.

3 Preheat the oven to 180°C/350°F/ Gas 4. On a lightly floured surface, roll out the pastry thinly and use to line a 20cm/8in flan tin (pan).

4 Put a circle of baking parchment in the base of the pastry case (pie shell) and fill with baking beans. Bake in the oven for 10–15 minutes until the pastry has set.

5 Remove the paper and beans and return to the oven for 5 minutes until the base is dry.

6 Fill the tart with the berries and sugar. Then return the tart to the oven and bake for a further 5–10 minutes until the pastry is golden brown.

7 Serve the berry tart warm with whipped double cream.

SERVES SIX TO EIGHT

INGREDIENTS
   500g/1¼lb fresh or frozen mixed
      wild berries
   200g/7oz/1 cup caster
      (superfine) sugar
   whipped double (heavy) cream,
      to serve
For the pastry
   300g/10oz/2½ cups plain
      (all-purpose) flour
   115g/4oz/½ cup unsalted butter
   50g/2oz/¼ cup caster
      (superfine) sugar
   1 egg, beaten

1 To make the pastry, put the flour in a food processor. Cut the butter into small pieces, add to the flour and then, using a pulsating action, mix together until the mixture resembles fine breadcrumbs.

VARIATION
Instead of cooking the fruit in the tart, you can bake the pastry case (pie shell) for 10 minutes more, until golden, leave it to cool, then brush the base with melted plain (semisweet) chocolate. Leave to set, then fill with fresh berries mixed with sugar, and serve. The chocolate will stop the berries from softening the pastry before the tart is served.

Per portion Energy 618kcal/2601kJ; Protein 8g; Carbohydrate 98.1g, of which sugars 43.3g; Fat 24.2g, of which saturates 14.9g; Cholesterol 60mg; Calcium 141mg; Fibre 3.8g; Sodium 177mg.

SWEDISH APPLE CAKE WITH VANILLA CREAM

SWEDISH APPLES ARE VERY SWEET AND IDEALLY SUITED TO THIS SUBLIME CAKE, ÄPPELKAKA MED VANILJKRÄM. APPLES FORM A SIGNIFICANT PART OF SWEDEN'S PRODUCE, SURVIVING THE COLD WINTERS WELL. KIVIK, A HARBOUR TOWN IN SKÅNE IN SOUTHERN SWEDEN, IS WELL KNOWN FOR ITS APPLE MARKET AND HOLDS AN ANNUAL FESTIVAL WHERE A HUGE PICTURE IS CREATED, MADE ENTIRELY OF APPLES.

SERVES SIX TO EIGHT

INGREDIENTS
115g/4½oz/½ cup plus 15g/½oz/
 1 tbsp unsalted butter
7 eating apples, peeled and cored
30ml/2 tbsp caster (superfine) sugar
10ml/2 tsp ground cinnamon
200g/7oz/1 cup sugar
2 egg yolks and 3 egg whites
100g/4oz/1 cup ground almonds
grated rind and juice of ½ lemon
For the vanilla cream
 250ml/8fl oz/1 cup milk
 250ml/8fl oz/1 cup double
  (heavy) cream
 15ml/1 tbsp sugar
 1 vanilla pod (bean), split
 4 egg yolks, beaten

1 Preheat the oven to 180°C/350°F/ Gas 4. Butter a 20cm/8in flan tin (pan) using 15g/½oz/1 tbsp of the butter.

2 Thinly slice the apples. In a bowl, mix them with the caster sugar and cinnamon.

3 Put the mixture in the prepared tin.

4 Put the remaining butter and sugar in a bowl and whisk them together until they are light and fluffy.

5 Beat in the egg yolks, then add the almonds and lemon rind and juice to the mixture.

6 Whisk the egg whites until stiff, then fold into the mixture.

7 Pour the mixture over the apples in the flan tin. Bake in the oven for about 40 minutes until golden brown and the apples are tender.

SERVING VARIATIONS
• Serve the apple cake with 300ml/ ½ pint/1¼ cups double (heavy) cream to which you have added 5ml/1 tsp vanilla sugar.
• Alternatively, serve with vanilla ice cream, which is particularly good if the cake is served warm.

8 Meanwhile, make the vanilla cream. Put the milk, cream, sugar and vanilla pod in a pan and heat gently. Add a little of the warm milk mixture to the egg yolks, then slowly add the egg mixture to the pan and continue to heat gently, stirring constantly, until it thickens. Do not allow the mixture to boil or it will curdle.

9 Remove the vanilla pod and serve the vanilla cream warm or cold with the apple cake.

Per portion Energy 541kcal/2254kJ; Protein 7.6g; Carbohydrate 39.7g, of which sugars 39.3g; Fat 40.3g, of which saturates 20g; Cholesterol 227mg; Calcium 122mg; Fibre 2.1g; Sodium 135mg.

CREAM LAYER CAKE

BLØTKAKE IS THE NORWEGIAN CELEBRATION CAKE, SUITABLE FOR ANY SPECIAL OCCASION BUT ESPECIALLY GOOD ON 17 MAY, THE NORWEGIAN NATIONAL DAY, WHEN THE CONSTITUTION WAS ADOPTED. THE POSSIBILITIES FOR THE PRESENTATION OF THE BASIC CAKE ARE NUMEROUS AND COOKS PRIDE THEMSELVES ON THEIR ELABORATE ARRANGEMENTS OF FRUIT AND WHIPPED CREAM.

SERVES SIX TO EIGHT

INGREDIENTS
    115g/4oz/1 cup plain (all-purpose)
       flour, to include 15ml/1 tbsp
       potato flour (optional)
    5ml/1 tsp baking powder
    4 large (US extra large) eggs
    90g/3½oz/½ cup caster
       (superfine) sugar
For the filling
    2 x 400g/14oz cans sliced peaches
       in natural juice
    raspberry jam
    1 quantity Vanilla Cream
       (see page 206)
    300ml/½ pint/1¼ cups double
       (heavy) cream
    5ml/1 tsp sugar
    3 varieties fresh soft fruit, such
       as raspberries, strawberries,
       bilberries or blueberries, or
       canned peaches

1 Preheat the oven to160°C/325°F/ Gas 3. Line a 23cm/9in round cake tin (pan) with baking parchment.

2 Sift the flour, potato flour, if using, and baking powder together.

3 Put the eggs and sugar in a bowl and whisk until pale and the mixture will form ribbons on the surface if lifted and allowed to fall back into the bowl.

4 Fold in the sifted flour until well combined. Turn the mixture into the prepared tin.

5 Bake the cake in the oven for about 40 minutes until firm to the touch and beginning to come away from the sides of the tin.

6 Leave in the tin for 5 minutes, then carefully turn out on to a wire rack to cool.

7 Carefully cut the cooled cake horizontally into three equally-sized rounds. Place the top round, upside down, on to a serving plate. Sprinkle with peach juice from the can.

8 Spread with raspberry jam, then add a layer of peaches and a layer of vanilla cream.

9 Put the middle cake round on top and repeat the layers, adding a final layer of peaches and vanilla cream.

10 Finally, add the bottom round of cake, upside down to give a perfectly flat top layer, and sprinkle with peach juice but do not use the jam, peaches and vanilla cream.

11 Whisk the cream and the sugar together until the cream just holds its shape.

12 Use the cream to cover the top of the cake, reserving a little, if you wish, to pipe on top.

13 Arrange the fresh soft fruit decoratively on top. Pipe the reserved cream, if you wish, around and between the different groups of berries. Alternatively, if fresh soft fruits are not available, decorate the cake with more canned peaches.

COOK'S TIPS
• Traditionally, Norwegians like to add sugar to their cream before whipping it.
• Avoid moving the cake rounds after they have been sprinkled with the peach juice as they could fall apart. Instead, have them in place on the serving dish before sprinkling with the juice.

Per portion Energy 363kcal/1513kJ; Protein 5.7g; Carbohydrate 35.2g, of which sugars 24.3g; Fat 23.1g, of which saturates 13.3g; Cholesterol 147mg; Calcium 64mg; Fibre 1.3g; Sodium 57mg.

KVAEFJORD CAKE WITH VANILLA CREAM

THIS IS A SUPERB EXAMPLE OF THE NORWEGIANS' LOVE OF ELABORATE GÂTEAUX AND SHOWS THEIR SKILL IN DEVISING DELICIOUS VARIATIONS. WHILE YOU CAN BUY PACKETS OF VANILLA CREAM, THE CLASSIC RECIPE HERE PRODUCES A MORE DELICIOUS RESULT. THE CAKE PROVIDES A PERFECT END TO A MEAL, OR CAN JUST BE SERVED WITH COFFEE.

SERVES SIX TO EIGHT

INGREDIENTS
- 115g/4oz/1 cup plain (all-purpose) flour
- 5ml/1 tsp baking powder
- 300g/11oz/1½ cups caster (superfine) sugar
- 90g/3½oz/scant ½ cup unsalted butter
- 4 eggs, separated
- 45–60ml/3–4 tbsp full-fat (whole) milk
- 60ml/4 tbsp roughly chopped almonds

For the vanilla cream
- 50g/2oz/¼ cup vanilla sugar or 50g/2oz/¼ cup caster (superfine) sugar and 5ml/1 tsp vanilla extract
- 25g/1oz/2 tbsp plain (all-purpose) flour
- 7.5ml/1½ tsp cornflour (cornstarch)
- 1 large (US extra large) egg, beaten
- 300ml/½ pint/1¼ cups full-fat (whole) milk
- 25g/1oz/2 tbsp butter
- 300ml/½ pint/1¼ cups whipping cream

1 For the cream, put the vanilla sugar or sugar and vanilla extract, plain flour, cornflour and beaten egg in a small bowl and blend together.

2 Heat the milk in a pan to just below boiling point, then gradually stir it into the flour mixture.

3 Rinse out the pan, then return the mixture to the cleaned pan and heat gently, stirring constantly, until the mixture comes to the boil. Immediately remove the pan from the heat and stir in the butter.

4 Transfer the mixture to a large bowl and cover with clear film (plastic wrap) to prevent skin from forming. Set aside to cool.

5 Whisk the cream until it holds its shape and fold into the custard.

6 Preheat the oven to 180°C/350°F/ Gas 4. Line the base of two 19cm/ 7½in sandwich tins (layer cake pans) with baking parchment. Sift the flour and baking powder together in a bowl.

7 Put 100g/4oz/½ cup of the sugar and the butter in a separate bowl and whisk together until pale and fluffy. Add the egg yolks, one at a time, beating well after each addition. Add the sifted flour, a little at a time, alternately with the milk.

8 Spread the mixture into the tins.

9 Whisk the egg whites in a separate bowl until they stand in soft peaks.

10 Whisk in the remaining 200g/7oz/ 1 cup sugar, a little at a time, until the mixture stands in glossy peaks.

11 Spread over the cake mixture in each tin. Sprinkle with chopped almonds.

12 Bake the cakes in the oven for 20–30 minutes until the cakes are slightly risen, the meringue slightly crisp and the almonds toasted. Leave to cool in the tins.

13 When the cakes are cold, remove from the tins and place one cake on a serving plate. Cover with the vanilla cream, then place the second cake on top and serve.

COOK'S TIP
The cake can be baked in a Swiss roll tin (jelly roll pan) instead of two sandwich tins, then cut in half before being sandwiched together with the vanilla cream.

Per portion Energy 605kcal/2526kJ; Protein 8.9g; Carbohydrate 63.8g, of which sugars 49.4g; Fat 36.7g, of which saturates 19.8g; Cholesterol 173mg; Calcium 156mg; Fibre 1.1g; Sodium 162mg.

WAFFLES WITH SPICED BLUEBERRY COMPOTE

THIS SWEDISH RECIPE, VÅFFLOR MED BLÅBÄRSKOMPOTT, REQUIRES A WAFFLE IRON. IF YOU PURCHASE ONE IT IS UNLIKELY THAT YOU WILL REGRET IT, AS WAFFLES ARE DELICIOUS WITH OTHER TOPPINGS. THE BLUEBERRY COMPOTE CAN ALSO BE SERVED WITH PANCAKES OR RICE PUDDING.

MAKES 20

INGREDIENTS
  25g/1oz/1 tbsp unsalted butter,
  plus extra for greasing
  350g/12oz/3 cups plain
  (all-purpose) flour
  350ml/12fl oz/1½ cups water
  475ml/16fl oz/2 cups double
  (heavy) cream, plus exta to serve
For the spiced blueberry compote
  200g/7oz/1¾ cups blueberries
  15ml/1 tbsp sugar
  5ml/1 tsp balsamic vinegar
  pinch of ground cinnamon
  pinch of ground cloves

1 To make the spiced blueberry compote, put the blueberries into a pan, then add the sugar, vinegar, cinnamon and cloves and poach for about 5 minutes until soft and liquid.

2 Bring to the boil and cook for a further 4 minutes to reduce the liquid. Either keep the compote warm, or cool and store in the refrigerator for up to 1 month.

3 To make the waffles, melt the butter. Put the flour in a large bowl and gradually beat in the water to form a smooth mixture. Add the melted butter.

4 In a separate bowl, whisk the cream until stiff, then fold into the mixture.

5 Preheat a waffle iron according to the manufacturer's instructions. Add a little butter to grease the waffle iron, then pour a little waffle mixture in the iron.

6 Cook the waffles until golden and crispy, keep warm and continue to cook the remaining waffle mixture, greasing the iron each time with a little butter. Serve hot with the blueberry compote and some extra whipped cream.

VARIATION
Instead of the blueberry compote, serve the waffles with lingonberry conserve.

Per waffle Energy 189kcal/787kJ; Protein 2.12g; Carbohydrate 14.52g, of which sugars 1.18g; Fat 14.03g, of which saturates 8.62g; Cholesterol 35mg; Calcium 41mg; Fibre 0,85g; Sodium 14mg.

NORWEGIAN PANCAKES

PANNEKAKER, NORWEGIAN PANCAKES, ARE CLOSELY RELATED TO FRENCH CRÊPES. THEY ARE SERVED WITH SUGAR AND CINNAMON FOR BREAKFAST, OR FOR DESSERT FILLED WITH LINGONBERRIES OR STRAWBERRIES AND CREAM, OR A SPOONFUL OF BLUEBERRY JELLY AND SOUR CREAM.

SERVES 12

INGREDIENTS
   25g/1oz/2 tbsp butter
   3 eggs
   115g/4oz/1 cup plain
    (all-purpose) flour
   350ml/12fl oz/1½ cups milk
   pinch of salt
   pinch of ground cinnamon
   vegetable oil, for shallow frying
   butter, jam or sugar and cinnamon,
    or fresh berries, such as
    raspberries, sour cream or whipped
    cream and icing (confectioners')
    sugar, to serve

1 Melt the butter. Put the eggs in a bowl and beat lightly together, then sift in the flour.

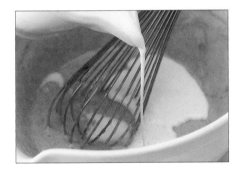

2 Add the milk, melted butter, salt and cinnamon to the egg and flour mixture and mix together to form a smooth, thin batter. Alternatively, this can be done in a food processor.

3 Leave to rest for 30 minutes to an hour until the flour has absorbed some of the liquid.

4 Heat a frying pan measuring about 18cm/7in. Add a little oil and when hot, add enough batter to swirl around the base of the pan in a thin layer.

COOK'S TIP
When turning a pancake over, don't try to flip it in the pan too soon. The secret is to make sure it is cooked before turning.

5 Cook the pancake until golden brown, then slip a metal spatula underneath and turn over or toss. Cook briefly on the other side until a spotted brown colour, then remove from the pan and repeat the process with the remaining batter.

6 To serve the pancakes, spread a line of butter across the centre of the pancake, add jam or sugar and cinnamon. Alternatively, add fresh berries and sour cream or whipped cream, roll up or fold over the pancake and dust with icing sugar.

Per portion Energy 105kcal/438kJ; Protein 3.5g; Carbohydrate 8.8g, of which sugars 1.5g; Fat 6.5g, of which saturates 2.1g; Cholesterol 54mg; Calcium 56mg; Fibre 0.3g; Sodium 43mg.

CLOUDBERRY SOUFFLÉ

THIS SWEDISH DISH, HJORTRONSUFFLÉ, IS UNDENIABLY SCANDINAVIAN. CLOUDBERRIES ARE RARE LITTLE GOLDEN RASPBERRY-LIKE BERRIES WITH AN EXQUISITE TASTE THAT ONLY GROW WILD IN NORTHERN SCANDINAVIA. THE JAM CAN BE FOUND IN SPECIALIST STORES.

4 Remove the sauce from the heat, leave to cool slightly, then stir in the egg yolks. Add the cloudberry jam and liqueur and turn into a large bowl.

5 In a large, separate bowl, whisk the egg whites until stiff then, using a metal spoon, fold them into the sauce.

6 Put the mixture into the prepared soufflé dish and bake in the oven for 20 minutes until risen. Serve immediately.

VARIATIONS
• The cloudberry jam could be replaced with another fruit jam.
• Replace the cloudberry liqueur with brandy or another fruit liqueur, if you like.

SERVES SIX TO EIGHT

INGREDIENTS
    50g/2oz/4 tbsp unsalted butter,
      plus extra for greasing
    60ml/4 tbsp plain (all-purpose) flour
    475ml/16fl oz/2 cups milk
    4 egg yolks and 6 egg whites
    275g/10oz/1 cup cloudberry jam
    30ml/2 tbsp Lakka (Finnish
      cloudberry liqueur)

1 Preheat the oven to 180°C/350°F/ Gas 4. Grease an 18cm/7in soufflé dish with butter.

2 Melt the butter in a pan, add the flour and cook over a low heat for 30 seconds, stirring to make a roux.

3 Slowly add the milk, stirring constantly, to form a smooth sauce. Cook until the sauce boils and thickens.

Per portion Energy 284kcal/1198kJ; Protein 6.7g; Carbohydrate 44.9g, of which sugars 37.4g; Fat 9g, of which saturates 4.7g; Cholesterol 118mg; Calcium 102mg; Fibre 0.2g; Sodium 129mg.

R I C E P U D D I N G <u>WITH</u> W A R M C H E R R Y S A U C E

At Christmas time in Denmark this warming winter pudding comes with a traditional surprise: whoever finds a whole almond in their serving wins a special prize! The prize is usually a plump little marzipan pig.

<u>SERVES SIX TO EIGHT</u>

INGREDIENTS
  1.5 litres/2½ pints/6¼ cups milk
  1 vanilla pod (bean)
  225g/8oz/1 cup short grain rice
  25g/1oz/2 tbsp caster
    (superfine) sugar
  25g/1oz/2 tbsp vanilla sugar
  50g/2oz/½ cup chopped
    blanched almonds
  1 whole almond
  250ml/8fl oz/1 cup double
    (heavy) cream
For the cherry sauce
  450g/1lb fresh or bottled dark
    cherries, stoned (pitted),
    cut into quarters
  90g/3½oz/½ cup sugar
  5ml/1 tsp lemon juice
  2 whole cloves
  30ml/2 tbsp cornflour (cornstarch)

1 Pour the milk into the top of a double boiler. Slit open the vanilla pod and scrape the seeds into the milk; add the pod. Bring the milk to the boil.

2 Add the rice to the boiling milk, lower the heat, cover, and cook for 2 hours, stirring occasionally, until almost all the milk is absorbed. Remove the lid for the last 10 minutes.

3 Remove the rice mixture from the heat and leave to cool slightly.

4 While it is still warm, stir in the caster sugar, vanilla sugar, chopped almonds and whole almond.

5 Transfer the pudding to the refrigerator until chilled.

6 Whip the cream until stiff and gently fold it into the cold rice pudding. Turn into a serving dish and chill until ready to serve.

7 To make the warm cherry sauce, put the cherries in a pan with 475ml/16fl oz/2 cups water, the sugar, lemon juice and cloves. Bring to the boil and cook gently, stirring, for about 20 minutes.

8 Transfer a small amount of the cherry juice to a small bowl. Add the cornflour to the juice and blend to a smooth paste.

9 Stir the cornflour mixture into the cherries and cook for 10 minutes more, until thickened.

10 Remove the sauce from the heat and allow to cool slightly. Serve drizzled over the rice pudding.

Per portion Energy 503kcal/2107kJ; Protein 10.7g; Carbohydrate 64.4g, of which sugars 38.3g; Fat 23.6g, of which saturates 12.7g; Cholesterol 54mg; Calcium 279mg; Fibre 0.8g; Sodium 96mg.

HONEY AND GINGER BAKED APPLES

NORWAY IS THE MOST NORTHERN COUNTRY TO GROW APPLES AND MOST ARE CULTIVATED IN THE HARDANGER VALLEY IN THE SOUTH. THERE ARE MANY NORWEGIAN VARIATIONS ON BAKED APPLES. THIS RECIPE IS BASED ON A FAMOUS DISH BY ANDREAS VIESTAD, THE NORWEGIAN CHEF.

SERVES FOUR

INGREDIENTS
  4 eating apples, such as Cox's
    Orange Pippin or Golden Delicious
  30ml/2 tbsp finely chopped fresh
    root ginger
  60ml/4 tbsp honey
  25g/1oz/2 tbsp unsalted butter
  60ml/4 tbsp medium white wine
  vanilla sauce, sour cream or double
    (heavy) cream, to serve
For the vanilla sauce
  300ml/½ pint/1¼ cups single
    (light) cream
  1 vanilla pod (bean), split lengthways
  2 egg yolks
  30ml/2 tbsp caster (superfine) sugar

1 To make the vanilla sauce, put the cream and vanilla pod in a pan and heat gently to just below boiling point.

2 Remove from the heat and leave to infuse for 10 minutes. Remove the vanilla pod.

3 Put the egg yolks and sugar in a bowl and whisk them together until pale and thick, then slowly pour in the cream in a steady stream, whisking all the time. Return the mixture to the pan and heat very gently until the cream is thick enough to coat the back of a wooden spoon. (If you draw a finger horizontally across the back of the spoon, the sauce should be thick enough not to run down through the channel.) Remove from the heat and leave to cool. Stir from time to time or cover to prevent a skin forming.

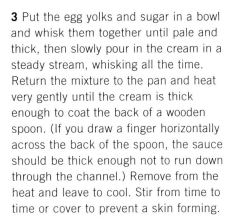

4 Preheat the oven to 160°C/325°F/Gas 3. Remove the cores from the apples leaving the stalk end intact, but removing the stalk. Fill each cavity with 7.5ml/½ tbsp chopped ginger and 15ml/1 tbsp honey.

5 Place the apples in an ovenproof dish, with the open end uppermost, and top each one with a piece of butter. Pour in the wine and bake in the oven, basting frequently with the cooking juices, for 45 minutes, until the apples are tender.

6 Serve the apples with the vanilla sauce, sour cream or double cream.

Per portion Energy 331kcal/1381kJ; Protein 4.3g; Carbohydrate 27.8g, of which sugars 27.8g; Fat 22.3g, of which saturates 13.2g; Cholesterol 155mg; Calcium 89mg; Fibre 1.2g; Sodium 68mg.

ALMOND PEARS

THIS OLD-FASHIONED SWEDISH BAKED DESSERT, MANDELPÄRON, IS A TEMPTING COMBINATION OF COOKED JUICY FRUIT AND A SPRINKLING OF GROUND ALMONDS. THE CREAM MELTS WITH THE JUICES AND GROUND ALMONDS TO FORM A DELICIOUS RICH SAUCE.

SERVES EIGHT

INGREDIENTS
8 large ripe pears
juice of 1 lemon
25g/1oz/2 tbsp unsalted butter
350g/12oz/2 cups ground almonds
475ml/16fl oz/2 cups double
  (heavy) cream

1 Preheat the oven to 180°C/350°F/Gas 4. Peel and halve the pears and remove the cores.

2 Put the pears into an ovenproof dish and sprinkle with lemon juice to stop them going brown.

3 Put a small piece of butter on top of each pear half.

4 Sprinkle the ground almonds evenly over the top. Bake in the oven for about 15 minutes, basting once or twice with the juice, until they begin to soften.

5 Meanwhile, whisk the cream until it is beginning to hold its shape. When the pears are cooked, pour over the whipped cream and serve immediately.

Per portion Energy 607kcal/2511kJ; Protein 10.5g; Carbohydrate 15.3g, of which sugars 14.1g; Fat 56.4g, of which saturates 21.8g; Cholesterol 81mg; Calcium 147mg; Fibre 5.7g; Sodium 23mg.

BAKING

Throughout Scandinavia baking and bakeries form an integral part of life. Stockholm has more bakeries than any other type of food store, and the sign of a golden pretzel has identified a pastry shop or bakery in Denmark since medieval times. In Norway, as in Sweden and Denmark, a cake, bun or biscuit is always accompanied by a cup of coffee. A large variety of savoury breads exist too, from Danish dark rye bread to the thin Norwegian potato bread, cooked in a pan, known as lefse.

TOSCA CAKE

ALMONDS ARE VERY POPULAR THROUGHOUT SCANDINAVIA AND THIS CAKE USES THEM IN A WONDERFUL, IRRESISTIBLE TOPPING. THE CAKE IS A GUARANTEED SUCCESS ON ANY COFFEE OR TEA TABLE. THE FOLLOWING RECIPE IS NORWEGIAN. FOR A LIGHTER EFFECT, USE HALF THE AMOUNT OF TOPPING.

SERVES TEN

INGREDIENTS
 50g/2oz/4 tbsp unsalted butter,
  plus extra for greasing
 115g/4oz/1 cup plain
  (all-purpose) flour
 7.5ml/1½ tsp baking powder
 pinch of salt
 2 large (US extra large) eggs
 150g/5oz/¾ cup caster
  (superfine) sugar
For the topping
 115g/4oz/½ cup butter, softened
 150g/5oz/1¼ cups blanched
  almonds, toasted and
  roughly chopped
 115g/4oz/generous ½ cup
  caster (superfine) sugar
 30ml/2 tbsp plain (all-purpose) flour
 30ml/2 tbsp single (light) cream
  or milk

1 Preheat the oven to 160°C/325°F/Gas 3. Butter and line the base and sides of a 20cm/8in round cake tin (pan) with baking parchment. Melt the butter and leave to cool. Sift together the flour, baking powder and salt.

2 In a large bowl, whisk the eggs until thick and pale, then gradually whisk in the sugar until the mixture falls in a thick ribbon.

3 Fold in the flour mixture and the cooled butter.

4 Pour the mixture into the prepared tin and tap lightly on a work surface to settle the mixture. Bake the cake in the oven for 30 minutes, or until just before the cake is cooked, when it is almost firm to the touch but needs another few minutes not to sink if removed from the heat.

5 Leave the cake in the oven and prepare the topping. Place the butter, almonds, sugar, flour and cream or milk in a pan and heat gently, stirring, until the butter has melted, then continue heating the mixture until it just reaches boiling point.

6 Preheat the grill (broiler) to medium-hot. Remove the cake carefully from the oven and spread the topping over the top, making sure that all the cake is covered. Place under the grill until the topping is golden brown, watching that the sides of the cake don't burn.

7 Stand the tin on a rack and leave to cool before carefully removing the cake from the tin.

Per portion Energy 389kcal/1626kJ; Protein 6.1g; Carbohydrate 40.2g, of which sugars 28.7g; Fat 23g, of which saturates 10g; Cholesterol 75mg; Calcium 82mg; Fibre 1.5g; Sodium 119mg.

CARDAMOM CAKE

FOR SCANDINAVIANS, CARDAMOM IS A FAVOURITE SPICE, AND ITS WARM FLAVOUR IS USED IN A VARIETY OF CAKES, BUNS AND OTHER DISHES. THIS CAKE IS A TRADITIONAL TEA OR COFFEE TIME TREAT IN NORWAY, AND IS DELICIOUS WITHOUT BEING ELABORATE OR TOO RICH.

SERVES SIX

INGREDIENTS

250g/9oz/1 cup and 2 tbsp butter, softened, plus extra for greasing
375g/13oz/3¼ cups plain (all-purpose) flour
45ml/3 tbsp baking powder
10 cardamom pods, seeds removed and finely crushed
250g/9oz//1¼ cups caster (superfine) sugar
3 large (US extra large) eggs, lightly beaten
150ml/¼ pint/⅔ cup milk
45ml/3 tbsp raisins
45ml/3 tbsp candied peel
15ml/1 tbsp flaked (sliced) almonds

1 Preheat the oven to 190°C/375°F/Gas 5. Butter a 1kg/2lb loaf tin (pan) and line the bottom with baking parchment.

2 Sift together the flour, baking powder and cardamom.

3 In a large bowl, cream together the butter and caster sugar until light and fluffy.

4 Beat in the eggs, a little at a time, then fold in the sifted flour.

5 Add the milk, a little at a time, folding in well after each addition.

6 Add the raisins, candied peel and almonds and fold in. Turn into the tin and bake in the oven for 50 minutes, until risen and firm to the touch. Turn out and cool on a wire rack.

Per portion Energy 786kcal/3295kJ; Protein 11g; Carbohydrate 103.2g, of which sugars 55.5g; Fat 39.6g, of which saturates 23.8g; Cholesterol 192mg; Calcium 179mg; Fibre 2.6g; Sodium 392mg.

PLUM CAKE

Seasonal cooking is an obvious necessity in countries of the far north with fierce extremes of climate. Traditionally, you ate what you could grow and stored food carefully to survive until the next harvest. Fruit trees were especially prized and apple, pear and plum trees still thrive in many areas of Scandinavia. These fruits are used in many ways in Danish cooking, as in this recipe, which is called blommerkage in Denmark.

SERVES TEN

INGREDIENTS
450g/1lb stoned (pitted) fresh plums, coarsely chopped, plus 9 extra plums, stoned and halved, to decorate
300ml/½ pint/1¼ cups water
115g/4oz/½ cup unsalted butter, softened
200g/7oz/1 cup caster (superfine) sugar
3 eggs
90g/3½ oz/¾ cup toasted, finely chopped almonds
5ml/1 tsp bicarbonate of soda (baking soda)
7.5ml/1½ tsp baking powder
5ml/1 tsp ground cardamom
1.5ml/¼ tsp salt
250g/9oz/2¼ cups plain (all-purpose) flour
15ml/1 tbsp pearl sugar, to decorate
250ml/8fl oz/1 cup double (heavy) cream
10ml/2 tsp vanilla sugar
10ml/2 tsp icing (confectioners') sugar

1 Place the chopped plums in a pan and add the water. Bring to the boil over a medium heat and cook for 10–15 minutes, until the plums are soft. Set aside to cool. You will need 350ml/12fl oz/1½ cups stewed plums for the cake.

2 Preheat the oven to 180°C/350°F/ Gas 4. Grease and flour a 24cm/9½in springform cake tin (pan).

3 Cream the butter with the caster sugar in a large mixing bowl until light and fluffy, then beat in the eggs, one at a time.

4 Stir in the stewed plums and the finely chopped almonds.

COOK'S TIP
Scandinavian pearl sugar, large crystals that have a pearly sheen, is used to decorate pastries, buns and cakes in Denmark. If you can't find it, you can use coarsely crushed white sugar cubes as an alternative.

5 Add the baking soda, baking powder, cardamom and salt and stir until blended. Gradually stir in the flour, a few spoonfuls at a time, and mix until well blended.

6 Pour the mixture into the prepared tin. Place plum halves around the circumference of the cake and place the remaining halves in the centre, cut sides down. Sprinkle the pearl sugar over the cake.

7 Bake for 1 hour, or until the top springs back when lightly touched. Cool in the tin for 15 minutes before unfastening the ring.

8 Beat the double cream until soft peaks form. Stir in the vanilla sugar and the icing sugar and beat the cream until thick.

9 Serve the cake either while it is still slightly warm or at room temperature, in slices topped with a dollop of whipped cream.

Per portion Energy 311kcal/1308kJ; Protein 6.4g; Carbohydrate 44.5g, of which sugars 15.9g; Fat 13.2g, of which saturates 7.4g; Cholesterol 89mg; Calcium 86mg; Fibre 2.4g; Sodium 102mg.

PRINCESS CAKE

A Scandinavian cookbook would not be complete without a recipe for that self-indulgent Swedish classic, the Princess Cake, or princesstårta as it is called in Sweden. With its distinctive light-green marzipan coating, it swells with whipped cream, sponge cake and jam. Traditionally, a pink rose crowns the top, but here fresh strawberries are used.

SERVES EIGHT TO TEN

INGREDIENTS
  200g/7oz/scant 1 cup unsalted
    butter, plus extra for greasing
  400g/14oz/2 cups caster
    (superfine) sugar
  3 eggs
  350g/12oz/3 cups plain
    (all-purpose) flour
  5ml/1 tsp baking powder
  10ml/2 tsp vanilla sugar
  a few drops of green food colouring
  250g/9oz good quality marzipan
    or almond paste (see below)
  icing (confectioners') sugar, to dust
  fresh strawberries, to serve
For the filling and topping
  3 gelatine leaves
  1 litre/1¾ pints/4 cups double
    (heavy) cream
  10ml/2 tsp sugar
  10ml/2 tsp cornflour (cornstarch)
  2 egg yolks
  10ml/2 tsp vanilla sugar
For the almond paste (optional)
  200g/7oz/1½ cups blanched almonds
  200g/7oz/1¾ cups icing
    (confectioners') sugar
  1 egg white

1 If you want to make almond paste to replace the marzipan, put the almonds in a food processor and, using a pulsating action, chop until finely ground. Add the sugar and egg white and mix to form a paste. The almond paste can be stored in a plastic bag in the refrigerator for up to 3 days until required.

2 Preheat the oven to 180°C/350°F/ Gas 4. Grease a 20cm/8in round cake tin (pan) with butter. Put the butter and sugar in a large bowl and whisk together until fluffy. Add the eggs and whisk together. Sift in the flour and baking powder, add the vanilla sugar and stir together.

3 Turn the mixture into the prepared cake tin and bake in the oven for 1 hour until golden brown and firm to the touch. Remove the cake from the oven and leave to cool in the tin. When the cake is cold, slice in half horizontally.

4 To make the filling, soak the gelatine leaves in cold water until soft or according to the directions on the packet. Put 500ml/17fl oz/2 cups of the cream, the sugar, cornflour and egg yolks in a pan and heat gently, stirring all the time, until the mixture thickens. Do not allow the mixture to boil or the eggs will curdle.

5 Pour the mixture into a bowl, beat in the soaked gelatine leaves and leave to cool but not set.

6 Put the remaining cream in a bowl, add the vanilla sugar and whisk until stiff. Fold the whisked cream into the cooled custard and, before it thickens, spread half the custard over the bottom layer of cake. Put the other cake layer on top and spread over the remaining custard.

7 Add a few drops of green food colouring to the marzipan or almond paste and knead until evenly coloured. Between two sheets of foil or baking parchment, thinly roll out the marzipan or almond paste into a round. Remove the top sheet of foil or baking parchment and, using a large plate at least 30cm/12in in diameter, cut the marzipan into a circle.

8 Using the foil or baking parchment to lift the marzipan, carefully place the marzipan circle over the top of the cake and tuck it down the sides of the cake so it looks like a green dome.

9 Sprinkle a little icing sugar on top to decorate and serve the cake with fresh strawberries.

Per portion Energy 326kcal/1512kJ; Protein 11.3g; Carbohydrate 11.1g, of which sugars 7.6g; Fat 9.7g, of which saturates 5.6g; Cholesterol 34.6mg; Calcium 19.5mg; Fibre 0.9g; Sodium 21.7mg.

CHOCOLATE GOOEY CAKE

THIS IS SWEDEN'S FAVOURITE CHOCOLATE CAKE. FOR PERFECT RESULTS IT IS ESSENTIAL TO UNDERCOOK THE CAKE SO THAT IT IS DENSE IN THE MIDDLE. MADE WITH ALMONDS INSTEAD OF FLOUR, CHOKLADKLADDKAKA IS GLUTEN FREE AND THEREFORE THE PERFECT TREAT FOR A COELIAC GUEST.

4 Add the pieces of butter to the chocolate and stir until melted.

5 Add the egg yolks, ground almonds and vanilla sugar and stir together. Turn the mixture into a large bowl.

6 Whisk the egg whites until stiff then fold them into the chocolate mixture.

SERVES EIGHT

INGREDIENTS
   100g/4oz dark (bittersweet) chocolate
      with 75 per cent cocoa solids
   5ml/1 tsp water
   100g/4oz/½ cup unsalted butter,
      plus extra for greasing
   2 eggs, separated
   175g/6oz/1½ cups ground almonds
   5ml/1 tsp vanilla sugar
   whipped double (heavy) cream,
      to serve

1 Preheat the oven to 180°C/350°F/ Gas 4. Grease a 20cm/8in shallow round cake tin (pan) with butter.

2 Break the dark chocolate into a small pan, then add the water and heat gently, stirring, until the chocolate has melted. Remove the pan from the heat.

3 Cut the butter into small pieces.

7 Put the mixture into the prepared tin and bake in the oven for 15–17 minutes until just set. The mixture should still be soft in the centre.

8 Leave the cake to cool in the tin, then, when cold, serve it with the whipped cream.

Per portion Energy 311kcal/1288kJ; Protein 6.8g; Carbohydrate 10g, of which sugars 9.3g; Fat 27.4g, of which saturates 9.9g; Cholesterol 75mg; Calcium 66.2mg; Fibre 1.9g; Sodium 97mg.

EASTER CAKE

THIS SWEDISH CAKE HAS AN INTENSE YELLOW COLOUR, WHICH MAKES IT A GOOD CHOICE FOR A CELEBRATION AT ANY TIME OF YEAR, PARTICULARLY AROUND EASTER. IT CERTAINLY MAKES A GOOD ALTERNATIVE TO THE SIMNEL CAKE THAT IS SERVED IN ENGLAND AT EASTER TIME.

SERVES EIGHT TO TEN

INGREDIENTS
400g/14oz good quality marzipan
   or almond paste (see below)
4 eggs, beaten
50ml/2fl oz/¼ cup fresh orange juice
100g/4oz dark (bittersweet) chocolate
   with 75 per cent cocoa solids
blueberries or redcurrants,
   to decorate
For the almond paste (optional)
200g/7oz/1½ cups blanched almonds
200g/7oz/1¾ cups icing
   (confectioners') sugar
1 egg white

1 If you want to make almond paste to replace the marzipan, put the almonds in a food processor and, using a pulsating action, chop until finely ground.

2 Add the sugar and egg white and mix to form a paste. The prepared almond paste can then be stored in a polythene bag in the refrigerator for up to 2–3 days until required.

3 Preheat the oven to 200°C/400°F/ Gas 6. Line a 20cm/8in cake tin (pan) with baking parchment.

4 Grate the marzipan or almond paste into a bowl. Add the eggs and orange juice and beat together until the mixture is fluffy. Put the mixture in the prepared cake tin.

5 Bake for 30 minutes until golden brown and firm to the touch.

6 Allow to cool slightly, then turn out (without inverting) on to a wire rack. While the cake is still warm, grate the chocolate over the top of the cake so that it melts.

7 Leave to cool. Serve decorated with fresh blueberries or redcurrants.

Per portion Energy 245kcal/1032kJ; Protein 5.1g; Carbohydrate 34g, of which sugars 33.4g; Fat 10.2g, of which saturates 2.8g; Cholesterol 77mg; Calcium 42mg; Fibre 0.8g; Sodium 38mg.

BIRTHDAY WREATH

In Norway, birthdays begin with a coffee tray taken up to the bedroom and this celebration wreath, fødselsdagskringle, often accompanies the coffee. It is best eaten on the day it is baked, but this is easily achieved as the wreath is allowed to rise overnight and then presented in the early morning, fresh from the oven.

MAKES ONE WREATH

INGREDIENTS
300ml/½ pint/1¼ cups milk
1 packet dried yeast
1 egg plus 1 egg yolk
30ml/2 tbsp sugar
450g/1lb/4 cups plain
  (all purpose) flour
225g/8oz/1 cup butter, chilled
For the filling
115g/4oz/1 cup ground almonds
115g/4oz/1 cup icing
  (confectioners') sugar
2 egg whites, lightly beaten
To glaze
1 egg yolk
15ml/1 tbsp milk
coarse sugar

1 Line a baking tray with baking parchment. To make the filling, put the ground almonds and the icing sugar in a bowl and then add enough egg white to make a soft marzipan.

2 In a pan, bring the milk to just below boiling point. Pour the milk into a large bowl and leave until lukewarm. Sprinkle in the dried yeast and leave for 15 minutes until frothy.

3 Add the egg and egg yolk, sugar and flour to the mixture and mix together to make a stiff dough that leaves the sides of the bowl clean.

4 On a lightly floured surface, roll out the dough into a rectangle, three times as long as it is wide. Cut the cold butter into thin slices and use to cover the bottom two-thirds of the dough.

5 Fold the top third over the middle and then turn the folded two-thirds over on to the bottom third. Turn the dough so that the folded edges are at the sides and roll out again to the same size rectangle. Fold again into three and roll out into a rectangle measuring 20 x 75cm/8 x 30in.

6 Spread the filling down the centre of the long length of the dough, then fold each side of the dough to the middle, over the filling, making a secure tube.

7 Place the dough and filling on the prepared baking tray and bend the dough into a wreath, tucking one end underneath a longer end, twisting this longer, upper end so that it sits in the middle of the circle.

8 Cover the wreath loosely with clear film (plastic wrap) and put in the refrigerator or a very cool place to rise overnight.

9 Preheat the oven to 230°C/450°F/Gas 8. Meanwhile, take the wreath out of the refrigerator or pantry and allow to stand at room temperature.

10 In a small bowl, beat together the egg yolk and milk and brush over the wreath. Sprinkle coarse sugar over the top.

11 Lower the oven temperature to 220°C/425°F/Gas 7 and bake for 20 minutes until golden brown. Cool on a wire rack.

Per wreath Energy 4779kcal/20001kJ; Protein 93.7g; Carbohydrate 524.6g, of which sugars 178.6g; Fat 271.1g, of which saturates 129.5g; Cholesterol 889mg; Calcium 1438mg; Fibre 22.5g; Sodium 1731mg.

ALMOND RING CAKE

*K*NOWN AS KRANSEKAGE IN *D*ENMARK AND KRANSEKAKE IN *N*ORWAY, TOWERS ASSEMBLED FROM STACKED RINGS OF MARZIPAN CAKE ARE SERVED AT FESTIVE OCCASIONS, AND AT SPECIAL 'ROUND' BIRTHDAYS AT THE START OF A NEW DECADE. SPECIAL SETS OF CAKE TINS, *15* OR *18* TO A SET, ARE OFTEN USED TO MAKE THE CAKE, BUT IF THESE AREN'T AVAILABLE, THE DOUGH CAN BE ROLLED BY HAND INTO RINGS.

SERVES 24

INGREDIENTS

For the cake
  250g/9oz/2½ cups blanched
    almonds, finely ground
  250g/9oz/2½ cups almonds with
    skins on, finely ground
  500g/1¼lb/4½ cups icing
    (confectioners') sugar, sifted
  3 egg whites
For the icing
  1 egg white
  175g/6oz/1½ cups icing
    (confectioners') sugar, sifted
  pinch of salt
  5ml/1 tsp double (heavy) cream

1 Preheat the oven to 200°C/400°F/ Gas 6. If using kransekage tins (pans), grease 16–18 tins.

2 To make the cake, combine all the ground almonds with the sugar in a large pan. Add the unbeaten egg whites and mix into a firm dough. Place the pan over a low heat and knead until the dough is almost too hot to handle.

COOK'S TIPS
• To enhance the almond flavour, lightly toast the blanched almonds in the oven at 160°C/325°F/Gas 3 for 10 minutes, turning once, before grinding them.
• The dough can be spooned into a piping (pastry) bag with a wide, round tip, and piped into the tins (pans).
• Any extra dough can be rolled into small shapes and baked along with the rings.

3 Roll out the dough into sausages about 1cm/½in in diameter and fit them into the prepared tins. Press the overlapping ends together to make a smooth circle. If you are not using tins, line two baking sheets with baking parchment.

4 Draw a 17cm/6½in diameter circle on the paper. Draw circles, each 1cm/½in smaller than the last, ending with a 5cm/2in circle. Roll the dough into sausages and fit one into each circle, piecing them together as necessary.

5 Bake the rings in the preheated oven for about 8 minutes, until the tops are a light golden brown. Remove from the oven and leave to cool in the tins.

6 To make the icing, beat the egg white until stiff, then stir in the icing sugar with the salt. Continue beating until the mixture is soft.

7 Stir in the cream and beat for 1 minute. Pour the icing into a piping (pastry) bag fitted with a 1.5mm/¹⁄₁₆in nozzle.

8 To assemble the cake, place the largest ring on a serving plate. Stack the remaining rings on top of one another with the smallest on top, adding a covering of icing each time, piped on in a swirling, looping pattern. Finish with a final swirl of icing. Add a Norwegian or Danish flag, if you like.

Per portion Energy 241kcal/1013kJ; Protein 5g; Carbohydrate 30.8g, of which sugars 30.3g; Fat 11.7g, of which saturates 1g; Cholesterol 0mg; Calcium 65mg; Fibre 1.5g; Sodium 15mg.

SWISS ROLL

ROLLED SPONGE CAKES, OR ROULADES, ARE POPULAR DESSERTS IN DENMARK, ACCOMPANIED BY STRONG BLACK COFFEE. THEY ARE EASY TO MAKE AND VERSATILE, WITH DELECTABLE FILLINGS THAT RANGE FROM FRESH FRUIT TO BUTTERCREAM. THIS RECIPE HAS A CHOCOLATE BUTTERCREAM FILLING.

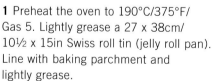

2 Sift together the flour, potato flour and baking powder in a mixing bowl. Whisk the eggs and 150g/5oz/¾ cup of the sugar together in a separate bowl until light and foamy. Gradually fold the flour into the egg mixture, continuing to beat until smooth. Add the water.

3 Spread the batter evenly over the prepared tin and bake for 10–12 minutes until golden brown. Sprinkle a clean dish towel with the remaining sugar.

4 To make the chocolate buttercream filling, cream the butter and icing sugar until light and fluffy. Stir in the egg yolk until well blended, add the cocoa and blend.

SERVES 12

INGREDIENTS
  50g/2oz/½ cup self-raising
    (self-rising) flour
  25g/1oz/¼ cup potato flour
    or cornflour (cornstarch)
  5ml/1 tsp baking powder
  3 eggs
  250g/9oz/1¼ cups caster
    (superfine) sugar
  30ml/2 tbsp water
For the chocolate buttercream filling
  50g/2oz/¼ cup unsalted butter
  90g/3oz/¾ cup icing (confectioners')
    sugar, sifted
  1 egg yolk
  30ml/2 tbsp unsweetened cocoa
    powder, sifted, plus extra
    for dusting

1 Preheat the oven to 190°C/375°F/ Gas 5. Lightly grease a 27 x 38cm/ 10½ x 15in Swiss roll tin (jelly roll pan). Line with baking parchment and lightly grease.

5 Turn the cooked cake out on to the prepared towel, remove the parchment, and trim the edges. While warm, roll the cake up with the towel inside. Set aside.

6 When the cake is cool, unroll it, spread with buttercream and roll up again, without the towel. Place the cake on a serving plate with the seam facing down, dust with cocoa powder and serve.

Per portion Energy 196kcal/826kJ; Protein 2.8g; Carbohydrate 35.1g, of which sugars 29.7g; Fat 5.9g, of which saturates 3g; Cholesterol 73mg; Calcium 34mg; Fibre 0.4g; Sodium 70mg.

COCONUT CAKES

THESE POPULAR, MOIST COCONUT CAKES, KOKOSTOPPAR, WHICH ARE SIMILAR TO COCONUT MACAROONS, ARE COMMONPLACE IN SWEDEN. THEY ARE BEST SERVED STRAIGHT FROM THE OVEN, BUT ALSO KEEP REASONABLY WELL IN THE FREEZER OR IN AN AIRTIGHT CONTAINER.

MAKES 15–20

INGREDIENTS
   1 vanilla pod (bean)
   120ml/4fl oz/½ cup double
     (heavy) cream
   200g/7oz/2⅓ cups desiccated (dry
     unsweetened shredded) coconut
   200g/7oz/scant 1 cup caster
     (superfine) sugar
   1 egg, beaten

2 Preheat the oven to 200°C/400°F/Gas 6. Line a baking sheet with baking parchment. Remove the vanilla pod from the cream and pour the cream into a bowl. Add the coconut, sugar and egg and mix together.

3 Spoon the mixture in piles on to the prepared baking sheet. Bake in the oven for 12–15 minutes until golden brown and a little crisp on top. Leave the cakes to cool slightly before transferring to a cooling rack.

1 Split open the vanilla pod and put in a pan with the cream. Heat gently until bubbles start to form round the edge of the pan, then remove from the heat and leave to infuse for 20 minutes.

COOK'S TIP
Don't discard the vanilla pod after you have used it to make the vanilla cream. Rinse it well, leave to dry and then keep it in a jar to use another time. Alternatively, put it in a jar of sugar to make vanilla sugar.

Per cake Energy 177kcal/740kJ; Protein 1.4g; Carbohydrate 14.9g, of which sugars 14.9g; Fat 13g, of which saturates 9.9g; Cholesterol 23.6mg; Calcium 16mg; Fibre 1.8g; Sodium 10.9mg.

GINGER BISCUITS

PEPPARKAKOR ARE FOUND ALL OVER SWEDEN. THERE IS EVEN A SWEDISH NURSERY RHYME THAT SAYS IF YOU ARE GOOD YOU WILL BE GIVEN PEPPARKAKOR BUT IF YOU ARE BAD YOU WILL BE GIVEN NONE! YOU CAN CUT THE BISCUITS INTO ANY SHAPE, BUT STARS AND HEARTS ARE THE TRADITIONAL FORMS.

MAKES ABOUT 50

INGREDIENTS
   150g/5½oz/½ cup plus 3 tbsp butter
   400g/14oz/2 cups sugar
   50ml/2fl oz/¼ cup golden
     (light corn) syrup
   15ml/1 tbsp treacle (molasses)
   15ml/1 tbsp ground ginger
   30ml/2 tbsp ground cinnamon
   15ml/1 tbsp ground cloves
   5ml/1 tsp ground cardamom
   5ml/1 tsp bicarbonate of soda
     (baking soda)
   240ml/8fl oz/1 cup water
   150g/5oz/1¼ cups plain
     (all-purpose) flour

1 Put the butter, sugar, golden syrup, treacle, ground ginger, ground cinnamon, ground cloves and ground cardamom in a heavy pan and heat gently over a low heat until the butter has melted.

2 Put the bicarbonate of soda and water in a large heatproof bowl. Pour in the warm spice mixture and mix well together, then add the flour and stir until well blended. Put in the refrigerator overnight to rest.

3 Preheat the oven to 220°C/425°F/ Gas 7. Line several baking sheets with baking parchment.

4 Knead the dough then roll it out on a lightly floured surface as thinly as possible. Cut the dough into shapes of your choice and place them on the baking sheets.

5 Bake the biscuits (cookies) in the oven for about 5 minutes until golden brown, cooking in batches until all the biscuits are cooked. Leave to cool on the baking sheets.

Per biscuit Energy 31kcal/130kJ; Protein 0.2g; Carbohydrate 5.8g, of which sugars 4.2g; Fat 0.8g, of which saturates 0.5g; Cholesterol 2mg; Calcium 5mg; Fibre 0.1g; Sodium13mg.

BERLIN WREATH BISCUITS

DESPITE THE GERMAN NAME, THESE BISCUITS ARE FROM NORWAY, AND ARE TRADITIONAL FAVOURITES FOR ENJOYING AT CHRISTMAS TIME. THEY ARE QUITE UNUSUAL IN THAT COOKED EGG YOLK IS USED IN ADDITION TO RAW EGGS AND THE RESULTING MIXTURE PRODUCES A VERY APPEALING TEXTURE.

MAKES ABOUT 48

INGREDIENTS
  2 hard-boiled eggs, yolks only
  2 eggs, separated
  225g/8oz/1 generous cup sugar
  475g/1lb/4½ cups plain
    (all-purpose) flour
  350g/12oz/1½ cups butter, softened
  coarse sugar, for coating

1 Put the hard-boiled egg yolks and raw egg yolks in a bowl and mash together. Beat in the sugar, a little at a time. Add the flour alternately with the softened butter, mixing well to make a stiff dough. Wrap the dough in clear film (plastic wrap) and put in the refrigerator for 2–3 hours.

2 Line a baking tray with baking parchment. On a lightly floured surface, using your hands, roll out pieces of the dough into strips the thickness of a pencil.

3 Cut into 10–13cm/4–5in lengths. Form into small wreaths by making a round loop and placing one end over the other.

4 Place on the baking tray and chill in the refrigerator for 30 minutes.

5 Preheat the oven to 190°C/375°F/Gas 5. Lightly beat the egg whites, brush over each wreath then dip into coarse sugar.

6 Return to the baking tray and bake in the oven for 10–12 minutes until very light brown.

7 Leave the wreaths on the baking tray for 2–3 minutes, then transfer them to a wire rack and leave to cool. Store the biscuits (cookies) in an airtight container.

COOK'S TIP
The dough will spread during cooking so make sure that the loops are large enough not to close up during baking. Chilling the wreaths in the refrigerator before cooking will help to stop the dough spreading too much.

Per biscuit Energy 107kcal/447kJ; Protein 1.1g; Carbohydrate 12.1g, of which sugars 4.5g; Fat 6.4g, of which saturates 3.9g; Cholesterol 24mg; Calcium 18mg; Fibre 0.3g; Sodium 45mg.

VANILLA RINGS

BLESSED WITH FINE INGREDIENTS – BUTTER, EGGS AND FLOUR – FROM THE COUNTRY'S PROSPEROUS FARMS, DANISH PASTRY CHEFS ARE RENOWNED FOR CREATING ARTISTICALLY SHAPED AND RICHLY FLAVOURED BISCUITS. THESE BUTTERY BISCUITS, VANILLEKRANSE, ARE A CHRISTMAS FAVOURITE.

3 Beat in the chopped vanilla pod or vanilla extract.

4 Gradually stir the flour, bakers' ammonia and almonds into the creamed mixture to form a soft dough.

5 Turn out on to a lightly floured surface and knead lightly until the dough is smooth.

6 Using a star piping nozzle or cookie press, form 5cm/2in diameter rings on the prepared baking sheets.

7 Bake the biscuits (cookies) for 8–9 minutes, until golden brown.

8 Cool the rings on a wire rack and store in an airtight container.

COOK'S TIP
Bakers' ammonia (bicarbonate of ammonia) is used by Northern European cooks to make biscuits light and crisp. It was originally obtained from ground reindeer antlers. Look for it in German or Scandinavian markets. As a substitute, use 5ml/1 tsp baking powder.

MAKES 72

INGREDIENTS
    400g/14oz/1¾ cup butter
    130g/4½oz/⅔ cup caster (superfine) sugar
    1 egg, beaten
    1 vanilla pod (bean), finely chopped, or 10ml/2 tsp vanilla extract
    450g/1lb/4 cups plain (all-purpose) flour
    1.5ml/¼ tsp bakers' ammonia (see Cook's Tip)
    115g/4oz/1 cup blanched almonds, finely chopped

1 Preheat the oven to 180°C/350°F/ Gas 4. Lightly grease two baking sheets.

2 Beat the butter and sugar in a bowl until light and fluffy. Beat in the egg.

Per biscuit Energy 78kcal/326kJ; Protein 1g; Carbohydrate 6.3g, of which sugars 2.1g; Fat 5.6g, of which saturates 3g; Cholesterol 14mg; Calcium 14mg; Fibre 0.3g; Sodium 35mg.

VANILLA CHRISTMAS BISCUITS

KNOWN AS VANILJEHJERTER, THESE NORWEGIAN HEART-SHAPED TREATS ARE A PERFECT CHOICE FOR CHRISTMAS. THEY ARE IDEAL WITH A CUP OF TEA OR COFFEE, OR CAN ACCOMPANY A FRUIT SALAD. A LITTLE BOX OF THEM WRAPPED WITH A BIG RED BOW ALSO MAKES A DELIGHTFUL PRESENT.

MAKES ABOUT 24

INGREDIENTS
225g/8oz/2 cups plain
  (all-purpose) flour
5ml/1 tsp baking powder
150g/5oz/10 tbsp butter,
  at room temperature
90g/3½ oz/½ cup caster
  (superfine) sugar
1 egg, lightly beaten
7.5ml/1½ tsp vanilla extract
120ml/4fl oz/½ cup milk

1 Sift the flour and baking powder together. Put the butter and sugar in a large bowl and beat together until light and fluffy. Add the egg and vanilla extract, then add the milk, alternating it with the sifted flour.

2 Mix together, then knead the dough lightly. Chill the dough in the refrigerator for 30 minutes.

3 Preheat the oven to 180°C/350°F/ Gas 4. Butter a large baking tray. On a lightly floured surface, roll out the dough to 1cm/½in thickness.

4 Using a heart-shaped cutter, cut out hearts and place on the prepared baking tray.

5 Bring the dough trimmings together, knead lightly, roll and cut out more hearts. Add them to the tray.

6 Bake the biscuits (cookies) for about 10 minutes until lightly golden brown. Leave on the tray for 2–3 minutes, then transfer to a wire rack and leave to cool.

COOK'S TIP
A pretty finish could be achieved by brushing the hearts with lightly beaten egg white, then sprinkling with caster sugar, before baking.

Per biscuit Energy 100kcal/420kJ; Protein 1.4g; Carbohydrate 11.9g, of which sugars 4.8g; Fat 5.6g, of which saturates 3.4g; Cholesterol 22mg; Calcium 24mg; Fibre 0.3g; Sodium 43mg.

SWEDISH DEEP-FRIED CAKES

THESE SMALL, DEEP-FRIED CAKES, CALLED KLENÄTER, WHICH ARE SIMILAR TO DOUGHNUTS, ARE AN ESSENTIAL PART OF THE CHRISTMAS CELEBRATIONS IN SWEDEN. THE CHARACTERISTIC SHAPE IS CREATED BY CUTTING A HOLE IN EACH STRIP AND THREADING ONE END THROUGH THE HOLE IN THE MIDDLE.

3 On a lightly floured work surface, thinly roll out the dough into a rectangle. Cut the rectangle into 1cm/½in strips, and then cut each strip into 5cm/2in pieces.

4 Cut a slit in the centre of each piece of dough, fold each piece in half and then put one end through the hole and press down to flatten the cake.

5 Heat the vegetable oil in a large pan or deep-fryer to 180°C/350°F or until a cube of bread, dropped into the oil, turns brown in 1 minute. Put the caster sugar on a large plate and set it aside.

6 Drop the cakes, in batches so that the pan is not overcrowded, into the hot oil and cook them, turning once with a slotted spoon, until they are golden brown and crispy. Remove the cakes and drain on kitchen paper.

7 Transfer the cakes to the sugar and turn them to dust them in the sugar, coating them on both sides. Serve them warm or cold.

SERVES SIX TO EIGHT

INGREDIENTS
15g/½oz/1 tbsp unsalted butter
350g/12oz/3 cups plain
    (all-purpose) flour
5ml/1 tsp baking powder
120ml/4fl oz/½ cup double
    (heavy) cream
5 egg yolks, beaten
vegetable oil, for deep-frying
200g/7oz/1 cup caster
    (superfine) sugar

1 Melt the butter and then leave to cool but not set.

2 Sift the flour and baking powder into a large bowl. Add the cream, egg yolks and melted butter and beat together to form a smooth dough. Leave the dough to rest for about 2 hours.

Per portion Energy 436kcal/1830kJ; Protein 6.3g; Carbohydrate 60.4g, of which sugars 27.1g; Fat 20.5g, of which saturates 7.9g; Cholesterol 151mg; Calcium 97mg; Fibre 1.4g; Sodium 23mg.

DANISH-STYLE DOUGHNUTS

THESE PLUMP, ROUND DOUGHY BALLS, ÆBLESKIVER, WHICH ARE WARM AND CRISP ON THE OUTSIDE AND DELICIOUSLY SOFT IN THE MIDDLE, DATE FROM THE 1600S, AND ARE COOKED IN A SPECIAL CAST IRON GRIDDLE. FOR A REAL SCANDINAVIAN FEEL, SERVE DRIZZLED WITH LINGONBERRY JAM.

MAKES 24 TO 30

INGREDIENTS
  250ml/8fl oz/1 cup milk
  15g/½oz fresh yeast
  50g/2oz/¼ cup unsalted butter
  25g/1oz/2 tbsp caster
    (superfine) sugar
  3 eggs, separated
  200ml/7fl oz/scant 1 cup single
    (light) cream
  225g/8oz/2 cups plain (all-purpose)
    flour, sifted
  5ml/1 tsp bicarbonate of soda
    (baking soda)
  1.5ml/¼ tsp salt
  10ml/2 tsp grated lemon rind
  5ml/1 tsp ground cardamom
  250ml/8fl oz/1 cup vegetable oil
  apple jelly or lingonberry jam,
    and icing (confectioners') sugar,
    to serve

1 Heat the milk to tepid and mix the yeast into it. Set aside.

2 Cream the butter with the sugar in a mixing bowl until light. Beat in the egg yolks and stir in the cream.

3 In a separate bowl, combine the flour, bicarbonate of soda, salt, lemon rind and cardamom. Stir the flour mixture into the egg yolk mixture, alternating with the yeast mixture, until well blended.

4 Beat the egg whites in a separate bowl until stiff peaks form. Gently fold into the flour mixture. Cover the bowl, and leave the batter to rest for 1 hour.

5 Heat the griddle over a low to medium heat. Test the temperature by sprinkling a few drops of water: if it jumps and sputters, the pan is ready. Add 10ml/ 2 tsp vegetable oil into each cup.

6 Pour batter into each cup, to within 3mm/⅛in of the top. Cook until the bottom is set and golden.

7 Use a metal knitting needle to rotate the ball a one-quarter turn. Repeat until the balls are golden brown all over. Take care not to pierce the balls.

8 Pile the æbleskiver balls on a plate and dust with icing sugar while still warm. Serve with spoonfuls of apple jelly, or drizzle with lingonberry jam.

Per doughnut Energy 118kcal/489kJ; Protein 1.8g; Carbohydrate 7.2g, of which sugars 1.5g; Fat 9.3g, of which saturates 2.6g; Cholesterol 27mg; Calcium 30mg; Fibre 0.2g; Sodium 23mg.

MAZARINS

Inside a Danish bakery or konditori the array of baked goods is astonishing. Influenced by 18th-century French, German and Austrian traditions, Danish pastry chefs created their own vast repertoire of baked goods, still beloved by contemporary Danes, including buttery little cakes, tartlets with jam, marzipan or custard fillings, puff pastries with chocolate and vanilla icing, and dozens of chocolate or almond flavoured biscuits. These tartlets are miniature Danish versions of a mazarin cake: a crisp pastry shell with an almond paste filling.

MAKES 12

INGREDIENTS
For the pastry
    150g/5oz/1¼ cups plain
      (all-purpose) flour
    25g/1oz/¼ cup icing
      (confectioners') sugar
    90g/3½oz/7 tbsp unsalted butter
    1 egg yolk
For the filling
    65g/2½oz/5 tbsp unsalted butter
    75g/3oz/¾ cup icing (confectioners')
      sugar
    2 small (US medium) eggs, beaten
    115g/4oz/1 cup ground almonds
    1 tiny drop green food
      colouring (optional)
For the icing
    200g/7oz plain (semisweet) chocolate
    25g/1oz/2 tbsp unsalted butter

VARIATIONS
Dust the tops of the mazarins with sifted icing (confectioners') sugar, or make a plain icing using 115g/4oz/1 cup icing sugar mixed with 10ml/2 tsp warm water and 2.5ml/½ tsp almond extract.

1 To make the pastry, sift the flour and icing sugar into a large bowl, then rub in the butter using your fingertips until the mixture resembles breadcrumbs.

2 Stir in the egg yolk and use your fingers to work the mixture into a soft, smooth dough.

3 Gather the dough into a ball, wrap it in baking parchment and chill in the refrigerator for 1 hour.

4 Roll out the dough to a thickness of 3mm/⅛in and use to line 12 oval-shaped, fluted tartlet tins (pans). Place the tins on a baking sheet and chill in the refrigerator while you make the filling. Preheat the oven to 190°C/375°F/Gas 5.

5 To make the filling, cream the butter and icing sugar until light and fluffy. Add the beaten eggs, a little at a time, stirring vigorously to mix.

6 Stir the ground almonds into the mixture, and add the green food colouring (if using). Spoon the almond filling into the prepared pastry cases. Bake for about 20 minutes, until the tops are light brown. Cool on a rack.

7 Break up the chocolate and melt it with the butter in a bowl set over a pan filled with water over a low heat.

8 Cool slightly, then spread over the cooled mazarins.

Per cake Energy 347kcal/1446kJ; Protein 5.3g; Carbohydrate 29.8g, of which sugars 19.8g; Fat 23.8g, of which saturates 11.4g; Cholesterol 78mg; Calcium 59mg; Fibre 1.5g; Sodium 105mg.

LENTEN BUNS WITH VANILLA CREAM

THOUGH VERY FEW DANES STILL OBSERVE THE LENTEN FAST, THE PRE-LENT HOLIDAY SURVIVES AS A FESTIVE, CARNIVAL-LIKE OCCASION. TRADITIONAL TREATS INCLUDE THESE PLUMP, YEASTY BUNS, KNOWN AS FASTELAVNSBOLLER, WHICH HAVE A SMOOTH CREAM FILLING AND VARIOUS TOPPINGS.

MAKES 24 BUNS

INGREDIENTS

For the buns

50ml/2fl oz/¼ cup tepid water

40g/1½oz fresh yeast

175g/6oz/¾ cup unsalted butter, softened

50g/2oz/¼ cup caster (superfine) sugar

2 eggs, plus 1 extra yolk

175ml/6fl oz/¾ cup milk

2.5ml/½ tsp salt

5ml/1 tsp ground cardamom

400g/14oz/3½ cups strong white bread flour

For the filling

3 egg yolks

45ml/3 tbsp caster (superfine) sugar

10ml/2 tsp vanilla sugar

15ml/1 tbsp potato flour or cornflour (cornstarch)

475ml/16fl oz/2 cups milk

pinch of salt

For the icing

1 egg white

150g/5oz/1¼ cups icing (confectioners') sugar, sifted

25g/1oz/¼ cup unsweetened cocoa powder, sifted

pinch of salt

5ml/1 tsp double (heavy) cream

30ml/2 tbsp pearl sugar, to decorate

1 Pour the tepid water into a bowl and stir in the yeast until blended. Cream the butter and sugar in a mixing bowl and beat until light and fluffy. Beat in one whole egg and the extra yolk.

2 Briefly warm the milk in a pan over a low heat, add the yeast mixture and stir into the creamed butter mixture. Add the salt and cardamom. Stir in the flour, a little at a time, and mix to a soft dough, adding more flour if necessary.

3 Knead the dough on a floured surface for 5–7 minutes, until smooth. Lightly oil a large bowl. Place the dough in the bowl, cover and leave in a warm place until doubled in size, about 1 hour.

4 To make the filling, whisk together the egg yolks and sugar in a pan until well blended. Whisk in the vanilla sugar, potato flour or cornflour and milk. Add the salt. Cook over a low heat, stirring, for 6 minutes, until the mixture thickens. Remove from the heat and leave to cool.

5 Grease two baking sheets. Turn the dough out on to a floured surface and divide into four. Cut each part into six pieces and shape into balls. Place on the prepared baking sheets. Make a 2cm/¾in well in the centre of each roll, and fill with a spoonful of the cream filling. Cover with clear film (plastic wrap) and leave in a warm place for 1½–2 hours.

6 Preheat the oven to 220°C/425°F/Gas 7. Beat the remaining egg. Brush it over the buns. Bake for 12–15 minutes, until golden. Cool on a wire rack.

7 To make the icing, beat the egg white until stiff. Stir in the icing sugar, cocoa and salt and beat until the mixture is soft. Stir in the cream and beat for 1 minute. Spread the icing over the tops of the cooled buns and sprinkle with pearl sugar.

Per bun Energy 186kcal/782kJ; Protein 3.9g; Carbohydrate 25.6g, of which sugars 12.2g; Fat 8.3g, of which saturates 4.6g; Cholesterol 67mg; Calcium 70mg; Fibre 0.6g; Sodium 77mg.

DANISH PASTRY

BUTTERY, FLAKY DANISH PASTRY, OR WIENERBRØD, IS UNRIVALLED THROUGHOUT THE WORLD AND IS ONE OF SCANDINAVIA'S MOST FAMOUS CREATIONS. USE THE HIGHEST QUALITY BUTTER YOU CAN FIND, AND KEEP THE PASTRY AS COLD AS YOU CAN WHILE YOU ARE MAKING IT.

MAKES TWO BRAIDS OR 16 PASTRIES

INGREDIENTS
For the pastry
    40g/1½oz fresh yeast
    150ml/¼ pint/⅔ cup milk
    120ml/4fl oz/½ cup double
      (heavy) cream
    50g/2oz/¼ cup caster (superfine) sugar
    2 eggs
    5ml/1 tsp ground cardamom
    5ml/1 tsp salt
    5ml/1 tsp vanilla sugar
    400g/14oz/3½ cups strong white
      bread flour
    340g/12oz/1½ cups unsalted
      butter, chilled
For the almond filling
    115g/4oz/½ cup unsalted butter
    90g/3½oz/½ cup caster
      (superfine) sugar
    50g/2oz/½ cup ground almonds
    45ml/3 tbsp double (heavy) cream
    2.5ml/½ tsp almond extract
    75g/2½oz/½ cup sultanas
      (golden raisins)
For the glaze
    1 egg
    30ml/2 tbsp milk
    flaked (sliced) almonds, to decorate

1 Blend the yeast with the milk in a small bowl. Heat the cream gently in a pan to barely lukewarm, 40°C/104°F. Stir the yeast mixture into the cream and leave to stand for 5 minutes.

2 Beat the caster sugar with the eggs in a large mixing bowl until the mixture is light and frothy.

3 Stir in the cardamom, salt and vanilla sugar. Add the yeast mixture and blend well. Gradually stir in the bread flour to make a soft dough.

4 Knead the dough in the bowl for 2–3 minutes. Cover and refrigerate for at least 1 hour (or up to 8 hours).

5 Turn the chilled dough out on to a lightly floured surface. Dust a rolling pin with a little flour, and roll the dough out to a 40cm/16in square about 1cm/½in thick.

6 Cut the butter into thin slices and place these side by side down the middle of the pastry square, ending about 2.5cm/1in from the edge of the dough. Fold over one side of the pastry to cover the butter, then the other side. Seal the ends. Wrap the dough with clear film (plastic wrap) and refrigerate for 15 minutes.

7 Unwrap the dough and roll out again to form a 40cm/16in square. Give the dough a quarter turn, then fold in thirds again, at right angles to the first folds. Wrap and chill for a further 15 minutes.

8 Repeat the rolling, folding and chilling steps twice more, then cover and leave to rest in the refrigerator for 15 minutes.

9 Meanwhile, preheat the oven to 200°C/400°F/Gas 6. Prepare the filling by combining the butter, sugar and almonds in a bowl. Stir in the double cream, almond extract and sultanas. Set aside. Line a baking sheet with baking parchment.

10 To make two Danish plaits, roll the dough out on a lightly floured surface to a 40cm/16in square. Cut the square into two rectangles and place them on the prepared baking sheet. Spread the prepared almond filling down the centre of each piece.

11 Make diagonal cuts about 2cm/¾in apart down each side. Alternating sides, fold the strips in a criss-cross pattern over the filling in the centre.

12 For individual pastries, roll out the dough and cut into 10cm/4in squares. Spoon about 15ml/1 tbsp of the filling into the centre of each square. Bake as a square, or fold opposite corners over to partially cover the filling. Repeat for each square, and place on the prepared baking sheet.

13 Cover with a clean dish towel and leave for 15–30 minutes for the pastry to rise slightly. Combine the egg and milk in a small bowl and brush over the pastry. Sprinkle with flaked almonds and bake for 15 minutes, until golden.

Per pastry Energy 436kcal/1814kJ; Protein 5.1g; Carbohydrate 32.8g, of which sugars 13.7g; Fat 32.5g, of which saturates 18.9g; Cholesterol 111mg; Calcium 78mg; Fibre 1.1g; Sodium 194mg.

LUCIA SAFFRON BUNS

THESE BUNS, LUSSEKATTER, ARE EATEN ON 13 DECEMBER, WHEN THE SWEDES CELEBRATE THE FESTIVAL OF SAINT LUCIA TO COMBAT THE EFFECTS OF A LONG DARK WINTER. THEY ARE FLAVOURED WITH SAFFRON AND ARE MADE EARLY IN THE MORNING OF THAT DAY.

MAKES 20

INGREDIENTS
  300ml/½ pint/1¼ cups milk
  130g/4½oz/9 tbsp unsalted butter
  a pinch of saffron threads
  50g/2oz fresh yeast
  700g/1½lb/6 cups plain
    (all-purpose) flour
  5ml/1 tsp salt
  150g/5oz/¾ cup caster
    (superfine) sugar
  40 raisins
  beaten egg, to glaze

1 Put the milk and butter in a pan and heat until the butter has melted. Remove from the heat, add the saffron threads and leave to cool until warm to the touch.

2 In a large bowl, blend the fresh yeast with a little of the warm saffron milk.

3 Add the remaining saffron milk, then add the plain flour, salt and caster sugar. Mix together to form a dough that comes away from the sides of the bowl.

4 Turn out the dough on to a lightly floured surface and knead for about 10 minutes until the dough feels firm and elastic.

5 Shape the dough into a ball, put in a clean bowl and cover with a clean dish towel. Leave to rise in a warm place for about 1 hour, or until the dough has doubled in size.

6 Turn out the dough on to a lightly floured surface and knead again for 2–3 minutes.

7 Divide the dough into 20 equal pieces. Form each piece into a roll, and then shape each roll into an 'S' shape and place on greased baking sheets.

8 Place a raisin at the end of each bun. Cover with a clean dish towel and leave the buns to rise in a warm place for about 40 minutes until doubled in size.

9 Preheat the oven to 200°C/400°F/ Gas 6. Brush the tops of the buns with beaten egg to glaze and bake in the oven for about 15 minutes until they are golden brown. Remove and leave on a wire rack to cool.

COOK'S TIP
These buns are traditionally made in any number of shapes. As well as the 'S' shape used here, they can resemble a cat, a braided wreath, a figure of eight or a crown. The latter represents the crown of St Lucia.

Per portion Energy 423kcal/1788kJ; Protein 9.2g; Carbohydrate 81.7g, of which sugars 15.1g; Fat 8.8g, of which saturates 5g; Cholesterol 20mg; Calcium 161mg; Fibre 2.8g; Sodium 69mg.

CARDAMOM BUNS

NORWEGIAN CHILDREN HAVE BEEN BROUGHT UP ON THESE BUNS, JULEBOLLER, WHICH ARE AN EXAMPLE OF NORWAY'S FONDNESS FOR THE FLAVOUR OF CARDAMOM. ON THE FIRST SUNDAY IN LENT, THE BUNS ARE CUT IN HALF, FILLED WITH WHIPPED CREAM AND THE TOPS COVERED IN SIFTED ICING SUGAR.

MAKES 24

INGREDIENTS
115g/4oz/½ cup butter
350ml/12fl oz/1½ cups milk
1 packet dried yeast
75g/3oz/6 tbsp caster (superfine)
  sugar, plus 2.5ml/½ tsp
  for the yeast
450g/1lb/4 cups strong white
  bread flour
2.5ml/½ tsp salt
10ml/2 tsp cardamom seeds,
  well crushed
beaten egg, to glaze

1 Line a baking tray with baking parchment. Melt the butter in a pan and leave until lukewarm.

2 Bring the milk to just below boiling point. Pour into a jug (pitcher) and leave until warm. Sprinkle in the yeast and the 2.5ml/½ tsp sugar and leave for 15 minutes until frothy.

3 Put the flour in a large bowl, add the remaining sugar, salt and crushed cardamom seeds and mix well together.

4 Add the milk mixture and the melted butter to the flour mixture and mix together to make a stiff dough that leaves the sides of the bowl clean.

6 Turn the dough on to a lightly floured surface, knock back (punch down) and knead for 2–3 minutes.

8 Preheat the oven to 230°C/450°F/ Gas 8. Brush the buns lightly with beaten egg to glaze and bake them in the oven for about 8 minutes until golden brown.

5 Knead the dough on a floured surface until it feels firm and elastic. Put the dough in a bowl, cover with a damp dish towel and leave in a warm place, for about an hour, or until doubled in size.

7 Divide the dough into 24 equal pieces and shape each one into a ball. Put on the baking tray and leave to rise for about 20 minutes until nearly doubled in size.

Per bun Energy 119kcal/499kJ; Protein 2.3g; Carbohydrate 18.6g, of which sugars 4.3g; Fat 4.4g, of which saturates 2.7g; Cholesterol 11mg; Calcium 46mg; Fibre 0.6g; Sodium 36mg.

FAT TUESDAY BUNS

Fat Tuesday Buns (or Shrove Tuesday Buns), called semlor in Swedish, are only eaten in January and February in Sweden, up until the beginning of Lent. They are so meltingly delicious it always seems a pity to restrict their availability until then. The recipe can incorporate ready-made marzipan, but an even better idea is to make your own almond paste.

MAKES 12

INGREDIENTS
  275ml/16fl oz/2 cups double
    (heavy) cream
  115g/4oz/½ cup unsalted butter
  40g/1½oz fresh yeast
  5ml/1 tsp ground cardamom
  30ml/2 tbsp sugar
  450g/1lb/4 cups plain
    (all-purpose) flour
  pinch of salt
  1 egg, beaten
  icing (confectioners') sugar,
    to decorate
  warmed milk, to serve (optional)
For the filling
  115g/4oz good quality marzipan
    or almond paste (see below)
  275ml/16fl oz/2 cups double
    (heavy) cream
For the almond paste (optional)
  115g/4oz/⅔ cup blanched almonds
  115g/4oz/ 1 cup icing
    (confectioners') sugar
  ½ an egg white

1 If you want to make almond paste to replace the marzipan, put the almonds in a food processor and, using a pulsating action, chop until finely ground. Add the sugar and egg white, and mix to form a paste. The almond paste can be stored in a plastic bag in the refrigerator for up to 3 days until required.

2 Pour the cream into a pan and heat gently until warm to the touch. In a separate pan, gently melt the butter.

3 In a large mixing bowl, blend the yeast with a little of the warmed cream and then add the remaining cream, melted butter, cardamom and sugar.

4 Add the flour and salt and mix together to form a dough.

5 Turn the dough on to a lightly floured surface and knead for about 10 minutes until the dough feels firm and elastic.

6 Shape into a ball, put in a clean bowl and cover with a clean dish towel. Leave to rise in a warm place for about 1½ hours until the dough has doubled in size.

7 Turn the dough on to a lightly floured surface and knead again for 2–3 minutes. Divide the dough into 12 equal pieces.

8 Shape each piece into a round bun and place on a greased baking sheet. Cover with a clean dish towel and leave to rise in a warm place until doubled in size.

9 Preheat the oven to 180°C/350°F/ Gas 4. Brush the tops of the buns with beaten egg to glaze, then bake in the oven for about 10 minutes until golden brown. Transfer the buns to a wire rack and leave to cool.

10 To serve, cut the tops off the buns and set them aside. Remove about half of the dough from inside each bun and put it in a bowl. Grate the marzipan or almond paste into the bowl and mix together with the dough. Replace the mixture in the buns.

11 Whisk the double cream for the filling until stiff, then top the buns with the whipped cream. Replace the tops. Sprinkle the icing sugar on top of each bun and either serve on individual serving plates or in a deep bowl with warmed milk, the traditional way of serving them in Sweden.

COOK'S TIP
When making the almond paste, you can blanch the almonds by popping them into boiling water, then sliding off the skins.

Per bun Energy 465kcal/1938kJ; Protein 5.3g; Carbohydrate 38.2g, of which sugars 9.6g; Fat 33.4g, of which saturates 19.9g; Cholesterol 96mg; Calcium 85mg; Fibre 1.3g; Sodium 69mg.

CHRISTMAS BREAD

THIS IS A RICH, DRIED FRUIT BREAD, WHICH IS TRADITIONALLY SERVED DURING THE CHRISTMAS CELEBRATION PERIOD IN NORWAY. IT IS OFTEN MADE AND GIVEN AS A SPECIAL FESTIVE GIFT, WRAPPED IN POLYTHENE AND TIED WITH A BIG RED BOW. IT IS CALLED JULEKAKE IN NORWAY.

MAKES TWO LOAVES

INGREDIENTS
    250ml/8fl oz/1 cup milk
    115g/4oz/½ cup butter
    120ml/4fl oz/½ cup warm water
    90g/3½ oz/½ cup caster (superfine)
        sugar, plus 5ml/1 tsp
    2 packets dried yeast
    1 egg, lightly beaten
    2.5ml/½ tsp salt
    2.5ml/½ tsp cardamom
        seeds, crushed
    500g/1¼ lb/5 cups strong white
        bread flour
    115g/4oz/½ cup candied
        peel, chopped
    150g/5oz/1 cup raisins
    beaten egg, to glaze (optional)
To finish
    melted butter or icing
        (confectioners') sugar
    glacé (candied) cherries
    nuts, such as flaked (sliced) almonds
        or mixed chopped nuts

1 First, grease two 450g/1lb loaf tins (pans) or a large baking tray and set them aside.

2 In a small pan, bring the milk to just below boiling point, then chop the butter into chunks and add it to the pan. Stir the mixture over a low-medium heat until the butter has melted completely.

3 Pour the mixture into a large mixing bowl and set aside to cool slightly, until lukewarm.

4 Put the water and the 5ml/1 tsp caster sugar in a small mixing bowl, sprinkle in the dried yeast and leave in a warm place for about 15 minutes until frothy.

5 Add the egg to the milk mixture, then add the yeast mixture, remaining sugar, salt and cardamom seeds. Add half the strong white bread flour and beat the mixture thoroughly.

6 Dust the fruit generously with some of the remaining flour and add to the mixture along with sufficient flour to make a stiff dough that comes away from the bowl and leaves the sides of the bowl clean.

7 Turn out the dough on to a lightly floured work surface and knead thoroughly until the dough feels firm and elastic.

8 Put the dough in a large bowl, cover it with a damp dish towel and leave in a warm place to rise until it has doubled in size.

9 Turn out the risen dough on to a lightly floured work surface, knock back (punch down) and knead again for 2–3 minutes.

10 Shape the dough into two equal-size loaves and place in the prepared tins. Alternatively, shape the dough into two rounds and put them on the greased baking tray. Leave to rise again until nearly doubled in size.

11 Preheat the oven to 180°C/350°F/ Gas 4. If you wish, brush the loaves with beaten egg to glaze.

12 Bake the loaves in the oven for 30–40 minutes until golden brown in colour. The loaves should sound hollow when knocked on the bottom.

13 Brush the cooked loaves with melted butter, dust with icing sugar or mix the icing sugar with water to create glacé icing and drizzle over. Decorate with glacé cherries and nuts. Leave to cool.

COOK'S TIP
If you use icing (confectioners') sugar to finish the loaves, dust them as soon as they come out of the oven. This way, the icing sugar partially melts and helps the cherries and nuts to stick to the bread.

Per loaf Energy 1889kcal/7972kJ; Protein 33.2g; Carbohydrate 333.5g, of which sugars 143g; Fat 56.3g, of which saturates 32.6g; Cholesterol 225mg; Calcium 658mg; Fibre 12g; Sodium 654mg.

DARK RYE BREAD

THE DANISH LOVE AFFAIR WITH RYE BREAD, OR RUGBRØD, WHETHER LIGHT, DARK, WHOLEMEAL OR CRISPBREAD, IS LEGENDARY. IT'S THE THING DANES MISS MOST WHEN THEY LEAVE HOME. THIS BREAD IS PERFECT FOR CREATING A SELECTION OF WONDERFUL DANISH OPEN SANDWICHES.

3 Add the butter and treacle to 250ml/ 8fl oz/1 cup boiling water and stir until the butter melts. Place the rye flour in a large mixing bowl and stir in the butter mixture. Add the yeast mixture. Stir in the caraway seeds and salt.

4 Gradually stir in the bread flour to make a soft, stiff dough. Knead the dough lightly in the bowl for 2–3 minutes.

5 Lightly butter a large bowl and place the dough in it. Cover the bowl and leave in a warm place for about 45 minutes until the dough has doubled in size. Preheat the oven to 200°C/400°F/Gas 6.

6 Lightly grease two 23 x 13cm/9 x 5in loaf tins (pans). Turn the dough out on to a lightly floured surface and knead again lightly. Form into two loaves and place in the prepared tins.

MAKES TWO LOAVES

INGREDIENTS
  40g/1½oz fresh yeast
  250ml/8fl oz/1 cup buttermilk
  40g/1½oz/3 tbsp butter
  120ml/4floz/½ cup treacle (molasses)
  350g/12oz/3 cups dark rye flour
  45ml/3 tbsp caraway seeds
  7.5ml/1½ tsp salt
  500g/1½lb/5 cups strong unbleached
    white bread flour
  15g/½oz/1 tbsp melted butter

VARIATION
Substitute 115g/4oz/1 cup rye meal for the same amount of rye flour to give the bread a coarser texture.

1 Blend the yeast with 250ml/8fl oz/1 cup warm water. Heat the buttermilk briefly in a pan over a low heat to barely lukewarm, 40°C/105°F.

2 Pour the buttermilk into the yeast mixture, stir and stand for 5 minutes.

7 Cut four diagonal slashes across the top of each loaf. Brush with melted butter. Bake for 45–50 minutes, until the crust is light brown and the loaf sounds hollow when the base is tapped.

Per loaf Energy 1975kcal/8371kJ; Protein 46.1g; Carbohydrate 398.4g, of which sugars 50g; Fat 33.1g, of which saturates 17.4g; Cholesterol 71mg; Calcium 940mg; Fibre 29.3g; Sodium 361mg.

THIN POTATO BREAD

THIS TRADITIONAL NORWEGIAN BREAD IS A TYPE OF LEFSE, WHICH ARE THIN, SLIGHTLY SOFT BREADS. THEY CAN BE EATEN BUTTERED AND SPRINKLED WITH SUGAR OR SERVED WITH HONEY OR LINGONBERRY OR CLOUDBERRY JAM. LEFSE CAN ALSO BE WRAPPED AROUND A HOTDOG OR FILLED WITH MEAT OR FISH.

MAKES ABOUT 35

INGREDIENTS
    1kg/2¼lb potatoes, peeled
    40g/1½oz/3 tbsp butter
    120ml/4fl oz/½ cup single
        (light) cream
    450–600g/1–1⅓lb/4–5 cups plain
        (all-purpose) flour
    salt

1 Cut the potatoes into chunks. Bring to the boil in a pan of salted water and simmer for 20 minutes until tender.

5 Heat a large ungreased frying pan or griddle and cook each bread over a medium heat until brown spots appear on the surface, turning once.

6 Put the cooked breads between two clean dish towels to stop them from drying out. Once they are all cooked, serve immediately.

2 Drain and put through a ricer or a sieve (strainer) into a large bowl. Add the butter, cream and 5ml/1 tsp salt and beat together. Leave to cool. When the potatoes are cool, add enough flour to form a firm dough.

3 On a lightly floured surface, knead until smooth. Divide the dough into pieces about the size of a large egg, roll into balls and put on a baking tray. Chill in the refrigerator for 30 minutes.

4 Roll out each ball of dough very thinly.

Per bread Energy 71kcal/301kJ; Protein 1.8g; Carbohydrate 14.7g, of which sugars 0.6g; Fat 1g, of which saturates 0.5g; Cholesterol 2mg; Calcium 23mg; Fibre 0.7g; Sodium 5mg.

THIN BREADS MADE IN A PAN

THESE THIN PANCAKES, KNOWN AS TUNNBRÖD, ARE SIMILAR TO TORTILLA BREADS AND ORIGINATE IN LAPPLAND IN THE NORTH OF SWEDEN, WHERE THEY WERE TRADITIONALLY BAKED IN AN OPEN FIREPLACE. IT IS POPULAR TO SERVE TUNNBRÖD WITH SAUSAGES AND MASHED POTATOES.

4 Cut the dough into 4–8 equal pieces, then roll each piece into a thin, flat round.

5 Put a round in the hot pan and fry for about 2 minutes, then turn over and cook the second side for a further 2 minutes.

6 Transfer to a large plate and cook the remaining rounds in the same way, stacking one on top of another. Leave to cool on the plate.

MAKES FOUR TO EIGHT

INGREDIENTS
  500g/1lb 2oz/4½ cups plain
    (all-purpose) flour
  5ml/1 tsp salt
  200ml/7fl oz/scant 1 cup milk

COOK'S TIP
These bread pancakes will retain their taste when served a day later.

1 Put a large heavy frying pan over a medium heat.

2 Put the flour and salt in a large mixing bowl then gradually add the milk and mix together, using a wooden spoon, to form a dough.

3 Turn the dough out on to a lightly floured surface and knead for about 2 minutes.

Per bread Energy 150kcal/637kJ; Protein 4.5g; Carbohydrate 33.2g, of which sugars 1.4g; Fat 0.8g, of which saturates 0.3g; Cholesterol 1mg; Calcium 78mg; Fibre 1.3g; Sodium 8mg.

HOME-MADE CRISP RYE BREADS

THESE TRADITIONAL SWEDISH CRISPBREADS, KNÄCKEBRÖD, WERE ORIGINALLY MADE WITH A HOLE IN THE CENTRE SO THEY COULD BE HUNG OVER THE OVEN TO KEEP DRY. NOWADAYS, THEY KEEP WELL IN AN AIRTIGHT CONTAINER. KNÄCKEBRÖD ARE ALSO SOMETIMES MADE WITH ROLLED OATS.

MAKES 15

INGREDIENTS
    600ml/1 pint/2½ cups milk
    50g/2oz fresh yeast
    565g/1¼lb/5 cups rye flour plus
      225g/8oz/2 cups, for dusting
    565g/1¼lb/5 cups strong white
      bread flour
    10ml/2 tsp caraway or cumin seeds
    5ml/1 tsp salt

1 Put the milk in a pan and heat gently until warm to the touch. Remove from the heat. In a bowl, blend the yeast with a little of the warmed milk.

2 Add the remaining milk, then add the rye flour, bread flour, caraway or cumin seeds and salt and mix together to form a dough.

3 Using the rye flour for dusting, turn the dough out on to a lightly floured surface and knead for about 2 minutes.

4 Cut the dough into 15 equal pieces, then roll out each piece into a thin, flat round. Place on baking sheets and leave to rise in a warm place for 20 minutes.

5 Preheat the oven to 150°C/300°F/ Gas 2. Using the rye flour, roll out the pieces of dough again into very thin, flat rounds. Return to the baking sheets.

6 Make a pattern on the surface using a fork or knife.

7 Bake in the oven for 8–10 minutes, turning after about 5 minutes, until hard and crispy. Transfer the breads to a wire rack and leave to cool. Store the breads in an airtight container.

COOK'S TIP
The Swedes use a special rolling pin with a knobbly surface to create the distinctive texture of this hard bread. An ordinary rolling pin is a good substitute, with the speckled texture created with the head of a fork or a knife end.

Per crispbread Energy 323kcal/1376kJ; Protein 9.2g; Carbohydrate 71.1g, of which sugars 2.4g; Fat 2.2g, of which saturates 0.7g; Cholesterol 2mg; Calcium 118mg; Fibre 7.3g; Sodium 19mg.

SUPPLIERS

SCANDINAVIA

H & W Linnevaror
(kitchen utensils and table linens)
Övre Husargatan 15/204
SE-413 14 Gothenburg
martin@how.se;
www.how.se

ICA ute i världen
(food specialities such as caviar, sill,
surströmming and chocolate)
niklas.gloggler@nara.ica.se
www.icasvensktmat.se

Jakob & Johan Dybvik As
(bacalao specialist)
Tingstadvika 5
6035 Fiskarstrand
Tel: +47 7019 9980
Fax: +47 7019 9990
sales@baccala.com
www.bacalao.com

The Northerner
(gifts, food and crafts)
Flöjelbergsgatan 16A
43133 Mölndal
Sweden
www.northerner.com

Norway Abroad
(mail-order food)
Henrik Ibsengate 100
0230 Oslo
Tel: +47 2212 3355
Fax: +47 2243 8877
www.norwayabroad.com

UNITED KINGDOM

Danish Food Shop
Operated by Bechman Ltd.
32 Haughgate Close
Woodbridge
Suffolk IP12 1LQ
Tel: +44 (0)791 509 5005
www.danishfood.net

Norwegian Church
(holds an annual food fair in November
with a wide range of Norwegian
ingredients)
1 Albion Street
London SE16 7JB
Tel: +44 (0)207 740 3900

Upper Glas Restaurant
The Mall, 359 Upper Street
Islington, London N1 0PD
Tel: +44 (0)207 359 1932
www.glasrestaurant.co.uk

Scandelicious
Visit: Borough Market, Southwark Street
London SE1 9AB
Contact: Scandelicious
4 Beaconsfield Road
Aldeburgh
Suffolk IP15 5HF
Tel: +44 (0)172 845 2880
www.scandelicious.co.uk

Totally Swedish
32 Crawford Street
London W1H 1LS
Tel: +44 (0)207 224 9300
shop@totallyswedish.com
www.totallyswedish.com

UNITED STATES

American-Swedish Institute
Bookstore and Museum Shop
2600 Park Avenue
Minneapolis, MN 55407
Tel: +1 (800) 579-3336
www.americanswedishinst.org

Anderson Butik
PO Box 151
120 West Lincoln
Lindsborg, KS 67456
Tel: +1 (800) 782-4132
imports@andersonbutik.com
www.andersonbutik.com

Berolina Bakery Pastry Shop
(cakes, pastries and fresh bread)
3421 Ocean View Blvd
Glendale, CA 91208
Tel: +1 (818) 249-6506

The Crown Bakery
133 Gold Star Blvd
Worcester, MA 01606
Tel: +1 (508) 852-0746
www.thecrownbakery.com

Distinctively Sweden
15 Messenger Street
Plainville, MA 02762
Tel: +1 (508) 643-2676
www.distinctivelysweden.com

Genuine Scandinavia, LLC.
(kitchenware, crockery and accessories)
958 Washington Street, #9
Denver, CO 80203
Tel: +1 (303) 318-0714
www.GenuineScandinavia.com

The Gift Chalet
(specializing in everything from
Scandinavia, including food)
8 Washington Street – Route 20
Auburn, MA 01501
Tel: +1 (508) 755-3028
GiftChalet@aol.com
www.giftchaletauburn.com

Ingebretsen Scandinavian Foods
1601 East Lake Street
Minneapolis, MN 55407
Tel: +1 (612) 729-9331
www.ingebretsens.com

Larsen Brothers Danish Bakery
8000 24th Ave NW
Seattle, WA 98117
Tel: +1 (206) 782-8285
www.larsenbakery.com

Nielsen's Authentic Danish Pastries
520 – 2nd Avenue North
Seattle, WA 98119
Tel: +1 (206) 282-3004
www.nielsenspastries.com

Nordic Fox
(restaurant featuring Scandinavian foods)
10924 Paramount Blvd
Downey, CA 90241
Tel: +1 (562) 869 1414

The Nordic Heritage Museum
Art Galleries, Immigrant Exhibits,
Museum Shop
3014 NW 67th Street
Seattle, WA 98117
Tel: +1 (206) 789-5707
www.nordicmuseum.net

Nordic House
3421 Telegraph Avenue
Oakland, CA 94609
Tel: +1 (510) 653-3882
pia@nordichouse.com
www.nordichouse.com

Norwill
(cookware, food and gifts)
1400 E Hillsboro Blvd #200
Deerfield Beach, FL 33441
Tel: +1 (954) 596-4506
Fax: +1 (954) 596-4509

Olson's Delicatessen
(Scandinavian foods and gifts)
5660 West Pico Blvd
Los Angeles, CA
Tel: +1 (323) 938 0742

Olson's Scandinavian Foods
2248 NW Market St
Seattle, WA 98107
Tel: +1 (206) 783-8288
www.scandinavianfoods.net

Scandia Food & Gifts Inc.
30 High Street
Norwalk, CT 06851
Tel: +1 (203) 838-2087
scandia@webquill.com
www.scandiafood.com

Scandia Imports
10020 SW Beaverton-Hillsdale Highway
Beaverton, OR 97005
Tel: +1 (800) 834-8547
www.scandiaimports.com

Scandinavian Marketplace
PO Box 274,
218 Second Street East,
Hastings, MN 55033
Tel: +1 (800) 797-4319
steve@scandinavianmarket.com
www.scandinavianmarket.com

Scandinavian Specialties
6719 15th Avenue NW
Seattle, WA 98117
Tel: +1 (206) 784-7020 or
+1 877-784-7020 (toll free)
www.scanspecialties.com

Signal Seafoods, Inc.
(Swedish crayfish delivered
to all of North America)
7355 SW 240th Place
Beaverton, OR
Tel: 001 (503) 626-6342
sales@crayfishparty.com
www.crayfishparty.com

Simply Scandinavian Foods
99 Exchange Street
Portland, ME 04101
Tel: +1 (207) 874-6759 or
+1 877-874-6759 (toll free)
www.simplyscandinavian.com

Viking Village
(Norway online store directory)
217 Ferry Street
Easton, PA 18042
Tel: +1 (800) 397-7180
Fax: +1 (610) 559-7187
viking.village@nni.com
www.vikingvillage.com

Wikström's Gourmet Food
5247 North Clark Street
Chicago, IL 60640
Tel: +1 (773) 275-6100
sales@wikstromsgourmet.com
www.wikstromsgourmet.com

IKEA

The international Swedish furniture
chain IKEA has sites in Europe, North
America, the Middle East and Asia
Pacific. Each store has a Swedish
food market, which stocks specialist
Scandinavian ingredients – from
Swedish meatballs to unrefined
hard bread and caviar spread.
Check the location of your nearest
IKEA store by visiting their website:
www.ikea.com

INTERNET SUPPLIERS

www.deli-shop.com

www.igourmet.com

www.swedensbest.com

www.swestuff.se

INDEX

ACKNOWLEDGEMENTS

The publisher would like to thank the following for permission to reproduce their images (t = top; b = bottom; r = right; l = left): 6t Ball Miwako/Alamy; 6b Andy Whale/Corbis; 7t Werner Forman/Corbis; 7b Anders Ryman/Corbis; 9t, 9b, 21b, 23tr and 25b iStockphoto; 10t and 11t Adam Woolfitt/Corbis; 10b Dave and Sigrun Tollerton/Alamy; 11b and 12t Arcticphoto/Alamy; 12b Leslie Garland Picture Library/Alamy; 13t Brother Luck/Alamy; 13b Mary Evans Picture Library; 14t Hubert Stadler/Corbis; 14b Gavin Hellier/Robert Harding World Imagery/Corbis; 15t, 16t, 16b, 18 and 19tr Chad Ehlers/Alamy; 17b Robert Harding Picture Library; 19tl Nordicphotos/Alamy; 19b Jason Lindsey/Alamy; 22b E. Petersen/Alamy; 23tl, 23b and 25tl Corbis.